AUTHORS IMPRINT

Dedicated to discovering and sharing knowledge
and creative vision, authors and scholars have endowed
this imprint to perpetuate scholarship of the highest caliber.

Scholarship is to be created...by awakening a pure interest in knowledge.

—Ralph Waldo Emerson

The publisher gratefully acknowledges the generous support of the Authors Imprint Endowment Fund of the University of California Press Foundation, which was established to support exceptional scholarship by first-time authors.

Pricing Beauty

Pricing Beauty

The Making of a Fashion Model

Ashley Mears

UNIVERSITY OF CALIFORNIA PRESS
Berkeley · Los Angeles · London

University of California Press, one of the most
distinguished university presses in the United States,
enriches lives around the world by advancing
scholarship in the humanities, social sciences, and
natural sciences. Its activities are supported by the UC
Press Foundation and by philanthropic contributions
from individuals and institutions. For more information, visit www.ucpress.edu.

University of California Press
Berkeley and Los Angeles, California

University of California Press, Ltd.
London, England

© 2011 by The Regents of the University of California

Photographs courtesy of Beowulf Sheehan, except as
noted.

Library of Congress Cataloging-in-Publication Data

Mears, Ashley, 1980-
   Pricing beauty : the making of a fashion model /
Ashley Mears.
      p. cm.
   Includes bibliographical references and index.
   ISBN 978-0-520-26033-7 (cloth : alk. paper) —
ISBN 978-0-520-27076-3 (pbk. : alk. paper)
   1. Models (Persons)   2. Modeling agencies.
   3. Fashion shows.   I. Title.
   HD8039.M77M43 2011
   338.4'774692—dc22

                                    2011006003

Manufactured in the United States of America

20 19 18 17 16 15 14 13 12 11
10 9 8 7 6 5 4 3 2

This book is printed on Cascades Enviro 100, a 100%
post consumer waste, recycled, de-inked fiber. FSC
recycled certified and processed chlorine free. It is acid
free, Ecologo certified, and manufactured by BioGas
energy.

To Jennifer

Contents

Illustrations

TABLES

Acknowledgments

A great deal of thanks are in order to many people without whom this project would never have left the runway. I thank my respondents for their time and generosity in interrupting their hectic schedules to share their stories and thoughtful reflections about their work. To my former bookers and managers, I am especially grateful. These pages are at times critical of the fashion world, but I hope they also show my respect for the work of modeling agents.

While at New York University, I was lucky to find a creative team of mentors—indeed, I think they are fine examples of "edgy." Thanks to Harvey Molotch, my intellectual muse, and to Craig Calhoun, who has such an inspiring mind. I am in continual awe of Judith Stacey for her generosity, guidance, and remarkable *style* as a sociologist; I could not have asked for more from an advisor.

Many other scholars have read and helped improve my work, among them Ann Morning, Dalton Conley, Caitlin Zaloom, David Garland, Howard Becker, Lynne Haney, Sudhir Venkatesh, and Richard Sennett. Viviana Zelizer warmly welcomed me into her field, and Joanne Entwistle gave me generous support during my time in London. When I was an undergraduate at the University of Georgia, I was fortunate to study with William Finlay, who gave me a push just when I needed it, and who continues to be a mentor.

In New York I had tremendously supportive friends who read (and then reread) many chapters: thanks to Noah McClain, Amy LeClair,

Jane Jones, Sarah Kaufman, Tey Meadow, Rebecca Glauber, Melissa Velez Owen Whooley, Harel Shapiro, Grace Yukich, Beowulf Sheehan, Melissa Aronczyk, Claudio Benzecry, Alexander Frenette, and Frederic Godart. Two writing groups were important forums to try out new ideas: the NYLON Research Network (formed at New York University and the London School of Economics), led by Craig Calhoun and Richard Sennett, and the Gender and Inequality Workshop at NYU, organized by the brilliant duo Sarah Damaske and Allison McKim. Magali Armillas-Tiseyra and Beth Kramer kept up the valuable tradition of "Grad Hall." Thanks also to Olya for her kindness and curiosity and to Dasha for her hilarious company.

Finishing the book was a challenge eased with the support of colleagues at Boston University, especially Sigrun Olafsdottir, Julian Go, and Emily Barman. I was helped just in time with the work of my undergraduate research assistant Laura Wing. My editor Naomi Schneider I thank for being an early believer in the project, and then for displaying such patience with me to the end.

Earlier versions of some of these chapters have appeared elsewhere. Parts of Chapter 2 and Chapter 4 appear in "Pricing Looks: Circuits of Value in Fashion Modeling Markets," in *The Worth of Goods: Valuation and Pricing in the Economy*, edited by Jens Beckert and Patrick Aspers (London: Oxford University Press, 2011), reproduced with permission from Oxford University Press. Parts of Chapter 3 appear in "Discipline of the Catwalk: Gender, Power and Uncertainty in Fashion Modeling," *Ethnography* 9(4): 429–56, reproduced with permission from Sage Publications. Data presented in Chapter 4 also appear in "How Do Cultural Producers Make Creative Decisions? Lessons from the Catwalk," coauthored with Frederic Godart, *Social Forces* 88(2): 671–92, reproduced with permission from *Social Forces* at the University of North Carolina Press. And portions of Chapter 5 appear in "Size Zero High-End Ethnic: Cultural Production and the Reproduction of Culture in Fashion Modeling," *Poetics* 38(1): 21–46, used with permission from Elsevier. I am grateful for permissions to use these materials.

This book was made possible with support from the National Science Foundation Doctoral Dissertation Improvement Grant, the NYU Graduate School of Arts and Sciences Dean's Dissertation Fellowship, the Mainzer Fellowship to the Center for Gender Studies at Cambridge, UK, and funds from the Morris Endowment at the Department of Sociology at Boston University.

Special thanks to Beowulf Sheehan, who kindly provided all photographs for this book except where noted.

Thanks lastly to my family for all the years of love and encouragement—and to my dad and Kathy, for countless bowls of saimin, to my mom, for late-night cups of tea, and also to Alexander Gilvarry for writing with me. And to my sister Jennifer, for a lifetime of friendship, this book is yours.

CHAPTER I

Entry

You've got a great look.

That was what he told me as I sat in a Starbucks in downtown Manhattan. I had come in search of a quiet table at which to crack open a social theory book, one of a number of texts I was assigned as a new graduate student in sociology at New York University. Instead I found myself seated across from a model scout who was handing me his card and telling me that I could be making a fortune as a fashion model.

While waiting in line for my coffee I overheard a man, flanked by two pretty young women at a nearby table, talking loudly about what it's like to work in the fashion modeling industry. He was in his forties, tan and balding; his two companions, who were listening to him intently, looked about twenty years younger. I took him to be a modeling agent out with two of his models, and I listened with feigned disinterest, having packed away my own modeling portfolio into my mom's attic just six months ago, content to start a new career in academia after what had been five years in the business, at first part time in college, mostly small stuff for local department stores in my hometown of Atlanta. Later, school vacations would be spent modeling in Milan, New York, Tokyo, and Hong Kong. It seemed a lifetime ago; I had just celebrated my twenty-third birthday, well past retirement age for a model, and the books weighing down my shoulders were a reminder of a new career ahead.

On my way out I passed their table, and the loud-talking agent stopped me: "Hey, which agency are you with?" The young women smiled at me.

I'm not with an agency, I told him. I quit modeling six months ago to become a full-time graduate student. He seemed to not hear me—"You're not with an agency? Why not?!" He began lauding my "look" and then asked for my phone number so that we could talk and he could "present" me to the agencies in New York. He introduced himself as Todd, a model scout, and he described his pretty companions as "girls" whom he had recently "discovered."[1]

Meeting Todd was simultaneously off-putting and intriguing. I arrived at grad school wanting to study the gender politics of beauty and the body, an interest that took root when, as a teenager modeling in New York, an agent told me to try to look as lean as possible. The going joke around his agency, he explained, was "Anorexia is *in* this season." As an undergrad studying sociology, I had fantasized about studying the modeling world from the inside, to determine how the industry arrives at such injurious beauty ideals. It's been a long tradition in the sociology of work and organizations to learn the ropes of an industry by working in it. But now, at the age of twenty-three, I was happily retired from a world in which I had been advised by age nineteen to lie about my age to seem younger. And yet here was this pushy scout, dangling a way for me to get my foot back in the industry's door.

Todd called regularly over the next few days and explained that his job as a scout was to scour North America in search of new talent for all the major New York agencies, which in turn would give him a cut of the commission for every successful new model he found. He lavished praise and extolled my potential to "make it big" in various articulations: "You have a very strong look, someone will like you. . . . I think you gotta real cool look, a New York look. . . . I'm super-selective. . . . You need outlets, can't study all the time. You can be a full-time student and full-time model. My top girls make $10,000 a day."[2]

And, finally, there was his tantalizing promise: "I can make it all happen for you in a few hours."

Well that all sounded very good, but when looked at sociologically, Todd's world began to open up questions I had never considered asking. What is a "look," and how is someone like Todd able to see value in it?

MEET SASHA AND LIZ

The very words "fashion model" conjure up images of rich, glitzy women in luxurious clothes strutting down catwalks and posing for world-famous photographers, the stuff of celebrity, fame, and fortune—glamour alive in the flesh.

Only it won't work out this way for the majority of women and men who enter the fashion modeling market. Consider two young women—I'll call them Sasha and Liz—making their way through modeling auditions in two fashion capitals, London and New York.

When Sasha was fifteen, she met a Japanese modeling agent at an "open call" audition in her hometown of Vladivostok, a harbor city in Southeast Russia. She can still remember the Polaroid picture the agent took of her: "I looked terrified!" She was invited to leave her grey port city that summer during school vacation to work as a model in Tokyo. It was an unlikely destination for a girl known as "Virus" at school for her thin body, so skinny in fact that she wore three pairs of stockings under her jeans to fill them out. Once in Tokyo she grew up fast, learning how to cook for herself, to budget her money, and to communicate in English, of which she could at first barely speak a word: "I remember standing outside the car asking my driver, 'Are you go me home?' He was like, 'What?'" She returned home with $5,000 in cash, "big money," she says now with a sarcastic smile, to the surprise of her friends and family, who put the money toward home improvements.

About the time Sasha was making her first $1,000, halfway around the world another teenager I'll call Liz was serving a plate of pasta to a couple of regular customers in an Italian restaurant in Pleasantville, New Jersey. The customers carried on with her as usual: "Oh, you should be a model!" The teen waitress, in her first job in her hometown suburb, demurred as usual, too interested in high school social life and sports. But the thought stayed with her until she moved to Manhattan at the age of nineteen to attend Baruch College, where she majored in nutrition, the cost of tuition defrayed by her middle-class family. In between classes, a scout stopped her on Fourteenth Street: "Have you thought about modeling?" This time, she said yes.

When I first met her at a magazine casting in New York, Liz was twenty-two years old, precariously balancing college classes with modeling castings, but doing neither activity well. Her grades were slipping, and she was perpetually in debt at her agency, which had advanced her the start-up costs of putting together her portfolio. Her teenage savings account quickly depleting, Liz made ends meet by waitressing and babysitting. She began to talk more and more frequently about moving to Los Angeles, a place, she's been told, where models can "cash out" on lucrative television commercial work.

Just as Liz contemplated leaving New York, Sasha was about to arrive. By the time she turned twenty-two, Sasha had traveled around the world, living in agency-owned "model apartments" for no more than three or four months at a time in cities such as Paris, Tokyo, and Vienna. After high school she attended a premier Russian university, only to drop out after one semester too enticed by the world's possibilities to sit still in a classroom. She made money too, as much as $50,000 one year, enough to support herself and to send substantial remittances home to her family in Vladivostok. However, when I met her in London at an audition for a cosmetics billboard, she was, in her words, "poor as a little mouse," renting a room in a photographer's flat in East London at £120 a week and scraping the bottom of her bank account. She was embarking on yet another journey, to New York, where she hoped her luck would change and her "look" would catch on in the fashion world.

Here we have two young women, both with brown hair, brown eyes, and fair skin. They have similarly lanky 5'9" size 2 bodies. Both are twenty-two years old, though they can (and do) pass as teenagers. Over the next few years, both will attend hundreds of castings in fashion capitals around the world. They have probably walked past each other in line at casting auditions in New York, though one doesn't know the other. They are two out of hundreds of thousands of contenders around the world chasing one of the most widely shared dreams among girls and young women. Both Liz and Sasha know, as their sea of competition knows, that the odds of having the right "look" to become the next top model are stacked against them.

Triumph and failure in a culture industry such as fashion modeling are enormously skewed. As in art and music markets, in fashion a handful of people will dominate the top of the hierarchy with very lucrative and visible rewards, while the bulk of contestants will barely scrape by, earning a meager living before they fade into more stable and far less glamorous careers. So extreme is the success of the winners that economists call these "winner-take-all" markets.[3] How, among the thousands of contenders worldwide, is any young woman like Sasha or Liz able to rise from the pack to become a winning commodity? What makes one model's "look" more valuable than the thousands of similar contestants? And just where does its value come from?

Success in markets such as fashion modeling might on the surface appear to be a matter of blind luck or pure genius. But luck is never blind, nor does genius work alone. Behind every winner in a winner-take-all market such as fashion modeling is a complex, organized production process. The secrets to success have much less to do with the models themselves than with the social context of an unstable market. There is little intrinsic value in a model's physique that would set her apart from any number of other similarly built teens. When dealing with aesthetic goods such as "beauty" and "fashionability," we would be hard-pressed to identify objective measures of worth inherent in the good itself. Rather, an invisible social world is hard at work behind the scenes of fashion to bequeath cultural value onto looks. The backstage of fashion reveals a set of players—models, agents, and clients—and the peculiar rules of their game that usually remain hidden behind the brilliantly lit runways, the glossy magazine pages, and the celebrated glamour of fashion.

This is precisely how glamour works: through disguise. Glamour, after all, has its roots in medieval Celtic alchemy. *Glamer* is a spell, a magic charm, that is cast to blur the eyes and make objects appear different from, and usually better than, their true nature.[4] As glamour is cast upon the model's look, all of her work—and the work of her agents, clients, their assistants, and their whole social world—gets juggled out of sight. This social world is enormously important in determining the realm of beauty and fashion ideals; after all, the relations of cultural production determine the possibilities of cultural consumption. Ultimately the clandestine world of fashion teaches us about much more than beauty and apparel; it holds lessons for the nature of modern work, markets, decision making, and new forms of racial and gender inequality. We usually can't see it, but there is an entire world of work that goes into producing that which appears to be a natural state: a model's "look." This is its story.

THE LOOK

A look is not the same thing as a quality commonly called "beauty." Neither Liz nor Sasha is best described as particularly beautiful. Sasha has big brown eyes and a small face framed by brown bobbed hair. She resembles the *manga* characters out of Japanese comic books. Liz is very skinny with imperfect teeth, thick, dark eyebrows, and almond eyes. Both describe themselves not as pretty but, to use a term that comes up often in the industry, "edgy."

The first designers to use live models in the early twentieth century noted that an ephemeral quality was the mark of a good model. French courtier Patou noted in the 1930s that his favorite model, Lola, was not necessarily beautiful. She sold clothes, Patou thought, because of her "great chic"—a seemingly spiritual quality.[5]

This ineffable quality is known as a model's "look." It is a special type of human capital—what sociologist Loïc Wacquant, in his study of boxers, calls "bodily capital."[6] Models sell this bodily capital to fashion clients, such as photographers, casting directors, stylists, and designers. Modeling agents, known as "bookers," broker the sale.

The term "look" seems to describe a fixed set of physical attributes, such as how a person actually looks. It's true that models conform to basic Western standards of attractiveness, for instance, youthfulness, clear skin, healthy teeth, and symmetrical features. Within this frame, they adhere to narrow height and weight specifications. The female model is typically at least 5'9" with body measurements close to a 34" bust, a 24" waist, and 34" hips. The male model is typically 6' to 6'3" with a 32" waist and a 39" to 40" chest. This framework is, as one stylist explained to me, a "good ol' formula" for a model.

But this formula does not, by itself, constitute a look. Beyond this basic physique, small and subtle differences lead clients to prefer one model over another. Models, bookers, and clients refer to these differences as a model's "look."[7]

Talking about the look proves exceptionally difficult for fashion insiders. Bookers and clients often grapple for the right words when asked to define a look. They struggle to explain that a look is a reference point, a theme, a feeling, an era, or even an "essence." A look is decidedly not the equivalent of beauty or sexual attractiveness. While bookers and clients talk about some looks as "beautiful" and "gorgeous," they are just as likely to value others they describe as "strange," "grungy," and "almost ugly." Bookers stressed the difference between people who are "just hot," that is, sexually attractive, and people who are appropriate as models, though the precise qualities that distinguish one from the other could best be described as "something special" or "something else."

Part of this "something else" is in the model's personality. Most models, bookers, and clients explain that a look is much more than the sum of a model's physical parts. It is the "whole package" of a model's being, including personality, reputation, on-the-job performance (including how one photographs), and appearance. In an industry predicated on appearances, personality is a surprisingly important factor for success. Alas, looks really can be deceiving.

I think of a look as a model's unique appearance and personality that will appeal to a particular client at a particular time, depending on the product being sold. To see the value of any given model's look, one may not simply lay eyes on the model, for a look is not a visible or an objectively identifiable quality inherent in a person. The look is in fact a system of meanings, such as a language or a code, tied to a social evaluation system. People learn to read and decipher this code in order to see distinctions between one model and the next, as well as their positions within the bigger fashion picture. It represents not just a person or an individual beauty but also a whole system of knowledge and relations among people and positions connected within an industry.

Looks are a type of commodity circulating in what sociologists call the "creative" economy, also called the "aesthetic" and "cultural" economy. The cultural economy includes those sectors that cater to consumer demands for ornamentation, amusement, self-affirmation, and social display. Products coming out of the cultural economy are inscribed with high levels of aesthetic or semiotic content in conscious attempts to generate desire for them among consumers. They provide social status and identity over and above their utility functions, hence their value is fluid and unpredictable. Lots of goods make up the cultural economy, such as art, music, television and film, and fashion.[8]

Models' looks are a prime example of cultural products. They are pure aesthetic content and are subject to wild, rapid fluctuations in value, which means that the people working in the modeling market face a high degree of ambiguity. Given all of this uncertainty, how does a person become a marketable look, as models try to do in the modeling market? How do bookers and clients determine their worth? And, finally, how do broader cultural understandings of value influence the worth of any particular look?

MODEL WORLDS

An investigation into the production of a look leads us into a social universe that usually goes unseen. It is a universe where intimate social ties guide economic transactions, where the poorest-paid jobs are worth more than thousands of dollars, where deception is integral to getting things done, and where mundane, taken-for-granted assumptions have enormous ramifications for pop culture and its mediascape of runways, commercials, billboards, and magazines.

The first step to understanding this world involves a little reverse magic to bring invisible actors into light. While models reap plenty of attention as pop culture icons, no model gets far without the campaigning

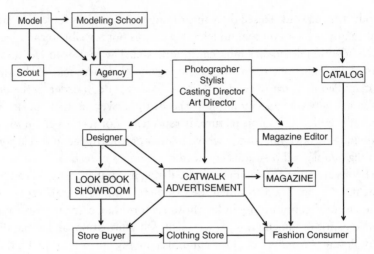

FIGURE 1.1. Production world behind the look

efforts of a booker and a few key clients. Networks of agents, scouts, assistants, editors, stylists, photographers, and designers constitute a production world that links models to fashion consumers. Scouts and agents "discover" raw bodily capital and then filter it to clients— photographers, designers, art and casting directors, stylists, and catalog houses. These clients "rent" models for short periods of time, maybe a few hours, days, or weeks, during which time they deploy this capital to appear in media outlets such as catalogs, showrooms, advertisements, magazines, catwalks, showrooms, and "look books," which are book- lets that feature a designer's new clothing collection. In these media outlets, models' images serve to entice store buyers and, ultimately, to seduce fashion shoppers, the final consumers of the look, into making a purchase, as shown in Figure 1.1.

Taken together, these producers constitute a world of backstage pro- duction, or an "art world," as sociologist Howard Becker calls it (1982). In an art world, the talent is one piece of the art-making process, but talent should not be privileged as the gravitational center. Creative goods such as music, art, or books do not mysteriously emerge from individual acts of artistic genius. They materialize from institutions, organizations, industrial field structures, and the everyday routines of people at work.[9] A work of art is as much the product of a whole series of intermediaries and their shared norms, roles, meanings, and routines as it is the creation of an individual artist. In other words, mundane processes of production are important in shaping culture.

An art world approach belies common sense; we're used to thinking that the best people rise to the top of any market, as popular media accounts unanimously celebrate. It is tempting to think that models are lucky winners in some "genetic lottery," as though their bodies were superior gifts of nature that automatically receive social recognition, and, indeed, some evolutionary psychologists echo this view.[10] Such explanations of the deservingly triumphant cannot account for the physical outliers—people such as Kate Moss, who at 5'6," is short by model standards, or Sophie Dahl, who reached fashion fame at a size 10, rather heavy compared to her catwalk counterparts. Nor does talent account for the hundreds of thousands of similarly built genetic lotto winners who will never receive social recognition—people such as Liz and Sasha and the thirty-eight other models I interviewed for this book. Their stories make sense only in the context of a whole web of producers, the relationships they form, and the conventions they share.[11]

Thinking about looks as part of a world of production rather than as an individual quality called beauty allows us to see how aesthetic judgments materialize from a collaborative process. The look is the result of people doing things together.

The Rules of the Game

Behind-the-scenes, participants may work together, but they do not necessarily work together harmoniously. Cultural producers struggle internally for power and recognition. Each is trying to "take all" implicitly at the expense of other contenders in a winner-take-all hierarchy.

These invisible players comprise a competitive world of high-stakes careers, and they calculate their steps according to two opposed logics: on the one hand, making money, and, on the other, creating art.[12] The producers most concerned with short-term economic profit are known as commercial producers. These models, bookers, and clients work predominantly in catalogs, television commercials, and print ads for goods such as toothpaste, electronics, and commercial clothing. Others are in fashion for fashion's sake. They are known as editorial producers, and you'll recognize their work in the high-end catwalks, magazines, and luxury-brand campaigns. Editorial producers follow an "anti-economic logic" by rejecting the pursuit of money, chasing after prestige instead.

That is, they are paradoxically willing to lose money in order to gain social esteem. This prestige may (but may not) pay off in the long run with huge financial gains. It is a gamble that underscores the entire undertaking of fashion; it is, as sociologist Pierre Bourdieu would call it, a rule of the game of fashion.

Producers tend to separate themselves into two broad social networks: those that work in editorial fashion, and those in commercial fashion. Producers in each network, or each "circuit," as I call them, think about fashion in distinctly different ways; they face different risks, they define success differently, and they pursue different types of payments.[13] When looking at the same models before them, bookers and clients will see them differently, that is, they will recognize valuable looks in systematically different ways. To navigate these nuanced differences, all producers socialize with each other, watch and imitate one another, and cultivate social ties and friendships that form the basis of the fashion modeling market.

Fashion producers are constantly conversing, circulating gossip by phone, text, and e-mail, gossip that spills out of their offices and studios and into happy hours, dinners, and late-night parties around downtown Manhattan and central London. On more than a few nights I found myself sharing drinks with bookers and models well into the early hours of the morning. "That's part of our job," a makeup artist once told me when I complained that there were too many social events on school nights.

The Problem of Pricing Beauty

Within their editorial and commercial circuits, bookers must figure out which clients prefer which kind of look, and both must determine how much models are worth. How do they determine the price of something as nebulous as a look?

Pricing is a particularly troublesome endeavor for cultural producers, because in most creative industries there is no clear correlation between price and quality. There are no standard price-setting indices that bookers use to figure out the worth of their models' time. A model's fee is contingent upon the meanings that bookers and clients make of his or her look, all of which vary among them and can skyrocket or tank over the course of one season.

The problem of pricing exemplifies a larger quandary faced by cultural producers, and, for that matter, people in any market. It is the problem of uncertainty, the inability to state in advance what one wants.

Modeling is like other "cultural" markets such as art, music, fashion, food, and film, where high uncertainty and inequality are the norm.[14] What makes these industries stand out from traditional sectors such as law, manufacture, and medicine is the exaggerated role of taste in determining value. A piece of art doesn't sell for its function but for its form, and that is largely a subjective matter, dependent upon the whims and sensibilities of buyers, critics, dealers, and the final consumers. In fashion modeling, bookers never know which looks will appeal to clients; meanwhile, clients never really know which models will be most successful in selling their products. This is because consumer demand is fundamentally unknown, a vexing fact of market life that advertisers and market researchers routinely attempt to remedy, but never with much success.[15] As the successful Hollywood screenwriter William Goldman once put it, "nobody knows anything" in a cultural industry. Because "nobody knows" what the next big thing will be, "all hits are flukes," and all flops are a surprise. Amid all of this uncertainty, fashion demands constant product renewal. The modeling market is constantly in flux, with "fresh faces" being "hot" one season and forgotten the next. Fashion is, after all, fundamentally about change.[16]

When faced with high levels of ambiguity—and no easy way to make decisions—producers are likely to turn to each other, relying on things such as gossip, reputation, shared histories, and conventions to make their decisions. All of this socializing and imitation has a cumulative advantage effect in which the "the rich get richer," exaggerating the inequality between the top and the bottom. Spurred by gossiping producers, successful goods accrue more success, while most entrants fail, leaving a wide gap between the winners and the losers.

The success of the few obscures what amounts to measly rewards for most. Linda Evangelista reportedly wouldn't get out of bed for less than $10,000 at the height of her career in the 1980s, and in 2009, Gisele Bünchen grossed $25 million in modeling contracts. Yet according to the *Occupational Employment Statistics*, in 2009 models earned an estimated median income of $27,330.[17] Earnings among models within an agency are enormously skewed, with some models in New York earning over $100,000 a year and others in debt as deep as $20,000. Average earnings are nearly impossible to predict, as any model's monthly income can fluctuate wildly. That's because, in addition to being poorly paid, work in the cultural industries is structurally unstable and on a "freelance" or per-project contractual basis. These are, sociologically speaking, "bad jobs" akin to irregular work arrangements in the secondary-employment sector, such as day laborers and contingent workers who piece together a precarious living.[18] These kinds of jobs require few skills and no formal education credentials, and the work provides no health or retirement coverage.

However, unlike other "bad jobs," cultural production is rich in cultural status. Though the odds of making it big (or making anything at all) are low, modeling is regarded as very attractive work, especially for women. In American popular culture, modeling is glorified as a glamorous and prestigious career for young women, as evidenced in teen fashion magazines.[19] Furthermore, the entry criteria are low, which results in overcrowding, with a great deal of struggle for success. Though the probability is slight, the possibility of hitting the jackpot is so deceptively attractive that modeling attracts more contenders than it should, creating a flooded market characterized by a taxing elimination tournament, similar to prizefighting.

To see if they have the right look or not, models are subjected to a systematic process of selection, or "filtering out," in which their agents arrange auditions or "castings" to meet prospective employers.[20] The job is, in effect, an intense series of job interviews with up to fifteen castings a day during busy seasons in major markets. The very few winners to emerge from the screening process can count their luck twice: once to enter the contest and again to win the prize. Models take these long odds against the clock of aging; from the day they sign up, their window of opportunity to "make it" is closing, especially for women. On average, most modeling careers last less than five years.

We now have the picture of a market that is highly volatile and turbulent, marked by uncertainty, imitation, inequality, and high turnover. Models attempt to embody the look, bookers scramble to find it, and clients chase the prestige of choosing it first. They are all vulnerable to losses as quick and enormous as their winnings, this is especially so for models. What determines if one model will rise to the top or settle at the bottom with the majority? Put another way, how do the goods in this market—the looks—attain value?

A look's value, I will show, develops out of social interaction among producers in the editorial and commercial circuits of fashion.[21] First, producers socialize within the fashion circuit to get a sense of which models are valued by other producers; they also carefully watch how models are systematically "filtered out" at castings in order to ascertain signals (and there are plenty) of a model's underlying worth. Top models result from an insular logic of distinction in the editorial world: in any given season, a set of powerful clients will somewhat arbitrarily champion a young woman (and very rarely a young man), which sets off a chain of positive feedback in the market, thereby creating a "winner" of enormous economic value who is no different from the other candidates in any obvious way, aside from her having been deemed valuable by the right people at the right time.

WHY STUDY FASHION MODELS?

Fashion models get a lot of attention. We read about them in popular presses, sensational journalism, historical accounts, and cultural and media studies. They are frequently critiqued as symbols of systemic gender, race, class, and sexual oppression. Yet for all the concern over their many meanings, fashion models have yet to be taken seriously as workers and as cultural commodities.[22] Although new sociological territory, fashion modeling can teach us much about how the realms of culture and economy shape one another.

This book traces the production of value in the modeling market in four stages. Chapter 2 lays out the history and architecture of the modeling market, with its crucial distinctions between the editorial and commercial circuits. Chapter 3 examines the work that models do in their various and often feeble attempts to become winners. We turn in Chapter 4 to the tastemakers, those bookers and clients who together negotiate which looks are valuable. Finally, in Chapters 5 and 6, we will see how cultural ideas about race and gender more broadly shape which bodies are perceived as worthy.

Working It

It takes work to model. Models do to the extreme what we all do at our jobs and in almost every facet of our social interactions: they *work it*. Chapter 3 examines how models put their best faces forward, project an idealized version of their selves, and succeed or fail depending on their arbitrary appeal to dozens of potential employers. They are part of a growing workforce of "aesthetic laborers," those workers whose bodies and personalities—the "whole person"—are up for purchase on the market. But unlike most workers, models do this without the guidance of a boss or the security of a safety net.

Though it has cultural cache, modeling is freelance work, meaning it is insecure and unstable. It is also, on the whole, low-wage work. Models

FIGURE 1.2. Front stage of fashion

FIGURE 1.3. Backstage of fashion

are part of a growing trend of informalization in the labor market; they navigate their individualized exposure to a ruthless market just like day laborers, domestics, and other casual workers in the expanding informal economy.

Brokering Culture

Having observed models up close in their work spaces—from their footsteps on the catwalk to their relentless diets—the next chapters zoom out to the cultural intermediaries who sell and buy looks. Chapter 4 examines how bookers and clients price models, a process that translates shared sets of cultural values into objective price value.

This translation of cultural into economic value has always been an important part of markets, but it is becoming more and more apparent to sociologists as the creative industries and "soft-knowledge"-intensive industries become central sectors of the economy. In London, for instance, creative industries accounted for about 800,000 jobs in 2007 with about £18 billion annual turnover. In New York the "creative core" of cultural production provided about 309,000 jobs (over 8 percent of all city workers in 2005), second only to London.[23] As of 2011, the fashion industry in New York alone employs 165,000 people and generates $9 billion in wages, $1.7 billion in tax revenue, and $55 billion in sales each year, according to the city's Economic Development Corporation,[24] which is to say that all of these industries matter. These are not marginal or frivolous sectors but are, in fact, huge engines of urban and, indeed, global economies.

The people who work in these industries are part of a new service class of "cultural intermediaries." They are what sociologist Paul Hirsch (1972) has called "gatekeepers," functioning as surrogate consumers charged with creating and disseminating aesthetic values, thereby shaping the wider field of possibilities of fashionable consumerist dispositions in the process. They play a crucial, if often an invisible, role in shaping the terrain of pop culture, from advertising designers, magazine editors, pop music producers, fashion designers and buyers, and art dealers.[25]

Even though we don't see them, bookers and clients wield enormous influence over which looks we come into contact with around the world. But just how do they know which models to filter in and out? What do they imagine consumers want? To answer these questions, we'll explore in Chapter 4 the cultures of production among bookers and clients, following their interpersonal relationships at the office to their interconnected social lives that bind them throughout the city and around the world. Their acts of valuation are inescapably rooted in preexisting social categories of race, gender, sexuality, and class.

Representing Bodies

Fashion produces powerful representations of idealized class, gender, race, and sexual identities. Chapters 5 and 6 examine how cultural values of race and gender set the terms for seeing some bodies as being worth more than others, for producers do not come to their jobs as blank slates but come seeped in culture. They draw upon and reproduce entrenched racist and sexist tropes of difference, but they do so unwittingly as they follow institutionalized production routines.

Models do much more than promote the sale of fashion. The model look promotes and disseminates ideas about how women and men *should* look. Fashion images are prescriptions for masculinity and femininity. Gender, we know, is a matter of active "doing," not mere passive being, so modeling can be thought of as the professionalization of a certain type of gender performance, one that interlocks with race, sexuality, class, and other social positions.[26]

Plenty of scholars from cultural studies, media studies, and feminist and intersectionality theory have analyzed the cultural meanings of fashion images and advertising. Feminist scholars have made the case that images of fashion models represent the objectification of women's bodies, defining and enforcing normative ideals of feminine beauty that disparage all women, especially working-class and non-white women.[27] In this sense, those women at the top of the display professions constitute "an elite corps deployed in a way that keeps millions of women in line."[28]

To discuss fashion model images in terms of their effects and patriarchal intent is to deal with one important part of the story. But it leaves out the production processes behind those images. If you were to look at an advertisement for designer clothes, you would not see how little the male model earns relative to the woman posing next to him. When watching a runway show you would miss the age-old tropes of sexuality that designers consider as they dismiss black women for their catwalks. The perfect image on the page of a magazine captures but a single moment in time, effacing the work and the inequalities that lie beyond the frame. If modeling is the professionalization of gender performance, then it is a prime site to see the construction of masculinity and femininity, as well as race, sexuality, and class.

Making Markets

Fashion is an excellent place to see the social side of markets because, as it turns out, how producers socialize with one another is explicitly tied to how they value a model's look.

Markets are not very social, however, in orthodox economic theory. According to neoclassical economics, markets are made up of self-interested, rational individuals who follow the forces of supply and demand. In the case of those particularly "deviant" or anomalous markets such as art, economists presume fixed personal taste, thereby imposing abstract logics onto a complex social realm, or they ignore these markets altogether as being frivolous peripheral markets, too far from the core economy to be taken seriously.[29] But there is no such thing as an anomalous market. Rather, there are just different types of markets that are organized around particular sets of social relations. Those economists who are breaking away from neoclassical orthodoxy, such as behavioral economists, are making gains in connecting economic decision-making to human and group psychological processes.[30] By contextualizing economic action in its social environment, previously taken-for-granted categories such as price become processes, and values become outcomes of messy negotiations and contested meanings. This book ultimately is about the contested negotiation and social relationships that underlie markets—not just fashion markets or culture industry markets but *all markets*.

ETHNOGRAPHY OF THE LOOK

To figure out what it means to have a "great look" in the modeling industry, I decided to accept Todd's invitation to meet with the agents. I arrived at 9:00 a.m. at the Gramercy Park Hotel and stood beneath the marquee, sheltered from a dreary drizzle, awaiting Todd to make my big day. There was already a small gathering of young people—nine teenage girls and three boys and a few of their parents—and when Todd arrived in a raincoat holding a Starbucks cup, we eagerly stood around him in a semi-circle to hear his welcoming remarks.

Todd began with instructions for following him to meet the bookers at a dozen agencies throughout the next two days, and then he cautioned, "You're all winners just for being here. . . . Just like anything else in life, it's super-competitive, and it doesn't come easy. They may spend five minutes talking with you and not really give a response, or they may glance you over for thirty seconds and then really like you. I don't know. Don't ask me because I won't tell you." At this point a few mothers chuckled from under their wet umbrellas. I heard it as nervous laughter to offset their growing anxiety over what was beginning to sound like a hard day ahead.

"You're all winners" is an obvious prelude to mounting rejection, and it was a taste of things to come in my fieldwork.

Todd arranged meetings with several different modeling agencies, and, among them, the bookers at Metro were the friendliest and most sympathetic (at least initially) regarding my school schedule.[31] Metro offered me a contract outlining two terms, exclusive representation and a 20 percent commission on all of my future earnings. By signing I agreed to be represented exclusively by Metro in New York, and to pay the company a standard commission of 20 percent from my bookings, plus an additional agency fee of 20 percent of my rates that would be charged to my clients. In exchange they agreed to promote and manage my modeling career. In this self-employment arrangement, agencies arrange opportunities for models to work in exchange for a cut of their success, but they are not liable for models' failures. Metro's accountant explained as much when he handed me the contract: "Here's where we don't promise you the moon and the stars, but we'll do our best to get you there." Within six months, my bookers at Metro introduced me to the owner of Scene Management, an agency of comparable size and repute in London. Scene's director offered me a similar contract and an invitation to work with the company in London. Two and a half years would be spent in participant observation, or, more like "observant participation," working for both agencies, during which time I would participate in the full range of modeling work, including five Fashion Weeks, hundreds of castings, and dozens of jobs in every type of modeling work—catwalk shows, magazine shoots in studios and outdoors "on location," catalog shoots, and fittings in the showrooms of Seventh Avenue, New York.

The day I signed, I attended castings to meet clients. Shortly thereafter, I met with a director at Metro and explained my interests in writing a dissertation based on my experiences in the field. After some negotiations, such as keeping the agency and its employees' identities confidential, I began to record observations. The owner of Scene agreed to similar terms. Usually I kept a small notepad tucked in the back of my portfolio and jotted down phrases just after a casting. When most models were changing from high heels into sneakers in the elevator, I was scribbling down notes. I normally transcribed all field notes within twenty-four hours, ending up with hundreds of pages of documents detailing each day.

As the project progressed, I became frustrated by the opacity of the casting process and how little information was made available to models about crucial decisions in their modeling careers. The terms for models' fees were unclear, and bookers sometimes explicitly instructed me not to discuss my rate with other models on the job, telling me that this was "nobody else's business." To figure out the logics of bookers and clients, I decided to interview them as well.

In my two years of modeling for Metro and Scene, I sat beside bookers at their table in the office, drank with them at their favorite pubs, and hung out with them backstage at fashion shows. As I was nearing the end of the participant observation phase of my research and withdrawing from modeling work, I formally interviewed a sample of bookers, managers, and accountants, speaking to a total of thirty-three employees: twenty-five bookers and six account managers, including two owners, in addition to two office assistants (identified in this book simply as "bookers" or "staff"). I recruited bookers and staff for interviews through my connections with Metro and Scene. These two samples of bookers and managers are representative of the array of staff members that one would encounter at any medium-size boutique agency in New York or London.

I then interviewed a snowball sample of forty models, twenty in New York and twenty in London, evenly split by gender, recruited from jobs and castings. Though there are disproportionately fewer men in fashion than women, I sampled an equal number of men and women for the interviews, because male models are rare voices and have received even less scholarly attention than their female counterparts.

To understand how casting decisions are made, I also interviewed a snowball sample of forty clients working in both cities. I recruited clients—designers, photographers, editors, stylists, and casting directors— whom I met at castings, backstage at fashion shows, or during photo shoots I attended. Thus while not a random sample, the clients in this study, like the models, worked across a wide range of status levels in the market, from middle-market catalog photographers to luxury-brand stylists.[32]

Like all fieldwork, this research required considerable time, which always seemed to be in short supply. From the moment I entered the field to my last few days, a sense of urgency was inescapable, especially at the agencies. One of my bookers, Ronnie, was often seated at his desk with one hand scribbling onto a notepad, the phone cradled to his ear, and his other hand punching computer keys. Most days I was lucky to receive only one hectic voice mail instructing me to "drop everything" and "rush" across town to a "really important" casting or a last-minute booking. It was often followed by a second, irritation-filled voice mail within ten minutes, reminding me of the importance of the first message.

This made for difficult conditions when scheduling interviews. Models frequently cancelled interviews for last-minute jobs and castings. When it was time to interview one booker in New York, scheduled a week in advance, she bristled into the meeting room ten minutes late and announced, "Mears, you gotta make it quick!" Clients were the most difficult to track down, given their erratic transnational schedules. I conducted one interview with a renowned photographer in the backseat of his chauffeured limousine on his way to London's Heathrow Airport en route to shoot in the States. But while scheduling proved difficult, I was surprised by the way models, bookers, and clients welcomed me into their offices, homes, and local coffee shops to generously share their time and stories.

This research was also, like modeling itself, physically and emotionally draining. There were daily brushes with embarrassment, humiliation, insecurity, rejection, and, more than a few times, anger. Scrolling through my field notes I am reminded time and again of such discomforts. There was one early morning at a casting for a body cream TV commercial in New York's SoHo neighborhood—a couple of hours before I would enter a graduate seminar room on social theory—where I was asked to dance around a film set in short shorts alongside two models who looked perhaps sixteen years old. After a pause in the dancing, the casting director asked the two models to stay for another round of auditions—"Except you," she quietly told me. "You can go."

Standing outside on the street a moment later, I scribbled in my notepad: *Feeling too old for this, wanting to quit. Almost there.*

But the fieldwork lasted over two years, far longer than I ever expected, partly because, like the models I interviewed, I couldn't seem to find a good time to quit. There were certainly dozens of moments, such as the body cream casting, when I wanted nothing more than to walk away from the project. And yet I too became seduced by the glamour of it all. I began to chase what Neff, Wissinger, and Zukin (2005) have referred to as the "Big Job." I found myself excited with each new booking and disappointed with each unresponsive casting. I became suddenly nervous when I met famous fashion photographers. I was actually giddy when I got the late-night phone call confirming that I would walk in a major Fashion Week show. I could not find a good time to quit the research because it always seemed like I was just around the corner from scoring my own Big Job. I signed up for this project with the goal of deconstructing a glamour industry, but I would find myself awestruck once inside. As an "observing participant," I witnessed and also *felt* the modeling market from a vantage point rarely accessible to academics.[33] This book follows the rich ethnographic tradition of accessing the social world from within, complete with all of the wonder and brutality of living through it.

Terms of the Market

A few definitions of fashion modeling parlance are in order. The main activities in which models participate are "tests," "go-sees," "castings," and "bookings." When a client, such as a department store, fashion designer, or a studio that shoots for various catalogs, is available to see models, it is called a "go-see." A "casting" is an appointment to meet with a client who has asked to see models for an upcoming job. When a go-see or a casting is a "request," clients invite specific models, as opposed to a "cattle call" casting, to which all available models in town are invited. Clients typically sort through models from the first casting and invite only a few to return to a "callback" or "fit-to-confirm" casting.

Typically at go-sees and castings the client will greet the model, either one-on-one or in a group setting. Models show their "book," or portfolio of pictures, and give the client a "composite card," which has on it a sample of their pictures, their name, the name of their agency, and their statistics. A model's "stats" include height, suit or dress size, measurements (bust, waist, and hips for women; waist, shirt, and inseam for men), shoe size, and hair and eye color. If interested, the client may take the model's picture, have him try on a sample of clothing, take his picture with a Polaroid camera, and, for runway bookings, ask to see his catwalk the length of the room and back. The model will usually leave a comp card with the client, bid farewell, and be thanked for coming. It is a quick, informal meeting.

After the casting, if the client wants to book the model for the job, then the client calls the model's booker to place the model on "option" for the job. An option is an agreement between the client and the booker that enables the client to place a hold on the model's future availability in rank order of interest, from first (strong) to third (weak) option. Similar to options trading in finance markets, the option gives the buyer the right, but not the obligation, to make a purchase. In the modeling field, options enable clients to place a hold on the model's time for twenty-four to forty-eight hours before he or she is actually confirmed for the booking. Unlike finance options trading, model options come free of cost; they are a professional courtesy to clients and also a way for agents to manage models' hectic schedules.[34]

"Tests" are photo shoots set up for the explicit purpose of making pictures to put in models' and photographers' books. "Bookings" are jobs such as photo shoots and runway shows. All of a model's daily activities, from testing to waiting in long casting lines, advance the goal of booking jobs. There are three main types of jobs: photo shoots for magazines, print advertisements, and catalogs; fashion shows on the catwalk, including Fashion Week; and showroom and "informal" fit modeling, where models try on garments in a designer showroom for a private audience of buyers looking to stock the racks at department stores and boutiques throughout the country.

The Agencies: Metro and Scene

Metro in New York and Scene in London are good sites for this research because they are both medium-size "boutique" agencies that rank among the roughly eighty or so "key" agencies around the world.[35] They are well-established agencies in the field, each with a broad representation of models who work in all sectors of the fashion industry, from high-end catwalk shows and campaigns to mass-market catalogs. Each agency has a handful of editorial superstars, one or two "supermodels," and a steady base of commercial models. At Metro, and to a lesser extent at Scene, models also work in informal and fit modeling, where the gritty production work happens and models try on newly manufactured clothes in an informal setting, such as a designer's showroom on Sixth Avenue.

Other "full-service" agencies in New York and in second-tier markets throughout the world represent a broader spectrum of looks, such as lifestyle, plus-size, petite, or ethnic models.

Metro has been in the business over two decades, represents over three hundred models (two hundred women and one hundred men), and employs over twenty people (primarily bookers and managers, with a

	Metro Models, New York	Scene Models, London
Size	Models: 200 women, 100 men 16 bookers, 3 accountants	Models: 100 women, 50 men 8 bookers, 2 accountants
Debt	Women: < $15,000 Men: < $2,000	Women: < $6,000 (≈£3,500) Men: < $900 (≈£500)
Models' Income	Women: $50,000–100,000 Men: $30,000–50,000	Women: $28,000–$80,000 Men: < $10,000
Annual Billings	Several million dollars	Several million dollars
Boards	Editorial; Women ("Money"); Runway; Men Boards	Women; Men Boards

FIGURE 1.4. Metro and Scene at a glance

few accountants and assistants). Roughly seventy models are in town and available for work at any given moment. Scene has twenty-five years in the business, with about one hundred and fifty models on the books, one hundred women and fifty men. Halfway through this research, however, Scene discontinued its men's board, replacing the fifty men with women models, an economically prudent decision, as we'll see in Chapter 6. Scene staffs ten employees, including accountants. Bookers expect roughly twenty to thirty models to be in town, depending on the season.

Despite Metro's larger size, both Metro and Scene earned a similar gross sum of several million a year in gross billings (based on the 2006 dollar-pound exchange rate). While structurally similar, the agencies differ in size, a fact that reflects, in part, their respective locations in the fashion industries of New York and London.

The Cities: London and New York

Fashion, like other culture industries, happens in cities, because cities enable the kind of social interaction necessary for culture industries to function.[36] Modeling clusters into the major "fashion cities" of New York, London, Milan, and Paris, where biannual Fashion Week designer collections receive global media coverage. Beyond these "top-tier" fashion cities, dozens of competing cities use fashion as a means of city and nation branding to position themselves as competitive cosmopolitan centers. A 2008 *New York Times* survey estimated 152 Fashion Weeks worldwide and counting, from Berlin, Antwerp, and Stockholm to Dubai, Hong Kong, Sri Lanka, and Zimbabwe.[37] Geographer Elizabeth Currid argues in her 2007 book *The Warhol Economy* that a global city's competitive advantage lies in the size and success of its creative industries. This makes fashion models literally a way for cities to put their best face forward in the global economic order.

Although they are both global cities and fashion capitals, London and New York vary in their type of fashion market. As a result of post-World War II development trajectories, London fashion today is a weak commercial enterprise with a stronghold in creativity and artistic concerns of "fashion for fashion's sake," while New York is widely regarded as a business center for fashion commerce.[38] The geographic divide between fashion-as-art and fashion-as-commerce maps onto the two circuits of the fashion market, the editorial and commercial circuits. New York is a place where models seek commercial success, while London is understood as a creative hub, an opportune place for editorial models to amass prestige. While these distinctions are crude in practice—New York offers editorial opportunities just as London provides lucrative commercial work—they orient players' understandings of the global modeling market. Studying both New York and London, with their opposing orientations toward prestige and profit, enables a fuller picture of the commercial and editorial circuits.

GLAMOUR AND SOCIOLOGY

Over the next three years, while I'm "working it" as a participant observer and collecting dozens of stories from industry insiders, Liz and Sasha radically divert from their similar starting points. One of them will be jolted into the upper middle class, earning $5,000 a day in catalog shoots and purchasing a home for her family, paid for in cash. She will rent a spacious apartment in downtown Manhattan, where she will study acting and prepare to enroll in college courses at an elite university in New York. The other young woman will end up broke and will move back home with her parents. She will forgo college entirely and work in showroom jobs for a few hundred bucks an hour here and there before training to become a yoga instructor. And though one of these two young women will advance economically on her journey through the modeling market, neither has a particularly glamorous story to tell about her work.

This is what glamour is all about—artifice and deception. If advertising is to entice consumers to purchase fashion and beauty products, then it is imperative that consumers do not see the amount and the kind of work it takes to promote their products. As Raymond Williams (1980) has noted, the qualities of most consumer objects are themselves not enticing enough to warrant purchase. They must be validated, he argues, "if only in fantasy, by association with personal and social meanings which in a different cultural pattern might be more directly available." This cultural pattern can be best described as magic.[39] Advertising is a magic system, and models are its magic wands.

Any magical act presupposes and produces a collective unawareness—ignorance, really—of its own arbitrariness.[40] Collective recognition of the look requires a collaborative misrecognition of its production, as though the look existed independently all along. So magical are cultural products that we see them in the realm of the spiritual, beyond the scope of scientific analysis. "You can't explain why someone likes you or not," a young male model from Paris once told me in London, regarding why clients choose him among the many other models for hire. "It's like, why do you like chocolate or coconut? You know, it's just in you. You can't explain it."

The sociological bet—and the stakes of this book—contends that, in fact, you *can* explain it. Beauty is neither in the model nor in the beholder. The value of a look lies in social relationships and cultural meanings that can be studied systematically. There is, in fact, an economy to this quality called beauty that models are thought to possess. Beauty, I will show, has a specific logic.

To unearth the relations of production in a glamour industry is to do the work of demystification. Sociology does this digging, this unearthing, of organizations and players and conventions that when put together constitute the social world. Sociologists demystify what may seem like miracles into mundane human interactions. In this way we are like hecklers in a magician's audience, the spoilers who reveal the backstage tricks, thus rendering perfect sense to what would be otherwise enchanted.[41] Ultimately we show the production of what appears natural. And this, I will argue, is *precisely* what gender, race, and class distinctions are—socially produced categories of difference that appear to be normal and natural ways of dividing up the world but are in fact products of a cultural system that legitimates and reproduces them.

In what follows I redirect the charmed gaze off of the glamour, moving out and away from the enchanted look in four analytic steps, beginning with the fashion field and models' labor practices within it, moving on to the tastemakers' strategic networking, and ending with cultural norms of race and gender. This book is an invitation to go behind the curtain to discover the clandestine process in the making of a fashion model, for as Erving Goffman said, the vital secrets of a show are visible backstage.

CHAPTER 2

Economics of the Catwalk

By any measure, JD had a great first year as a model. As a sophomore university student living in his hometown of Manchester, UK, he caught the train to Kings Cross Station every week or so to shoot a booking arranged by his high-fashion modeling agency in London. He was twenty years old and making more in a month that he had earned all his life in part-time retail jobs. His first booking was a high-fashion campaign that paid £10,000 for one day's work. Not bad, considering he didn't even want to model, but he had gone along with his friends into a scouting competition.

JD saw modeling as a steady cash flow requiring minimum effort. It was "easy money," a term I heard often as models spoke of what appeared to be an extraordinarily favorable effort-to-rewards ratio, at least when looked at in the short term. Easy money just kept streaming into JD's bank account. He began to turn down campaigns that paid "only" £800 a day—"Stupid!" he says now. He might complain of such a paltry rate to his booker "Can't you just get me another campaign?" to which his booker would patiently explain, "Campaigns are hard to get, JD, not everyone gets them," but to no avail. JD measured a job's worth in monetary terms alone, and he couldn't get his head around working for "free":

"You know like they'd call me up like 'You got *Dazed and Confused*! You have to do it!' Well how much does it pay? Nuthin'? I'm not doing it! I'm not coming down from Manchester for some bullshit I'm not getting paid for, *Dazed and What*?!"

Dazed and Confused, it turns out, is a leading fashion magazine celebrated around the world as a launching pad for famous designers, musicians, and models. He turned down many similarly prestigious editorials and campaigns: *i-D* magazine, a photo shoot in Tokyo for Issey Miyake, and the couture collections featuring a top female model: "It was with some really famous model girl, but again I didn't know who she was, Anouck?"[1] The jobs he did accept with glee paid high day rates and were considered cool among his friends and family back in Manchester:

"But then when I got *Sportswear Now*," he recalls, "I was like, 'Yeah man, *Sports Now*! My boys can see me in the window!' It's just a shit sporting goods store, but for me back in Manchester village everyone's like, 'Yeah man, you did *Sports Now*!' And I'm like turning down *Vogue*. That's why I made a mistake. Because I turned down really big jobs."

What goes up inevitably comes down, and rather quickly in a market like modeling. *Vogue* lost patience, and Miyake lost interest. The phone stopped ringing; JD's flush streak went dry. He went from booking one job a week to one a month, and now maybe he'll book a few jobs for the whole year.

At twenty-two years old, JD has finished university with honors in computer sciences. He lives in central London and is looking for work at advertising firms, where he hopes to some day produce advertisements and cast models himself. These days he attends castings on the rare occasion a client requests him, but his modeling career is pretty much over. As it happened, the stylist on the *Dazed and Confused* booking was a famous figure in menswear, and after being turned down not once but *three times*, he has blacklisted JD from any future jobs. "Now I'm never requested for any casting," JD says, shaking his head. "Stuff like that— big mistake I made."

. . .

What counts as a "big job" in fashion modeling? Is it the amount of money? The public exposure? The prestige of the client? Two years ago JD thought the obvious: a big job paid big bucks. That was his big mistake. The blunder is not so much in turning down work but in not being able to discriminate among different types of worth beyond their immediate cash value. It is a problem of undervaluing fashion elites and overvaluing cash. This is the inability to see the long-term payoffs beyond the short-term profits, to separate symbolic from economic rewards, to recognize the prestigious names in the fashion industry, and to understand their connections to each other. The problem is, in short, an illiteracy of the fashion field and its guiding logics.

The look exists in a cultural production field, in the way Pierre Bourdieu defined it, as a distinct social universe with its own rules, logics, and capitals that function independently of—even opposite to—those of the economy.[2] Within this field, looks, like other cultural products, fall into two distinct yet overlapping spheres that can be loosely thought of as avant-garde or "editorial," on the one side, and mass market or "commercial," on the other. The two spheres are personified in JD's short career: *Dazed and Confused* on the editorial end, and *Sportswear Now* on the commercial end, and between them there exists a cultural gap. The people who work predominantly on each end form networks, what sociologist Viviana Zelizer would call "circuits of commerce." Zelizer means commerce here in the old sense of the word, when commerce meant conversation and mutual exchange.[3] A circuit is a type of social network organized around economic activity, but it's not *just* a network, because it features specific understandings, practices, information, obligations, rights, symbols, and media of exchanges.[4]

We can think of editorial and commercial fashion as "circuits of value" because players in each share different measures of success and value. Editorial and commercial producers have distinctive understandings of what counts as good taste, good work, and fair payment. In fact, a large sum of money from catalog clients, when looked at from the editorial circuit, is worthless compared to the few hundred dollars to be earned on a magazine shoot. Editorial and commercial producers share different ideas about what counts as the "look" at all. Within this field, models, bookers, and clients all grapple for better footing in what amounts to a prestige hierarchy. The fashion field, from a sociological point of view, looks at times like a battlefield.

As one little pawn passing through fashion's structure, the twenty-year-old JD couldn't understand the origins of his own market value, as he had yet to be socialized into the field of fashion. This chapter would have proved useful to him back in Manchester, as it provides a map of the fashion world with its typology of good work and corresponding looks and pricing schemes. But to understand the complex meaning structure of the global field of fashion, we must first understand how it emerged.

THE FIRST MANNEQUINS

The fashion model first appeared in the late nineteenth century, when the Englishman Charles Frederic Worth showed his designs on live "mannequins" in his Paris salon in the 1850s.[5] They were young women usually drawn from the workshop floor, or from among the *demimonde*. When the first women appeared to model dresses in courtier showrooms, they elicited an ambiguous tension around what, exactly, was for sale, the dress or the woman wearing it. Fashion modeling was neither a sought-after occupation nor a socially esteemed one. Because models displayed their bodies for money, they were considered morally suspect, like actresses and sex workers. Indeed, Victorian society condemned fashion as the art of disguise and the practice of hypocrisy, as illustrated in widespread social fears of the villainous "painted woman" who hides her devious intentions beneath a cosmetic veneer. When the London dressmaker Lucile showcased the first mannequin parade in the late 1800s, she recruited her models from working-class London suburbs. Before courtiers like Coco Chanel became more selective of their mannequin's appearances by the 1910s, the chief concerns for models were "slenderness and good manners."[6]

With the rise of mass production and the spread of consumer culture, fashion shows grew into semiformal events with fixed dates, so by 1920, models became fixtures in designers' salons, typically modeling before an audience of aristocratic clients at tea. American department store Wannamakers adopted the European fashion show in Philadelphia in 1910, showing new fashion on live mannequins during lunchtime in the store restaurant.

As fashion grew internationally, designers' demand for models also grew, and modeling rose as a celebrated job for women. Modeling became an important new work option for women seeking upward mobility in the 1920s, though it was (and is) rather poorly paid and informal labor.[7] The first modeling agency was opened in New York in 1923 by John Robert Powers. To overcome the stigma of "model," he preferred the moniker "Powers Girl." The first model search by French designer Jean Patou in 1924 brought in five hundred American applicants, of which six lucky girls were chosen as models. Across the Atlantic, Lucie Clayton's modeling agency opened in London in 1928.[8] With agency representation, models' fees increased. By the 1930s, American models earned $65/week for photographic work and $40/week for wholesale modeling in fittings and showrooms on Seventh Avenue. In the 1940s and 1950s, popular models drove up these wages, especially Queens-born Dovima, whose own photographic rate soared from $25/hour to $60/hour, making her known as "The Dollar a Minute Girl."[9]

At the time, women like Dovima worked in a split market as either runway or photographic models. Runway models worked the catwalk shows, fittings, and showrooms for fashion houses and were most prevalent in Europe, where *mannequins de cabine*, or "house models," worked full time to fulfill the needs of courtier salons. Photographic models, on the other hand, posed for magazines and catalogs, and they were the most visible, and hence the most prestigious, of all models. Photographic models were also paid more money, and, like runway models, they worked on a quasi-permanent basis for magazines such as *Vogue* and *Harper's Bazaar*, which at the time paid hourly rates comparable to catalog houses.

By the 1960s, on the heels of the youth and pop cultural explosions in Europe and America, fashion radically decentralized from "class fashion," in which Parisian haute couture dictated global style from the top down, to "consumer fashion," driven from the bottom up by lifestyles and subcultures. Paralleling a broader social shift of relaxing social rules, couture's role as the sole purveyor of legitimate taste gave way to multiple influences of things such as rock-and-roll and street styles.[10] Eager to crack the youth and mass markets so captivated by boutique designers, couture houses introduced luxury *prêt-à-porter*, or ready-to-wear, labels. In 1961 Pierre Cardin produced a menswear ready-to-wear show in Paris, and in 1966 Yves Saint Laurent opened his *Rive Gauche* ready-to-wear boutique. The grand splendor of the department store gave rise to boutique shopping, and the closed guild system of haute couture's golden era faded into "classless" fashion. Now the growing middle classes could buy a piece of elite fashion via an affordable prêt-à-porter design. Meanwhile, high fashion began taking design cues from "street" styles, with new trends following a pastiche of inspirations. The upper classes lost the authority to define fashionable style, as early social theorists Thorsten Veblen and Georg Simmel had supposed. Throughout Western consumer society, as in fashion, homogeneous class cultures declined, and in their place numerous "niches" or subcultures of different consumer tastes emerged, crisscrossing socioeconomic backgrounds.[11]

Much of the couture side of the business since the 1960s has become a "loss leader," meaning couture loses money but generates the publicity and prestige around the brand.[12] In 1975 *Maison Christian Dior*, the house of Christian Dior, developed revolutionary brand licensing as a way to augment its profits through the sale of accessory items. Couture houses in the early twentieth century had contracted out perfume, such as the famous Chanel No. 5, introduced in 1921. Dior expanded the practice by contracting worldwide manufacturers of home, beauty, and accessory products, which, in exchange for the right to use the prestigious Dior name, paid royalties to the *Maison*. Belts, bags, sunglasses, perfume, candles, linens, you name it—cheap but quality-controlled mass-manufactured goods emblazoned with the Dior logo—were produced and sold around the world. The "Christian Dior model," as it became known, is now the dominant business strategy for fashion houses.[13] The transformation toward branding demanded a new type of fashion model, one that could both walk the catwalk and pose in magazines and advertising. This new model, the editorial model, bridged the photographic–runway divide, and her career ascended to celebrity heights.

The Blow-Up

As ready-to-wear fashion mushroomed, the modeling industry grew too throughout the 1960s. As fashion shows became larger events, designers looked to hire renowned models as a means of increasing their press coverage. In the early 1970s agencies in Milan raised show fees from $50/hour to $200/hour, and photographic stars such as Jerry Hall and Pat Cleveland took to the catwalks soon after. Magazine stars replaced *mannequins de cabine*, who were pushed off the runways and consigned to the backstage work of fittings and showrooms.

With magazine stars appearing on catwalks in the major fashion cities, models quickly gained international notoriety with soaring rates and celebrity status. Models became the stars of pop films such as *Blow Up* (1966) and the symbols of "youthquake" culture. Diana Vreeland, editor-in-chief at American *Vogue*, raised models' profiles by printing their names in editorial spreads in the late 1960s, and other fashion magazines followed suit.

Magazines at this time ended the practice of employing a regular crew of models. Magazine pages became career launching pads for new talent; as such, their rates dropped from approximately $50/hour to $100/flat day, where they remain to this day.[14] Photographic work in commercial advertising and catalogs, however, remained a source of steady and average pay for the majority of models who worked in neither prestigious catwalk shows nor high-end fashion magazines. Thus the divide between photographic and runway modeling reconfigured into the split between editorial and commercial modeling.

By the 1970s Ford Models' Lauren Hutton became the most highly paid model for Revlon cosmetics at a famed rate of $200,000 for twenty days of work a year. Designers in Milan in the 1970s and 1980s paid models an average of $2,500 a show and upward of $10,000 for catwalk stars.[15] Fashion Week was broadcast worldwide via television and satellite in the 1980s, at which point fashion shows began to look like rock concerts: long lines of attendees snaking around velvet ropes, paparazzi cameras flashing, and front rows studded with Hollywood stars.

The fashion industry itself was undergoing massive industrial changes in the 1980s. With globalization, new flexible manufacturing enabled clothing to be quickly and cheaply produced in global commodity chains—retailers and fashion brand corporations in Paris and New York started to outsource manufacture overseas to decentralized production networks in developing countries. The results, argues Sean Nixon in his study of British menswear, were more segmented markets that could quickly respond to subtle shifts in consumer tastes.[16] Most recently, mass retailers such as Topshop and H&M have been able to sell cheap copies of designer prêt-à-porter in just two to four weeks after their catwalk debuts, a practice called "fast fashion," for its rapid turnout of new styles.[17]

With an expanding range of niches to brand, advertising has transformed from a mode of delivering fact-oriented messages into a dream vehicle, crafting elaborate sets of emotional meanings and values around products. This "creative revolution" in advertising, seen first around 1970 in the UK, marked a move toward "image-led" or "aspirational" advertising. This new code of promotion pushes "emotional selling points" by linking consumer goods to lifestyles and symbolic meanings.[18] Traditional fashion advertising used to be about the presentation of clothes, but with these global changes in fashion and advertising, clothes developed into one piece in the whole stylistic package of a fashionable "look," of which the fashion model plays a critical part.

Under the regime of image-led advertising, fashion modeling ballooned into the "supermodel" bubble in the 1970s and 1980s, with star models commanding fees upward of $40,000 for each catwalk appearance.[19] With few supermodels and multiple deep-pocketed buyers, models' fees skyrocketed as their agents played designers off one another.

Linda Evangelista, of the "The Trinity" (with Naomi Campbell and Christy Turlington), famously would not get out of bed "for less than $10,000 a day." In the 1990s supermodels grossed millions of dollars annually. In 2010 three models made it into *Forbes* magazine's "Celebrity 100" list of the world's most powerful celebrities: Gisele Bünchen, with $25 million, Heidi Klum, with $16 million, and Kate Moss, with $9 million.[20] Over the course of the twentieth century, the model went from a degraded shopgirl to an iconic millionaire.

Models in a Digital World

The market since the 1990s has experienced dramatic change. With the Internet and digital technology, global networks of scouts and agencies have unprecedented access to clients and models around the world. Many bookers who began their careers in the 1980s remembered the Berlin Wall as a scouting barrier; it has since given way to a huge influx of Eastern European models who now compete with young women and girls from other heavily scouted areas such as Latin America. Modeling agencies have accordingly gone international—Elite Model Management currently has over thirty branches worldwide, from Atlanta to Dubai—and these "one-stop" beauty shops are able to cater to clients around the world.[21] Agents now snap pictures and videos on digital cameras, and they can e-mail these as virtual casting packages to clients anywhere around the globe.[22]

With the increased capacity to find and sell models, agencies have proliferated around the world. In New York alone their numbers were higher than ever on the eve of the financial crisis. As Wissinger reports, the Manhattan business Yellow Pages listed 30 agencies in 1950; 41 in 1965; 60 in 1979; 95 in 1985; 117 in 1998; and 132 in 2002.[23] In 2008 only 120 agencies were listed, a dip perhaps indicative of the recession.

More agencies equate to more models. The supply of bodily capital has swelled in the last two decades, something bookers in particular bemoan, claiming that there are more models and fewer jobs today than ever before. Kath, a booker since 1991, exclaimed that the numbers of models have increased, "Double, triple! Oh my God a bazillion! How many agencies! I don't even know." The precise number of models in any given market is impossible to obtain, since models are constantly on the go, working in fashion markets around the globe.[24] According to Models.com, about ten "top" modeling agencies cover the majority of fashion bookings in New York; each of these agencies represents between one hundred and fifty and six hundred models. Nonimmigrant US visas rose to eight hundred models in 2003, and a 2008 House bill proposed to allot one thousand foreign models into the United States each year so as not to compete with other specialty workers, namely computer engineers.[25] Metro bookers estimated that approximately three thousand to five thousand models flock to New York during a Fashion Week show season. One survey in the UK estimated that just over 80 percent of all models in London Fashion Week are foreign workers.[26]

The fashion industry has also received greater attention in pop media outlets, such as *Vogue* magazine's website extension, Style.com. Launched in 2000 by Condé Nast Publications, Style.com showcases every designer outfit sent down the catwalk each Fashion Week season. Reality TV shows increasingly highlight the fashion industry with competitions to be the next top fashion designer, hairstylist, magazine editor assistant, and, of course, fashion model.[27] With more publicity, agencies are besieged with young women and men who dreaming to model. At Metro, dozens of hopeful candidates line up for a chance to impress bookers during open call on weekday afternoons. At Scene, young people constantly wander into the lobby each day for a chance to meet the agents. A steady flow of e-mails and letters containing snapshots floods the in-boxes of assistants at both agencies. The vast majority winds up in the trash.

Greater fame has brought lesser individual fortune. While growing in size, the industry has contracted individual profits. Supermodels and their high fees have been replaced with thousands of eager competitors, lower rates, and the rapid turnover of sometimes seasonal modeling careers. Modeling rates on the whole have plummeted, a function of oversupply in combination with advertising's dwindling power to capture audiences. Technologies such as TiVo, in which television audiences can record shows without commercials, have diminished the power of television advertising, slashing models' rates for TVCs (television commercials). In the 1980s worldwide TV commercials paid initial fees upward of $1 million, with residual payments, or "use fees," paid each time the commercial aired; a few hundred dollars for a 30-second spot could amount to checks made out to agencies for thousands of dollars every few months. TV commercials yielded lofty sums for extended lengths; they were the golden goose egg for fashion modeling agencies. Since the early 2000s, international commercial rates slowly sunk to averages closer to about $15,000 total in 2008, with "buyout" usage, meaning clients pay this one-time fee regardless of its scale, usage, or airtime.[28]

High-end fashion campaigns are no longer the sole provisions of models either, now that celebrity culture has catapulted Hollywood stars and pop singers into the new spokespersons for fashion and cosmetic campaigns. It wasn't until the late 1990s that actors began to endorse commercial or fashion products, except in overseas markets such as Tokyo so as not to tarnish the image of a serious actor. Fashion magazines have followed suit. A decade ago, ten out of twelve American *Vogue* covers featured models; in 2008, just one model, Linda Evangelista, graced the cover.[29] These jobs, once the pinnacle of a model's fashion career, are in ever-shorter supply.

Finally, rates since 9/11 have stagnated. September 11, 2001, was the first day of Fall Fashion Week in New York, and the shows were cancelled and collections went unsold in a year that was particularly damaging for the whole advertising industry. Models' rates absorbed the economic shock, and bookers have had difficulty raising them since. By bookers' estimates, some clients now pay just half of what they did before 9/11, and clients are resistant to attempts to raise rates.

Against this backdrop of global oversupply and shrinking rates, agencies were suffering even before the 2008 global economic crisis. To cope with lower rates, they took on more models in pursuit of the next face that would break out from the pack, secure rare multimillion-dollar contracts, and rise to fame and fortune. The trouble is, finding the next big look is unpredictable, so agents have intensified the search to reach as many candidates as possible. The candidates are tried out for brief periods, only to be "dropped" when it seems unlikely that they are a winning ticket. From the bookers' standpoint, the cycle speeds up each season.

"*Ohmygod* there are so many more models today. It's insane!" said Rachel, a New York booker. "Everyone's scouting tenfold. The rates aren't as high as they used to be, so everyone's competing for more jobs, so everyone's thinking, the more models you have the more money you can make the more jobs you can get"—she paused, seemingly out of breath. "Even this last show season there were just like, tons and tons of girls in this city."

A modeling career is considered short term: any given model has low expectations for longevity, so modeling is viewed as less of a career than it is a stint. Agencies have a high turnover rate for models, with twenty-five in and out each year at Metro, and ten new faces added and old ones dropped at Scene, like a revolving door. Models' tenure at these agencies ranges from a few months to a couple of decades; on average, most models last about five years.

The result, as Helen, a senior booker at Scene, remarked, is a much different market than when she began three decades ago (and, in her view, it's a less interesting one). Young people are now scooped up, tried out, and spit out in rapid succession. "Everybody's looking for the Kate Moss and Natalia Voldinova," said Helen. "The girl that is going to make the mega bucks. And the fact is, you can't tell whether you've got it or not until way down the line, so everybody just keeps on searching and everybody gets scouts."

Helen looked exhausted as she spoke these words; her business has become a disheartening one. She continued: "I find it really tough. They take people from places, and it's a lot of wasted time and a lot of people [are] sent home [and told], 'Oh, you're no good.' I think it's a shame."

With lower rates and more competition, Metro and Scene are like mice running on a wheel. Though both agencies experienced economic growth and expanded their offices throughout the early decade of 2000, relative to their competitors they are scrambling to keep up. The rise of editorial modeling as distinct from commercial modeling laid the tracks for a race in which agencies would hustle to find that rare fresh face, inflating supply and deflating rates in the process.

Venturing into London on the train from Manchester two years ago, JD didn't see his precarious position amid a broader structural transformation. His brief career with £10,000 fashion campaigns rode on a wave of the globalized economy, a flooded market, dwindling rates, accelerating fast fashion, and a centuries-old career in twilight, now reduced to a fleeting spotlight that shines on fewer and fewer stars.

ARCHITECTURE OF THE MARKET

Looks, like any works of art, cohere into genres. Producers can name these different forms with considerably more ease than they can define their content. For instance, Billy, a New York photographer of six years, quickly rattles off "known" types of looks: "Yeah, there's the crackhead skinny guy. The buff Abercrombie dude. You have the, like, Dolce & Gabbana gay guy," and so on. Among the many colorful descriptions that producers named, here is a sampling:

the tarted-up housewife, ephemeral bohemians, apple pie, the drug addict, yoga fit, the L.L. Bean guy, high-end hipster chicks, little tweety birds, the Brazilians, the Belgians, and Russian baby dolls

The typologies are endless. These different types come in and out of vogue along with fashion trends, so that one look becomes "the look" for particular segments of fashion at any given moment.

But their movement is not random. There is an economy to this jumble of looks, and it follows an anti-economic logic.[30] In this economy, some of the most desirable jobs pay the smallest sums of money, while those with the largest cumulative earnings suffer the poorest stature. It is the "economic world reversed," as Pierre Bourdieu put it, because here, the losers win. And they can potentially win *big*.

The Economic World Reversed

Producers of the look, like producers in any field of cultural production, have a complicated relationship to profit; some of them embrace economic principles, while others reject monetary pursuits. This depends on their location in the editorial or commercial circuits. Within these circuits of value, models book different jobs, earn inversely related amounts of prestige and income, and face varying levels of risk. They also have distinct looks that everyone claims to be able to see. Editorial models have an unusual or, to use industry parlance, an "edgy" look. Commercial models are widely described as "soft" or "classic" looks. Each look appeals to different audiences; just as in avant-garde art circuits, editorial looks are produced for other producers, that is, editors, stylists, and fashion insiders, while commercial looks are produced for mass consumption. A commercial look generates immediate economic returns, but at the expense of long-term profits. Meanwhile, the value of an editorial look matures over the long term—that is, if it doesn't evaporate into thin air from one season to the next.

Models who specialize in editorial work, so named after "editorial" pages that showcase editors' opinions, book predominantly magazine shoots and catwalk shows. These are by far the poorest-paid jobs in modeling. But payment in a cultural production field takes several forms, and in modeling, not all monies are equal.[31] Though editorial jobs pay low immediate economic returns, or "economic capital," they are rich in prestige, or "symbolic capital." Prestige is valuable in its own right, as it enables one to "make a name for oneself" and grants authority to consecrate

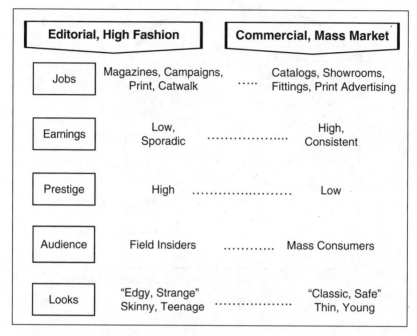

Editorial, High Fashion		Commercial, Mass Market
Jobs	Magazines, Campaigns, Print, Catwalk ·····	Catalogs, Showrooms, Fittings, Print Advertising
Earnings	Low, Sporadic ·················	High, Consistent
Prestige	High ····················	Low
Audience	Field Insiders ············	Mass Consumers
Looks	"Edgy, Strange" Skinny, Teenage ················	"Classic, Safe" Thin, Young

FIGURE 2.1. Editorial and commercial worlds in the fashion field

"good taste." Agencies and models are betting against the odds that symbolic capital will eventually pay off in the long run should the model score a luxury-brand campaign. This is the occupational jackpot, which can pay millions of dollars, renewable for several years.

Commercial jobs, such as print advertising, catalog shoots, television commercials, and informal fittings and showroom modeling, pay very well in the short term with consistently high day and hourly rates. Steady and predictable, commercial bookings pay the bills for models and bookers alike, but at a cost: this is by far the least prestigious type of work. Those models with steady above-average earnings are valuable economic assets to the agencies, yet they are symbolically worthless. They do not earn the symbolic status required to book campaigns, and a model who becomes "known" for commercial work is essentially out of the running for the jackpot. The penniless editorial model, meanwhile, enjoys a high cultural status but rarely adds to (and often detracts from) his or her agency's financial books.

In her study of the aesthetic economy, Joanne Entwistle documents this trade-off among fashion models and buyers at Selfridges department

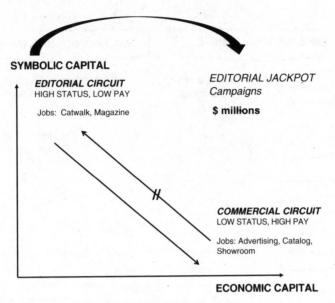

FIGURE 2.2. Structure of the field of fashion

store, noting the valorization process from editorial to commercial spheres, and Patrik Aspers has found a similar tension in his study of fashion photographers in Sweden. The hidden cost of steady commercial work, they find, is its toll on symbolic capital, which in the long run hinders financial gain. This means that, paradoxically, producers have an *incentive* to reject economic *incentives,* and they have an *interest* in economic *disinterestedness.*[32]

In theory, editorial and commercial circuits are polar opposites, but in practice, fashion's circuits are leaky systems; they have blurry and overlapping edges. Models move between editorial and commercial circuits, adapting their look to particular clients. Clients are also dynamic; an editorial client may book a commercially pretty model, or a commercial catalog might gravitate toward an edgy one. High-end catalogs such as *Barney's* and *Neiman Marcus* present edgy looks to mass audiences, and the *Victoria's Secret* catalog is highly prestigious yet targeted to middle-market consumers.

Generally, however, the value of a model's look emerges from the interplay between two distinct circuits. Picture this relationship along two axes, as shown in Figure 2.2.

Models working at the far end of the Economic Capital axis earn high rates in catalogs, showroom, and commercial advertising but are essentially "stuck" there, in the land of "cheesy" catalog jobs, unable to move up into editorial work. Models working at the far end of the Symbolic Capital axis earn less money in magazines and catwalk jobs, but their prestige can translate into higher rates in commercial jobs as they move along the Economic Capital axis, and they can, so they hope, hit the jackpot by booking lucrative campaigns.

The Beauty World Reversed

There are physical differences between editorial and commercial models, albeit faintly detectable to the outside observer. Commercial models at both Metro and Scene are likely to be older and larger in body size than editorial models. Commercial women range from size 2 to size 6, while editorial "girls" range from size zero to size 4. The colloquial term "girl" somewhat accurately describes the majority of female editorial models, who range from age thirteen to twenty-two, significantly younger than commercial models, who are typically at least eighteen years old and progress into their thirties and beyond. Editorial "boys" tend to be slim, with 28" waists and 36" chests, whereas commercial men are "hunks in trunks," with 32" waists and 40" chests. The hunks are older, ranging from eighteen to fifty and up, while editorial boys range from sixteen to their mid-twenties.

Beyond these physical differences, editorial and commercial models vary enormously in how they are *seen*. Bookers, clients, and models describe commercial looks as conventionally attractive. Commercial women, whom bookers affectionately refer to as "money girls," are just that: they look like, and earn, a million bucks. They work predominantly in showrooms and for catalogs and commercial print advertising, jobs that pay the bills for models and agents alike. The commercial look is, variously stated, cheerleader pretty, manicured, wholesome, classic, clean, all-American, and glamazon. They are attractive, of course, but with widespread appeal, a "better-looking version of the girl next door," as a Metro booker said. This "girl next door" is not necessarily white, but as these terms imply, she is coded as middle class. Commercial men are similarly "handsome," and "classically nice, regular-looking guys," as one booker explained, and "they're probably the guys that would make very good boyfriends." Commercial models are, very relatively speaking, "normal," and their normality translates into reliably high, steady earnings.

Within this "safe" commercial genre are models who specialize in showroom work, that is, fittings and informal runway presentations, and those who specialize in catalog work. Of most importance for showroom models are precise body measurements between sizes 4 and 8, as clients hire them mostly to aid in the construction and sale of sample garments. Catalog models embody norms of mainstream prettiness that are appealing to the average shopper in middle America:

> Like definitely pretty, like a girl that would be walking down the street and you go, "Yeah, she is hot." You know, heads are turning. That's what I think is catalog. Clean, all-American, very wholesome. But usually if a man from middle America thinks she is hot, then that is sort of catalog. (Bre, New York booker)

In contrast to the "everyday smiley catalog girl" or the "generically" handsome guy, the editorial model is seen as "unique" and "strong." An editorial model is typically described as having an unusual or, to use a term that comes up often in the business, an "edgy" look. Producers define edgy as an "atypical" or an "odd" kind of quality.

Everyone in the field had a tough time putting edgy into words. Beyond its rudimentary physical markers of youth and skinniness, edgy is an amorphous quality, perhaps most easily defined negatively. Edgy is *not* commercially pretty but is code for a look that departs from conventional norms of attractiveness. It is the uncanny, sitting on the border between beautiful and ugly, familiar and strange, at once attracting and repulsing its viewer. As Clive, a New York stylist, explained, "You know the really, really good girls? They are freaks. Absolute freaks! Not as people, but physically, they are freakish. . . . But even though it is freakish, it is very attractive."

While producers cherish an edgy look, they realize its value may not be recognizable to field outsiders:

> An editorial model generally has a more, um, strong look. . . . At school she was probably considered very ugly by her classmates. And some people, like my mom or whoever, might look at a picture of her in *Vogue* and say, "What's she doing modeling? She's strange-looking." And she *is* strange-looking, but she's strange in a great way. (Fria, London booker)

When classification schemes are not automatically obvious—"soft," "edgy," "classic"—how do the classifiers discern between types of looks? How do bookers manage the "biography" of their models when boundaries between markets are fuzzy? The answer has to do with the people for whom models are intended to appeal. A social hierarchy of consumers corresponds to this classification and hierarchy of looks. The commercial look is presumed to resonate with a field of mass consumers. With its soft and "boring" beauty, commercial models appeal to middle America, frequently expressed as "the Midwest" or "Ohio." Apple pie, as one booker put it, works best at the mall. In contrast, the edgy look is presumed to resonate with the field of restricted production, that is, other high-end fashion producers, such as the readership of avant-garde magazines.

For example, *i-D* magazine boasts that its readers are "opinion formers and industry style leaders . . . they are able to predict trends, influencing the mass market and define brand credibility."[33] While the editorial look functions to build brand identities and communicate prestige, the commercial model simply moves merchandise. Along similar lines, Italian sociologist Lucia Ruggerone found in her study of Italian designers that working in high fashion means devoting oneself to the production of brand identities and aesthetics—and things like "edginess"—that are at best only weakly linked with salable products and final consumers.[34]

Editorial looks are consciously *not* meant to make cultural sense to consumers in "Ohio" but, rather, to field insiders, presumably in New York and other fashion capitals. (This is not an intended slight to Ohio; producers also referenced the Midwest, and more generally, "middle America," Nebraska, Illinois, and their own mothers as examples of commercial consumers.) Precisely because it does not thrive amid these mass-market audiences, editorial fashion has an elevated status. The more types of people with whom a model can resonate, the less exceptional she is, hence the lower value, perceived or real, attached to a commercial look. Here we can take a lesson from the art world: as a general rule, the credit attached to any cultural product tends to decrease with an increase in the size and social spread of its audience.[35]

Thus modeling exemplifies the classic tension between art and commerce, and models show us how producers navigate the age-old antithesis.[36] Because art is esteemed to be superior to the vulgar material interests of the market, it carries a moral authority, a sort of credibility transferrable to products through branding and lifestyle advertising. The editorial look confers a cultural authority and a form of credit to a handbag, perfume, or a pair of heels, masking cheap consumer products with the distinctiveness of a luxury-brand identity.

Editorial fashion is both the "economic world reversed," in Bourdieu's terms, and the *beauty world reversed*. The winners—by any rational economic measure *and* mainstream beauty contest—lose. That is, the "pretty" and well-paid catalog model is shut out of the long-term prestige contest, and, symbolically at least, she is snubbed.

Of course, the differences between "edgy" and "soft" are, like the look itself, contingent and self-reinforcing. An editorial model deemed prestigious enough to appear in a Prada campaign will, by virtue of her appearance, become a prestigious editorial star. Likewise, "commercial" is a self-fulfilling label, such that the model seen as commercial by her agents will do catalog work that defines her look as commercial. She will tailor her look to fit with catalog clients' expectations, whether or not she prefers an editorial career. Indeed, bookers complain that for any model, the proverbial grass is always greener across the circuit. Editorial models, often broke, always want to do catalog work, and commercial models, feeling slighted, want to pursue high-fashion work. Should a model become too pushy in disputing her categorization, bookers are likely to "drop" her, terminating her contract. The things that we believe to be real, sociologists often say, we *make* real in their effects, and if there's one lesson I immediately learned in fashion, it's the power of beliefs.

Belief in the Game

Fashion's producers believe in the unique existence of the look, be it "edgy" or "classic," because, put simply, they have to. A belief in the rules of any game is a precondition to playing it. To indulge doubt, to question if one model *really* looks all that different from the next, is to question the purpose of the whole enterprise, and to exit the game. Producers must believe in what they are doing, that one look *is* meaningfully different from the next, and that "good taste" *does* exist and is essential to creating good fashion. They believe, in short, in making fashion for fashion's sake. By believing in these rules, producers forget that they are following social conventions; they operate under the illusion that this game of fashion exists independently of their belief in it.[37]

All producers act under this *illusio*, this belief in the autonomous quest for "the look." Models want to be it, bookers strive to find and sell it, and clients want to choose it. But victory—of being, brokering, or choosing a winner—seems more magical for producers in the editorial than in the commercial circuit.

Let me explain.

Because "edgy" editorial looks exist primarily to communicate brand images and "push the envelope" of artistic innovation, they are harder to identify and sell than those "safe" and "normal" commercial looks, which (almost) never go out of fashion. Editorial producers thus face greater subjective unpredictability and the inability to state in advance what they want. In the commercial circuit, decisions are more transparently predictable—a look is normal enough to appeal to mainstream consumers—than in the editorial circuit, where the criteria for deciding on one "edgy" look versus another are ambiguous. This ambiguity means that there is an inability to make predictions in the editorial circuit. Editorial models cannot predict their earnings next year (or next month, for that matter). Bookers cannot predict if their new editorial model will catch on. And clients cannot assess whether an editorial model will make their fashions seem more or less fashionable.

Working in the commercial market is a relatively safe and predictable process. Producers have greater ability to state in advance what it is that they're looking for in a model. There are incremental steps from one job to the next, and though of course the odds are still stiff—few people in the world will ever star in a JCPenney's advertisement—it seems as though there is no real challenge of "making it" in the commercial circuit, simply because there is nowhere to excel to. Catalogs and showrooms, with their safe, steady earnings and "normal" looks, seem like straightforward and transparently decided jobs. There is no commercial winner who seizes all of the rewards, since there is nothing symbolically worth winning in the commercial circuit. Without the potential for hitting the jackpot, there is no magic. The commercial circuit breaks this aspect of the *illusio*, or belief, in the game.

This is in contrast to the editorial circuit, where there are no intermediary steps from one job to the next but rather leaps with uncertain landing places. The rewards are great but the struggles to reach them are treacherous and ridden with ambiguities. One has the sinking sensation that one may not make it to the next step, which means that when one *does*, well, how extraordinary! With great stakes and unpredictability, the winner in the editorial winner-take-all game seems to have achieved something not only impossible but also miraculous, as though by magic.

THE MONEY TRAIL

Most people tend to see legal tender, such as dollar bills, as "real money," while nonmonetary exchanges such as "gifts" and "trades" are the extras, mere "perks," on the margins of serious economic transactions. But nonmonetary payments are crucial to the pricing system in the aesthetic economy. Cash is just one recognized type of currency, and not necessarily the most valued kind. Payment could come in forms ranging from thousands of dollars to a free handbag, pictures, the promise of publicity, and the association with high-status clients such as *Vogue* and photographer Steven Meisel.

Such unique payments do not correspond to hours worked or effort expended; rather, the range of acceptable tender varies by social standing and by circuit. People in editorial and commercial fashion share an awareness of the proper matching of media, transactions, and status, and they work hard to ensure that appropriate matches are made. Appropriate matches are important to maintain because they mark positions in fashion's hierarchy.[38] Following fashion's money trail requires first considering the symbolic meanings of sums.

Cash Value

In the editorial circuit, where uncertainty is at its highest and risk is steepest, models either win big or they don't win anything at all; there is not much of a middle class. This goes for work in prestigious magazines, catwalks, and campaigns.

The average editorial shoot hovers around $100 a day. *Vogue* magazine pays about $150 (£75 in the UK) for a day's work of eight hours, plus an extra $300 for appearing on the cover. A few publishers pay up to £120 and $225 for a day of magazine shooting. Many magazines in New York and London pay nothing at all, though lunch and snacks are often provided (see Table 2.1).

Editorial models also work for low wages in the most visible and celebrated of a model's work, the catwalk. While top models can command upward of $20,000 a show—not bad, considering a fashion show lasts thirty minutes at the most and requires four hours of preparation time in rehearsals, fittings, and hair and makeup—the vast majority of models receive little or no pay for their labor. On average, models earn about £280 a show in London (about $500), while the average rate for a typical fashion model in New York is about $1,000 a show. Each season, a handful of models is chosen by a few high-end designers such as Calvin Klein, Jil Sander, and Dior to walk "exclusively" in their shows; exclusivity fees can reach six-figure deals.

Finally, editorial models compete for luxury-brand campaigns, the prize of the market. This is the highest echelon of success in the industry, only reached through the risky route of editorial work and only reached by few. Like the catwalk, clients who book models on exclusive fashion or fragrance campaigns pay extra to ensure sole rights to their new

TABLE 2.1   RANGE AND AVERAGES OF WOMEN MODELS' EARNINGS PER JOB

	Women Models		
Job Type	Minimum	Average	Maximum
Fragrance Campaign	$100,000	$100,000	$1,500,000
Luxury-Brand Campaign	40,000	100,000	1,000,000
TV Commercial	15,000	50,000	100,000
Commercial Advertisement	10,000	30,000	50,000
Top-Level Catalog	7,500	10,000	20,000
Average Catalog	2,500	3,000	7,500
Low-Level Catalog	1,000	2,500	5,000
Showroom/Day	400	1,000	2,000
Showroom/Hour	150	250	500
Fashion Show	0	1,000	20,000
Editorial Shoot	0	100	225

model's public exposure. Campaigns can potentially pay several millions of dollars, depending on the exclusivity rights, place, and length of use; exclusive worldwide, multiyear campaigns earn the most money. Among the models I interviewed, women reported astronomical fees upward of six figures, and men reported campaign rates of $50,000 and rumors of exclusive fragrance contracts with houses such as Dior for $100,000.

The consistent money is in the commercial sphere. Catalogs, showrooms, and commercial print advertisements provide the bulk of a model's income. Catalog work is the "bread and butter" of a modeling career, with day rates that begin at $1,000/day for new models, peak at $20,000/day for top models, and average about $3,000/day for most. Catalog retailers often book models continuously for days in a row and weeks at a time, often shooting "on location" in exotic locales, providing the models' transportation and hotel expenses in addition to paying a percentage of the day rate for models' travel days. I interviewed some women who earned up to $10,000 a day on catalog jobs, but most considered $5,000 to be a high catalog rate.

Print advertising includes photo shoots for nonluxury fashion and nonfashion clients such as alcohol, cigarettes, and mass-market, "high-street" retailers. These rates range, on average, from about $5,000 to $50,000.

Metro has another commercial board called the Showroom board, which specializes in informal showroom modeling and fittings. It is consistently high-volume work with small rates, on average about $200/

hour, but for several hours, days, and weeks at a time. Some of the established showroom models have rates up to $2,000 per eight-hour day. This adds up to lucrative sums. In fact, the Showroom board brings in well over half of all earnings to Metro. The highest consecutive earner, year after year, at Metro is a showroom model who has the precise size 8 body needed to fit clothing for a major American retailer. She makes $500/hour and works every day; to my surprise, I learned that she was fifty-two years old at the time.

Showroom models may advance to "house models" at major fashion houses in which they work exclusively for a designer's showroom on fittings and informal presentations, and sometimes they appear in the Fashion Week collections. While still lower in status than the editorial model, a designer's house model is generously paid between $150,000 and $300,000 annually. A house model becomes intimately close to the design team, which can have added benefits. Most notably, I learned that the longtime employer of one house model custom designed for her a wedding dress as a bridal gift.

A separate runway division does not exist at Scene or at most other agencies in London, where clothing production is on a much smaller scale compared to New York.[39] The London equivalent of the showroom is the hair show. Hair modeling is big business in the UK, the home base of multinational salons. Hair shows entail the grooming, trimming, or dyeing of models' hair before a live audience of salon professionals and press, and these shows are routinely held throughout the year and provide a reliably steady flow of income to agencies. London hair shows pay between £300 and £500 a day and can last two to three days at a time during a "hair convention." Hair shows, however, do not offer reliable earnings comparable to showroom work, as models can only do so much to their hair before endangering their look.

A final type of commercial job is the television commercial, which is very lucrative but sporadic. One model in my sample reported earning $20,000 to do a department store commercial for fur coats, and another booked a shampoo commercial that totaled $100,000, plus residuals. Metro and Scene occasionally arranged commercial auditions when invited by commercial clients, but for the most part they arranged for models to work with talent agencies that specialize in TV commercials.

If we break down these earnings by hourly rate, we end up at $12.50/hour for an eight-hour editorial job, $166/hour for the catwalk (an average five-hour, $1,000 runway show), $200/hour for showroom work, $343.75/hour for catalog work (an eight-hour, $2,750 catalog), and $2,287.50/hour for advertising.[40]

Consider, for example, *i-D* magazine in London, one of the most sought-after editorial clients for a model. A day of shooting *i-D* does not pay models. It does not cover taxi fare, nor does it cover the cost of the magazine, about £10, which models must buy to put tear sheets—ripped out pages of a magazine—in their portfolios to showcase their work. In the end, models *lose* money by working for *i-D*. In contrast, a day of catalog work, say, at JCPenney, starts at about $2,500 minimum for a woman, and an hour of showroom or fitting pays $150, with a minimum of four hours, or $600. Agents hedge their bets that the *i-D* shoot will boost a model's profile with symbolic capital such that, in the long run, she will hit the campaign jackpot, and eventually those campaign earnings will far surpass foregone catalog or showroom earnings. But this is a risky bet, bookers admit, and prestige, accountants are quick to remind, doesn't pay the bills.

In addition to making less money, editorial models have less time in the game. With the rapid turnover of "fast fashion," a model's editorial popularity can be as brief as two or three seasons before her bookings "fall off," as one booker put it. Commercial looks can maintain steady work for lengthier periods of up to ten years, such that the lifetime earnings of the showroom or catalog model likely surpass those of a typical editorial model.

But participants are not in editorial fashion for the money alone, and I found, time and time again, that $150 from *Vogue* was seen as more special than $1,500 from Target. The classic sociologist Georg Simmel has claimed that money has an "empty quantitative nature" and only takes on meaning beyond its objective number in big quantities, since large sums fire our imaginations with "fantastic possibilities." Viviana Zelizer has since countered that small sums (and, in fact, all monies) also have distinctive meanings, as in the case of the *franc symbolique*, a token sum of money advocated in civil-law countries to be paid to parents as compensation for the accidental death of a child. Contrary to Simmel's original theory—formed in response to growing fears over market capitalism's dehumanizing potential—small sums can carry enormous symbolic weight.[41] It's not the quantity but the social qualities that a payment invokes.

Paid in Promise and Prestige

When asked why magazine and catwalk clients pay so little, many bookers simply state, "Because they can." Because editorial clients pay models in the form of publicity and symbolic capital, there is no need to attract models with further incentives. High-fashion and avant-garde titles also offer models the chance to shoot with top photographers such as Steven Meisel, Mario Testino, Steven Klein, and Patrick Demarchelier, all recognized giants in fashion whose very names function as additional capital bolstering a model's reputation.

For the most part, models accept this logic, understanding that the eventual economic rewards will make up for their immediately low wages. "Some magazines can change your career," Clare, a twenty-five-year-old model working in London told me, remembering how her rates climbed after she first appeared in British *Vogue*. "It sounds really extreme, but there are definitely some shoots that can take a girl from being just another model to being, you know, the top billing for the shows and campaigns."

While some campaigns can yield astronomical fees, others pay surprisingly little. Some of the most prestige fashion houses notoriously pay the smallest sums of money. Rachel, who specializes in booking New York's editorial work, explained:

> I remember when we were booking a girl at the other agency; we were just in shock that the rate was so low. Like any of these people, like Prada. A girl can go to Prada and work every day for a thousand dollars a day. That's nothing! *Nothing*. So the more prestigious the job, the less the money.

As bookers know, prestige is its own currency. Bookers know that prestigious clients *know* that they don't have to pay their models much, if anything at all, because they provide models with valuable symbolic capital to start up any model's career:

> Armani is not the greatest of campaigns, but whatever, Armani can turn around and build a girl's career or build a guy's career; there's a relationship between the client and the model [that] hopefully mutually benefits both of them, whereas nobody builds their career on the Pepsi ad. (Ivan, New York booker)

Brand-name fashion, as opposed to brand-name soda, adds value to a model's reputation and, hopefully, his or her lifetime earnings. Models also work for pictures and exposure in magazines, though these forms of payment are rife with problems. A client may never send the pictures, as promised, or the pictures might not run in the magazine, as promised.

The promise of future success can—and in fact most likely will—go unfulfilled. The prestige of editorial work, however, has lingering social benefits. Several years after quitting the field, the bookers at Metro still fondly refer to the few high-profile Fashion Week shows I managed to secure.

Will Work for Clothes

"Did you get to keep the clothes?"

That question often is asked when my research comes up in casual conversation. Impeccable style is part of our cultural imagination of fashion models, whose wardrobes, we think, must be filled to the brim with fabulous freebies and gift bags. But offerings of clothes, shoes, and handbags, like any gift, do not come free of charge. These "perks" of modeling are not mere extras on the sidelines of the "real" economic transactions. Perks are in fact central forms of payment and are a recognized transaction media loaded with symbolic meaning. They mark social status for models and clients alike.

Gifts of clothing are most frequently "given" during Fashion Week, where many designers pay in "trade," the term for a system of paying models in clothes. Designers of all levels, from bare budget start-ups to established retail giants, *can* pay in trade, but generally only new designers in the early stages of their careers barter with last season's leftovers when hiring models. These "gifts" of clothing can vary widely. During my two years in the field, I received everything from hand-delivered valuable couture pieces to crumpled T-shirts available for pickup out of an old box. After I walked in one small show for a new label, the designer directed the models to her work studio upstairs where we each were told to pick out two items from an enormous pile of rumpled clothes, belts, and bags spread across a large conference table; seventeen models proceeded to pillage through the pickings in a frenzy. Two weeks after walking in a major celebrity-studded show for one famous designer, I received a bag full of five samples from the designer's past collection, all expensive pieces, but ill-fitting nonetheless. These pieces, usually, became gifts of my own to pass on to friends.

Payment in trade is a haphazard arrangement, quite likely to go unfulfilled. Many designers never send clothes as promised, or they send damaged or unwanted clothing. In one instance, I shot for thirteen hours for the look book of an up-and-coming designer who promised a wonderful embroidered jacket, which was never to be seen, nor was the designer heard from again; her company went bust. On the opposite end, at yet another Fashion Week show, models submitted an online form to request their favorite item from the collection, which arrived two months later, accompanied by a personalized thank-you note.

Such an irregular system of payment would never be permitted from catalog clients. Precisely because they enable greater access to prestige and high-status names in fashion, editorial clients are able to forgo the monetary payments expected of their commercial peers. Thus the perk marks the client's high social status. Clients may or may not come through on promises of barter, because they have already paid models with the opportunity to appear in coveted catwalks and shoots.

Just as perks mark the prestige of editorial clients, they also signify the low status of novice models. Supermodels do not pick T-shirts out of a box for their efforts; such an arrangement is inappropriate to a supermodel's social standing. Top models can command tens of thousands of dollars for each catwalk appearance, while newcomers must accept any payment. This is the logic of barter in showrooms, where new models are hired to fit clothing in exchange for store vouchers. On the eve of a major designer's Fashion Week show, I was hired to work in a showroom to "build looks," which involves trying on the designer outfits that would be worn the following day by highly paid top models. For four hours of work, I received $750 store credit to the designer's shop in SoHo, where I learned that the average cost of a dress is $800 and my store credit would be reported as taxable income. For novice models with lesser social standing, these trades are considered integral parts of their development.

More seemingly peripheral perks are the so-called "freebies" that models enjoy by participating in other service and entertainment industries. As a model I received free haircuts from chic Manhattan salons, deeply discounted gym memberships, and scores of "free" dinners and drinks at nightclubs in New York's Meatpacking District. But, as Marcel Mauss has noted, no gift goes unreciprocated.[42] The gift creates obligations; it enrolls receivers into the obligation to reciprocate. A gift signifies an exchange relationship, and with every free drink, haircut, and gym discount, models pay with their bodily capital by inadvertently advertising these goods and services. Consider how gifts of clothing are good advertising for designers:

So you've modeled for the client because you're attractive in the client's eyes, and the client knows you to be a good vehicle for selling those clothes. And now, you were paid in the clothes, so you put those clothes on and go out in them, so what are you doing? You're selling those clothes all over again! What a great idea for the client! (Leonard, New York staff)

At one casting with an hour wait in line, models received a "free" pair of designer jeans, but with a catch: models had to walk out of the casting wearing them, a clever marketing strategy to have dozens of models in uniform denim at the height of Fashion Week, turning Manhattan's streets into a conspicuous catwalk. There is no such thing as a free lunch for models, who pay for their freebies with their looks.

Hence, editorial models, for all their prestige, are likely to be broke compared to their commercial counterparts. These pricing schemes are naturally difficult to explain to field outsiders. I met one young Eastern European woman whose editorial career was soaring in London, though she had little to show for it. Even worse, she had trouble explaining to her parents why she needed to borrow money, despite her full work schedule. I could sympathize. My own father had recently remarked, upon learning that I received a bag full of sample clothes for walking in a fashion show, "That and a buck will get you a cup of coffee."

Where Does the Money Come From?

I was surprised to find more than a few stylists, photographers, and designers in straits as dire as the editorial models. Photographers and stylists frequently lose money on magazine shoots, paying for studio and equipment rentals and lunch and transportation costs out of pocket. How do high-end clients manage to pay exorbitant campaign jackpots in the face of these losses? Where, in other words, does the money come from?

Following the catwalk from start to finish reveals a surprisingly complex money trail. Fashion Week shows are particularly expensive for designers. In New York, a single-show budget can run into hundreds of thousands of dollars: $50,000 to rent space in Bryant Park Tents (now Lincoln Center), $100,000 on production costs, including hair and makeup, dressers, set design, lighting and music, and another several thousand to pay models.[43] The immediate profits of this costly venture are zero. Catwalk shows do not generate direct returns on investment for most designers, but, rather, they are brand-building strategies for future success. Many catwalk designs are not practical, or wearable, creations,

FIGURE 2.3. The photo pit

nor are they intended to be. Historically, the most dramatic showpieces in the salons never actually went into production, because their purpose was to generate publicity and prestige for the courtier. Today, for instance, the famous Italian design house Dolce & Gabbana reportedly sells about 75 percent of its clothing line well *before* its new designs hit the runway, a common designer practice known as pre-collection sales.[44]

The catwalk is a costly public relations stunt, an exercise in branding. Shows are important image-making mechanisms, which can either gain or lose the attention of international editorial presses, thereby generating sales down the line for the brand's diffusion line products such as perfume and prêt-à-porter labels. The high-end stuff has a relatively small profit margin, but it creates the image that affixes to licensed products such as perfume, sheets, and sunglasses, where the real money is made. As Moore notes, couture collections featuring $10,000 gowns are rarely profitable. A designer's ready-to-wear collection sells at premium prices, with typical net margins of profit between 25 and 50 percent, whereas diffusion line products such as sheets, candles, and even branded bottles of water have much higher net margins.[45] With an eye toward cultivating a brand and carving out an identity in a crowded marketplace, the catwalk becomes a stage to impress field insiders. For example, a new designer in London takes pains to cast the right edgy look for his catwalk in order to impress the "really intelligent" audience, namely, influential magazine editors:

> It is important for like the really intelligent audience, people who work at Vogue and W and, you know, the editors for different magazines, that you're presenting a really modern package and that they see modern potential in you. (Victor, London designer)

With a good presentation and the right models, a show can gain the attention of buyers and presses, giving a brand the media coverage and buzz necessary to underwrite financial backing for distribution and, perhaps eventually, global franchises and product licensing.

The editorial circuit is thus a house of cards, a tenuous set of cultural meanings upon which the whole industry rests. The widely publicized successes of a handful of editorial superstars attracts new talent to enter the contest, seduces current models to work for irregular compensation, and entices clients to bet big against personal financial losses. To make ends meet, editorial models travel to other fashion cities, where they hope to "cash out" on caches of symbolic capital.

On the Heels of Global Circuits of Value

All modeling markets are rooted in cities, which anchor the kinds of unique communities and networks necessary for cultural industries to function. Different cities have different histories and norms, all of which set the tone for how "the look" happens regionally. London and New York are two comparative cases in point.

As a city, London is a famed hub of creativity. As a fashion capital, it is oriented toward cutting-edge design and editorial production, but it has a historic weakness when it comes to the commerce part of the industry. With roots in couture fashion and a traditional focus on serving an elite market segment, British designers tend to have a narrow product range, effectively shutting themselves out of the diffusion product lines where the profit margins are high. Markets tend to be path dependent— once a direction is set, early developments will set the future course along the initial path, which becomes "locked in" by cooperating institutions, actors, and norms.[46] As a result of this path dependence, the London fashion market is a smaller and less corporate enterprise compared to other fashion capitals such as New York and Milan.

In theory, then, London is an edgy model's ideal destination. As Anna's London agent had told her excitedly when she visited from her home base of New York:

"I really think you're gonna work really well here because you're very London, very i-D looking, and blah, blah, blah." You know i-D magazine . . . it's kind of like quirky, edgy, pretty, but still like, editorial basically.

Most clients and bookers paid lip service to this idea of a "London look," a specific edge tailored to London's history of subcultural style, rock and roll, and its urban cool and creativity. They described this look with reference to British post-punk designers. As Billy put it: "That Alexander McQueen, Stella McCartney, Vivienne Westwood. The base of it is rock, like Sex Pistols, updated with classic elements." Others terms that producers used to describe the "London look" or the "English look" were "experimental," "progressive," "gritty," and "offbeat," and for men in particular they deployed descriptions such as "messy hair," "rock star" "drug addict," "very, very, very skinny" and "Peter Doherty."[47] Models with this kind of look come to London to build their portfolios with some of the most prestigious avant-garde magazines in the business, among the most frequently mentioned were i-D, Pop, Dazed and Confused, and the now defunct legendary titles The Face and Arena.

While rich in cultural kudos, there is not as much opportunity to make money in London as in fashion cities such as New York or Milan. London Fashion Week, for example, grew from fifteen catwalk shows and fifty exhibitors in 1994 to forty-nine shows and over two hundred exhibitors in 2007. London Fashion Week brings in approximately £100 million in revenue to the city. New York, however, hosts over two hundred and fifty shows (seventy-five of which are "major" designer labels) and generates an estimated $773 million in revenue, prompting several London bookers to describe their city's fashion industry as "tiny."[48]

The catwalk fees in London are uniquely standardized and cheap. London designers pay minimums set by the Association of Modeling Agents (AMA), a loose network of the "major" agencies in London, which books up to 90 percent of the market share of fashion modeling jobs. As of 2008, the AMA minimum rates were set according to the degree to which designers had established themselves, from £100 charged to new designers showing their collections for the first time to £345 charged to fourth-season (and higher) designers. According to the British Fashion Council, about 35 percent of all designers in London are showing for the first, second, or third time, in keeping with London's reputation as a fashion city with new and emerging talent, not a hub of large global fashion brands like New York.[49] As a result, catwalk models are paid less at London Fashion Week than other fashion capitals' fashion weeks, about $500 (£283) versus $1,000/show in New York and $2,000/show in Milan and Paris. Men and women models report that Milan is the only fashion capital where they expect to earn money in the Fashion Week shows. However, at the time of my research, London was an appealing market for the strength of the pound, which fluctuated from $1.8 to $2.0 per £1 between 2005 and 2006. Even a low-rate catalog job, at £1,000/day, was high by New York standards with the favorable exchange rate.

Whereas London is oriented toward artistic concern for "fashion for fashion's sake," New York is widely understood as the center of the fashion industry. It earned this title when creative designers and their production houses shifted across the Atlantic during World War II, with the resulting devastation of the European fashion industry.[50] With its origins in mass-market sales and ready-to-wear production, New York was always a clothing manufacturing hub. Following the Nazi occupation of Paris, New York rose in the ranks from a "rag trade" industry to a serious creative design capital. The Council of Fashion Designers of America was established in 1960, with the explicit aim of shifting New York's fashion industry image from business to art.

Although the sewing factories once lining Seventh Avenue have in recent years relocated overseas, New York remains the dominant center of the fashion world in terms of design and marketing. American designers were quick and effective to adopt wide diffusion line products and franchise operations. Fashion retail sales in the United States dwarfed those in the UK. Geographer Christopher Moore estimated that the twelve major American international designers totaled about $15 billion in 1998, compared to total sales of $3 billion from UK international designers. American sales were due largely to global fragrance, cosmetic, and household product licenses and international franchises. In Moore's terms, American designers became the "McDonald's of fashion"; they perfected a corporate formula to sell merchandise through franchised licensing agreements.[51]

Perhaps because of this deliberate intertwining of commerce and creativity, few people I interviewed identified a distinct "New York look." It could at best be described as edgy, tempered with commercial appeal, a reference to the traditional sportswear influence in American apparel. After all, American *Vogue*, most clients explained, is far less edgy than its European cousins, such as French *Vogue*. Models come to New York to meet with some of the biggest designers, photographers, magazine editors, and stylists in the world. A few stated bluntly that New York is the place to go for money, but most expressed a more comprehensive goal: they come to New York to "make it," and more than a few expressed the classic Frank Sinatra lyric: "If I can make it there, I'll make it anywhere."

But even in a plentiful market like New York, models are cautious of overstaying their welcome. Claire, a British model for eight years, explained why she travels between New York, London, and Paris: "I stay in London for a while and do some jobs, and then I know I have to move again, because they get bored of me here!" John, a catalog model of three years from Oklahoma, who makes about $50,000 a year, keeps a rotating residence in New York during summer and fall, Miami in the winter, and a stop in Chicago in between. In one year alone, for example, he lived in six different apartments across America.

Models are always on the global go in search of new tear sheets to improve their books and new clients to impress with their existing ones. Models in need of new pictures and editorial prestige head to Paris,[52] London, and Singapore; they head to Munich, Miami, Tokyo, and Hong Kong for a dependable jolt of catalog cash; to LA for television commercials; to Milan for catwalk exposure and catalog money; and so on.

Together with their agents, models calculate the costs and benefits of foregoing one form of earnings over the other. Tokyo is a prime example where commercial interests prevail. It is the only Asian city closely connected to the global high-fashion circuit.[53] Bookers from around the world send their models to Tokyo for purely economic ends; it is ostensibly a fail-safe market for models to "cash out." Unlike magazines in Europe and North America, Japanese magazines pay models lucrative catalog rates, starting between $1,000 and $3,000/day. Year round in Tokyo, with the exception of August and December holidays, there is a constant demand for foreign models in both editorial and commercial work, with a large stock of Japanese fashion designers, product advertisers, magazine editors, runway casting directors, and catalog clients hiring foreign, or *gaijin*, models. Local agencies in Japan attract international models by offering short-term contracts with guaranteed minimum payouts. Contracts range from four to eight weeks for gross amounts between $10,000 and $50,000, depending on the model's status.

The trade-off for high earnings is lost prestige. Japanese tear sheets bestow little symbolic value, and they are not commonly used in model's portfolios in Western fashion capitals, with the exception of *Vogue Nippon*. In fact, one day when I was chatting with the bookers at Metro, I sat beside a graphic designer at work on his computer carefully Photoshopping Japanese Kanji characters out of a magazine page. Removing the Asian characters, or "cleaning it up," as he called it, will make the picture acceptable to put in the model's portfolio. A magazine editorial with Asian script is not suitable to show to New York clients, because it is too closely aligned with the model's profane moneymaking endeavors.

SURVIVAL AT THE AGENCIES

Metro and Scene both identify as "boutique" agencies, which means that they are relatively small and specialize in editorial looks, whereas other "full-service" agencies, such as international powerhouse IMG, manage multiple divisions, such as plus size, television, celebrity and sports stars, children, and older "lifestyle" models. Boutique agencies are tailored to a niche, which is a firm's attempt to differentiate its products from competitors.[54] Agencies fill a niche by specializing in a particular type of look. Though they likely cater to all kinds of clients, agencies promote their niches as a means of self-identification in a crowded market, as one booker noted:

> Metro has a look. Scene has a look; they all do. My agency is expensive commercial. *Sports Illustrated, Victoria's Secret.* Our guys are apple pie and beautiful smiles and wonderful eyes. (Ivan, New York booker)

Agencies are like delicatessens, remarked one stylist, and each offers an exotic "taste of the month." Though both agencies I studied sustain growth via high-volume "bread-and-butter" jobs in showrooms, hair salons, and catalogs with safe and reliable commercial looks, both identify as specialized editorial agencies. Metro promotes itself as a boutique agency with "cutting-edge" looks that push boundaries and break beauty cannons. Scene similarly promotes itself as a "funky" boutique agency that discovers new and "quirky" looks.

Despite Metro's larger size, both agencies were taking in several million dollars a year in total billings (based on the 2006 dollar-pound exchange rate).[55] This gross includes the agency fee of 20 percent charged to models' clients that goes directly into agency proceeds, and agencies take 20 percent of the remaining amount in commission from models' earnings.[56] For example, I booked a two-day catalog shoot that paid $1,600 gross to me, minus Metro's 20 percent model commission of $320, so my net pay was $1,280. Metro then charged an additional 20 percent agency fee to the client, so the total invoice to the client was $1,920, and the agency's net profits totaled $640.

An agency also accrues commission when its models travel to other markets, in which case the original agency claims "mother agency" status. Mother agencies have the responsibility to place their models with agencies in other markets, and in exchange, they earn commissions for work done in those markets. Plane tickets and other travel expenses are typically advanced by the host agency, to be repaid with the models' future earnings. Mother agencies in Europe can take a 10 percent cut from their models' gross rates on jobs booked through other agencies, which amounts to 25 percent of the host agency's proceeds.

Striking a Balance

Like all cultural production organizations, modeling agencies must find a balance between earnings and prestige in order to survive.[57] Editorial jobs are important for generating image and hype, which are vital to secure catalog clients and high-end advertisements such as fragrance and cosmetic campaigns. No agency can afford to have too many purely editorial models, because they sap money and resources that the models are unlikely to repay. This is especially dangerous for smaller agencies such as Metro and Scene, which can't afford to incur too many losses. Nor can an agency have too many commercial models before repelling high-status luxury-brand campaign clients and their cadres of networked photographers and stylists. Commercial jobs pay the bills for models and bookers alike, but they detract from an agency's image of cool. Everyone at an agency is well-versed in the tradeoff between being prestigious and making money. We can visualize the estimated financial implications of Metro's boards in the graph (see Figure 2.4) that follows.[58]

As Metro's earnings curve depicts, about 20 percent of its models are in the red, meaning they are in debt to the agency's investments in their careers. These are editorial models whom bookers are hoping will hit the jackpot, which at Metro recently amounted to a half million dollars for an exclusive fashion campaign.[59] But these "hits" are few and far between, and for every editorial winner at Metro, roughly fifty models have negative accounts due to accumulating career start-up costs such as

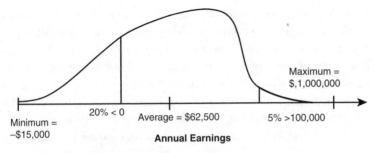

FIGURE 2.4. The distribution of models' annual earnings at Metro

pictures, composite cards, and even plane tickets and visa sponsorship. Heather, a booker in New York, used Devan, a superstar editorial model with cropped hair and tattoos, as an example:

> An editorial model like Devan is a great example of this, because she is not a pretty girl. You could not book her for a L'Oreal hair campaign. You cannot book her for something that the public is going to look at and find her beautiful. It's just not gonna happen. So I'm sure when she first started she was doing nothing but editorial, not making any money at all. So she got very lucky, and she is one of the lucky girls that do such great editorial that it led her to landing big campaigns that then paid the money. (Heather, New York booker)

Most boutique agencies like Scene and Metro have, at any given time, only one or two models like Devan at this level. By the time this book goes to press, they will probably have been dethroned and replaced.

The relatively small size of both Metro and Scene means that the agencies cannot take too many risks on unprofitable models. At Metro, approximately sixty out of its three hundred models have debts ranging from a few hundred dollars to $15,000. Scene has fewer models in the red (figures were not available); it tries to keep models' debts under £2,000 ($3,480), with rare exceptions creeping up to £3,500 (about $6,000).

To recoup its losses, Metro counts on the top 5 percent of its models who bill more than $100,000 annually, such as high-demand fit models, top-billing "money girls" and men, and the occasional editorial superstar. As a manager at Metro explained:

> You just have to make sure that the winners win strongly enough to account for the losers. That's exactly what an agency is doing. I've just said that we've got 20 percent of the agency losing, we're still investing in those people— making them cards, getting them tested, there is money being spent on them. You've gotta recover that money somehow. (Leonard, New York staff)

Metro's profits come from the bulk of models in between these two ends: about 200 men and women whose earnings have a smaller distribution, ranging from a few thousand dollars to $100,000. Their work includes showrooms, fittings, catalogs, and "direct bookings." Agencies handle a considerable amount of direct bookings, which are local one-off jobs arranged for models who are based in other markets. These earnings tend to be small and sporadic compared to the bread and butter of the agencies, the crossover models. Crossover models are the mainstay of any agency. They have a malleable look that can be edgy enough for a magazine and classically relatable for catalog clients. If the editorial model is broke but cool and the purely commercial model is rich and dull, then the majority of models are a mix of both. Lopping off the two extreme ends of earnings are the majority of models who do middle-range magazine editorial shoots and make middle-range earnings. They shoot for commercial fashion magazines such as *Elle* and *Glamour*, book steady catalog work, and score occasional small campaigns. They also work regularly with "magalogue" (from "magazine" and "catalogue") clients such as Saks Fifth Avenue, Neiman Marcus, and Barneys, which produce thick, glossy catalogs shot to resemble magazine editorials. Such a crossover model is likely to earn, on average, $60,000 a year in New York and $87,000 (£50,000) a year in London.[60] Both agencies concentrate on building up a steady stream of revenue from these crossover models.

This business plan of losses, wins, and steady earnings has proved more or less successful for both agencies, yet accountants at both agencies seemed to think that business performance could be better if only the financially draining editorial models could be dropped. This raises the question: Why do agencies even bother with editorial models? The question is integral to understanding how looks accrue value, even as they lose profit.

In Faster Pursuit of Less Money

When I returned to Scene in the fall of 2006, the agency had recently incorporated, with investments from a London billionaire and socialite. I arrived just in time to attend the agency's Fashion Week party, held in the investor's glitzy townhouse in Regent's Park. The party was a lavish scene, with an open bar, gourmet food, and a DJ. One room featured an art installation of light bulbs arranged in an enormous euro sign. Beneath the bright glow of the giant illuminated euro, I started to talk with the agency accountant. He very quickly began to recount horror stories of his days at the office when models come to him asking for their paychecks. Though they may have worked frequently in recent weeks, they are still "in the red," and models often greet this news with hostility, or tears. The accountant's tales of financial misery seemed surreal in the billionaire's shining house.

Later, when I interviewed the accountant, it appeared that most of his trouble was with the editorial models, who seem to be perpetually in the red. If fact, he couldn't understand why bookers like editorial looks at all, as he explained in our interview:

> The bookers, you know, they're more, I don't know what the word is, you know, I can see it from a money point of view and they see it from just a "new model look" coming in, and you know, just enticing the photographers with these new girls. I guess because people just want something new.

Sometimes the accountant encourages the bookers to pursue more catalog models, "but I'm just told to shut up and get in the back." It's not easy being an accountant in an economic world reversed.

Given the greater earnings and steadier, safer salaries of commercial work, it would seem that all modeling agencies would pursue this circuit exclusively, dropping their unprofitable edgy looks. Indeed, accountants at both agencies, frustrated by the "anti-economic" logic of editorial jobs, repeatedly told me that they could not understand why all models don't exclusively work for catalogs. At Metro, one accountant shook his head in dismay when I asked how much money editorial brings into the agency. His colleague, the managing accountant, sighed and said that catalog work isn't "cool enough." The stakes of the editorial bet are annoying to accountants, who are more focused on agency incomes and expenditures. At Metro, accountants divulged their doubts about why they should invest in editorial models, especially the more extreme edgy ones:

> Sometimes I wonder. Sometimes we have girls that are so clearly not, like, going to fit the mold, you know. They have this edgy look that is basically strictly an editorial look. You know this girl's never doing a Calvin Klein ad or anything like that. And a lot of the time you see these girls that have a huge debt, but you know, I digress. I mean it's not my decision. I'm not a scout. I'm the accountant. (Joe, New York staff)

Though they hit the jackpot few and far between, agencies still play the editorial contest because it generates prestige and cultural kudos, which then exalts *all* of the agencies' models. First, editorial stars attract the best new talent to an agency. Such is the case of Scene, which represents a famous top model:

It's such good PR that she's on our books, it was virtually *worth*—but we didn't know when we took her on what she would be like. . . . You know when you've got schoolgirls wanting to be a model and they see, or you know, you've got Naomi Campbell on the books, you know, that might tend them to come here or to an agency with Kate Moss. (James, London staff)

Models generally agree. The more reputable and prestigious the agency, the better their chances are of booking bigger jobs. Models are therefore likely to change agencies at least once during their careers in their search to fit into the right niche at the most prestigious agencies they can find. Likewise, the better an agency's reputation, the better models it will attract. Winning supermodels generate a great public image for their agencies, especially as the public never gets to see the hundreds of models who remain in the red.

When it comes to the catwalk, agents, like the designers they service, don't expect to see profits immediately. Agencies don't put much stock in catwalk revenues. One agent in London explained, "London Fashion Week takes a lot of effort but represents less than 1 percent of my sales."[61] The shows are vital, however, in generating prestige for models and agencies alike, for whom the catwalk is an "endorsement," as one casting director put it. As a former agent and scout told me, the shows are a launching pad into editorial notoriety: "A girl gets noticed if she has a really great show season." Her agency will get noticed too.

While the returns on editorial investments are not calculable, they are generally believed, by models, bookers, and clients alike, to be worth it. This worth is not just premised on future earnings but on symbolic rewards valued in their own right, such as experience and "fun."

Belief, we know, is produced and sustained by the game of fashion, which was itself backed by a flush economy in the boom of expanding finance capital and rising real estate values—a boom gone bust in 2008, sparking the recession that would cripple luxury goods markets around the world. This is, in fact, the epilogue to our story: the slowdown of the modeling market in the wake of the recession, which ultimately drove Scene to close its doors, giving up participation in the game for good before the turn of 2010.

A BAD JOB

"Do you make a lot of money?"

This question tended to come up when discussing my research even more frequently than inquiries about my wardrobe. Unfortunately, the answer is quite a letdown. Average earnings for most models are barely enough to make rent in a city like New York.

Unpredictable, poorly paid, and without benefits, modeling is, in sociological terms, a "bad job," akin to day labor. Across America, models earned a median of about $27,330 in 2009.[62] Among the models I interviewed, incomes ranged from a male model in debt for $1,000 at his agency to a female commercial model who grossed $400,000 in a year. Since their earnings fluctuate wildly from month to month, models had difficulty estimating their annual earnings.

The casting, the most time-consuming undertaking of a model, is unpaid work, though it demands considerable investment. Attending castings is a time-consuming and expensive endeavor in cities like London, where metro travel cards cost £7 a day, or about $12, in addition to the expense of on-the-go food purchases. Models have to be available for last-minute castings and jobs at all times of the day every day unless they "book out" ahead of time to request specific times off. This means models frequently work with little advance notice on weekends and, sometimes late into the night on photo shoots.

Models' paychecks are also subject to substantial deductions in the form of commissions. Models' commissions vary across fashion cities and by international tax codes. Agencies in Paris take a 20 percent commission, plus 40 percent in tax withholding, so models keep 40 percent of their gross earnings. Likewise, non-US models in New York pay 20 percent commission to agencies and are by law subject to 30 percent tax withholding, keeping 50 percent of their gross pay. Metro has its models sign an "Independent Contractor's Agreement," which states that models recognize that they are independent contractors and not employees, and therefore they are responsible for paying taxes on income that Metro reports to the Internal Revenue Service (IRS). I quickly realized that what got reported as one's income, however, was significantly more than what the model actually got to keep. As it turns out, this "bad job" is also an expensive one.

An Expensive Job

Modeling requires extensive and expensive start-up and maintenance costs. These add up quickly. Overall, Scene was more cautious with expenses than Metro, but both agencies charged high fees for a range of things one would never imagine, from daily bike messengers who shuttle books to clients around the city, to the actual costs of the portfolio,

TABLE 2.2 AN EXPENSIVE JOB IN NEW YORK AND LONDON

Monthly Expenses			One-Time Expenses		
	New York	London		New York	London
Housing	$1,200	£960	Test Shoots	$400	£ ~
Pocket Money	400	300	Prints	300	200
Cards	200	100	Agency PR	200	50
Bikes	200	50	Portfolio	80	80
FedEx	100	20	Catwalk Lessons	75	~
Website	15	20	Chauffeur	~	285

housing, comp cards, and "Agency PR," which involved a press kit billed to each model who appeared in it (see Table 2.2).

The cost of housing, the biggest expense for a model, is particularly high among New York agencies when considering the cost per bed. One New York booker explained that his agency owns one downtown two-bedroom apartment with two bunk beds in each room, for a total of eight beds, plus a sofa bed in the living room. At peak times, such as Fashion Week, nine models may live in the apartment at one time, but regardless of how much or how little privacy is available, each model pays the set rate of $250 a week, or $1,000 a month. This means that, when fully occupied, the agency receives $9,000 a month from its tenants, about twice the amount the apartment would be worth on the New York rental market. At Scene in London, bookers arranged for models to stay in private rooms in residential flats owned by associates of the agency for £120 a week, or £480 (about $830) a month.

These expenses are billed against models' prospective earnings and are automatically deducted from their accounts. At Metro, foreign models can be in debt as much as $10,000 before they even begin castings in New York, considering start-up costs such as a visa ($1,800), a flight ($1,000), several test shoots, photograph prints, composite cards, a chauffeured car, and accommodations. This means that models will not see their first paycheck until they book a greater amount than the sum of their debts.[63] A model who leaves an agency with a debt is legally bound by contract to repay it, though accountants explained that they don't bother to pursue these debts, since failed models are an unlikely source from whom to recoup losses. Instead, agencies write off negative accounts as business expenses. However, models' negative accounts will by law transfer to their next agencies should they attempt to model elsewhere, which is unlikely, as agencies are hesitant to represent models with existing negative balances from prior agencies. In other words, once in debt, everywhere in debt. What looks like indentured servitude is a routine part of the independent contractor agreement.

In the end, several models reported earning far less than they expected. This was especially true for male models, whose rates tend to be lower than women's. Although Ethan, a twenty-two-year-old from Nashville, booked dozens of jobs during his six months in New York and lived frugally on the floor of a friend's Harlem apartment ($225 a month), he still ended up leaving his agency with a debt of $1,000. He explained:

> Men's modeling is really like a racket, how it works. . . . Like I do catering to make money, and there are other models who have big billboards, huge campaigns, making $20,000 a shoot. They still don't have enough money to live, because they owe so much back money that it's all gone. So they still end up catering with me. I cater with people who are in, like, billboards and have campaigns and stuff like that.

The catwalk is a case of economic hardship. For all their prestige, Fashion Week shows can be costly ventures for the hundreds of unknown faces competing for a break, especially in London, where each show pays, on average, about £280 (less than $500). The estimated costs of participation for a foreign model are considerably high, at about $3,200 (or £1,600, including a £600 flight, £400 visa, £500 weekly living expense, and £100 show composite card). At busy times, Scene arranges a chauffeured car service to help models get through their many castings. In my own experience, the charge for one day of this service was £285 (about $500), which took the entire earnings from two shows to repay.[64]

Getting Paid (or Not)

Like gifts of clothing, cash payments are slow to come, and they might not come at all. Designers and advertisers are risky liabilities to agencies because they too face a turbulent market. Demand for fashions can change quickly, investors may suddenly pull financial backing, and fashion labels, boutiques, and advertising start-ups can, and frequently do, go bust without notice. Also common are clients who are in good financial standing but who have bad habits when it comes to paying on time, or at all. At Scene, clients are legally obligated to pay invoices within thirty days of using one of their models. Within sixty days, if the client has not paid, Scene's accountants engage in the tedious task of "debt chasing," which involves multiple phone calls, e-mails, and persistent follow-up on errant clients, all the while trying to placate irate models and managers who are waiting to get paid. "You'll be on it, chasing someone, and it's a nightmare, and finally you get paid," said James, an accountant. "But there's another one [coming] up, so you got to go do it again." Added to this, James notes, is "the pressure of the models, screaming, 'Where's my money!' I've got [the owner] saying, 'Why isn't the money in? We've got bills to pay!' "

After chasing debts to no avail, both agencies can resort to suing delinquent clients, though this is rare, since lawyer fees are usually greater than the sums of money owed. In New York, some of the biggest magazine publishers are known for the worst payment records, but, given the relatively small amounts of money at stake, agencies rarely chase debt with magazine clients.

Some agencies have a policy of advancing earnings to models within one week of the booking. However, if a client fails to pay within ninety days, then the agency will rescind the money from the model's account until paid in full by the client. Hence, the agency pays its models for doing a job, but if a client reneges on the agency, then the model must return the funds. In an effort to reduce its own risks posed by delinquent clients, Scene pays models only after receiving the client's payment. Scene does offer to advance owed monies to models at a rate of 5 percent, and, like a bank, the money is recoupable. In other words, if the client doesn't pay up, then the model takes the loss, not the agency.

Given high expenses and client delinquency, a model's money can be slow to arrive. Such was my case: I signed my contract with Metro at the start of the year in the mid-2000s and began working on editorials, shows, and small catalog jobs by the end of the month. I did not get my first check, for $181.06, until mid-April (prior to this I received voided checks clipped onto a page-long list of expenses).[65] Earning money within three months of working was, an accountant told me, a good turnaround and quicker than most models got paid.

By the end of my first year in the field in New York, the year I gave nearly every hour of free time to my bookers, I calculated my total earnings and losses. I grossed $18,660, and out of that amount paid $3,732 in commissions to the agency and $3,608 in expenses. My take-home pay for the year was $11,318—about half of the yearly stipend I received as a graduate student.[66]

SOCIAL ALCHEMY

With an anti-economic logic, the pursuit of editorial stardom is an exercise in delayed gratification. But patience is a learned virtue, one the likes of which JD, our Manchester lad, had yet to acquire at the age of twenty. It takes socialization into the field to recognize the complex types of non-monetary values, such as "free" pictures, clothes, and name affiliation to top models, designers, and magazines.

Today, JD has the hang of the editorial and commercial circuits. In fact, he has completely reversed his attitude toward money. When asked if he would shoot an editorial in *Dazed and Confused*, he nearly leapt out of his seat and said:

> *Ohmygod* yes! Basically, like a rate on *Dazed and Confused* is probably nothing, but I like fashion. I like advertising, and I would love to be in a picture . . . just to be part of it. Sometimes I open some people's books who just do editorials, and they're like, "Yeah I got no money, I got nothing." But at the end of the day, I wish I was in that masterpiece . . . You're a lucky bastard!

Unlike the rational actor we expect to see in markets, even in Pierre Bourdieu's analysis of capital—symbolic, cultural, and social capitals are, after all, means to secure ultimate economic ends—JD has become a fool for symbolic rewards. He is now a devotee of fashion for fashion's sake. The prestige is no perk. It has become a source of personal pride. This, JD explains, is the only reason he continues to model: for the chance to be a part of something magical.

But the magic, we will see, is an illusion created by the producers' collective misrecognition of their playing a prestige game. Belief in the editorial game, the *illusio*, keeps the producer committed to the production of the "edgy" look, an ambiguous achievement that when at last it happens, it appears as if by magic! The miraculous "look" that leaps up to the editorial jackpot is no supernatural talent. It is a product of organized and orchestrating producers: models, bookers, and clients struggling among themselves and with each other. In this struggle, the value of the look and the *belief* in that value are continuously generated. Like all miracles, the look is born out of social alchemy.

Alas, JD's window of opportunity to be a part of this alchemy has closed. His time to take an interest in economic disinterestedness is over, and now he looks for a steady office job in advertising, the very industry that has discarded him. Timing, producers frequently told me, is everything in the modeling market. This is true for the model and for all the pieces of the larger puzzle in the production of the look—the timing of bookers' and clients' sales and purchases; the timing of fashion trends and their resonance with cultural tides; and the timing of the model's arrival upon and assimilation into the industry. Models must first get a handle on what it means to work in a field where timing and chance haphazardly determine careers.

CHAPTER 3

Becoming a Look

THE HEELS

Two weeks after signing the contract with Metro Model Management, I received an e-mail on a Saturday afternoon from Heather, an encouraging and very friendly booker. It read:

> Hi sweetie! . . . You have a bunch more castings on Monday. You have been requested to see Michael Stevens. That is SO HUGE!!!! If you don't know, he is the most important photographer that can turn you into a huge star in an instant. . . . So you should definitely come to the agency first thing before you go anywhere.
> xo, Heather

Prior to this, all I could think for the past several days was that I had signed up for this research at the wrong time, Fashion Week. Already in my second week of go-sees and castings, I had crisscrossed the city to meet with dozens of clients, posed for two test shoots and one catalog, and skipped two graduate seminars. Next week was Fashion Week, I was on option for several shows, and I faced a solid lineup of more back-to-back castings that promised waiting in long lines in SoHo, Chelsea, Midtown, and back again. I was exhausted. It looked like my graduate studies were headed for disaster, and I was already thinking up new research projects.

But then I received this e-mail and felt the familiar jolt of excitement that would keep me in the field for the next two and half years, that promise of possibility that pushed me to arrive early at the agency on Monday morning.

So there I was, sitting in the lobby of Metro's sleek Manhattan office, watching several of the bookers trickle in for a new day's work. They are an ordinary-looking bunch: thirty-something, average bodies in jeans and slacks and sneakers. They greeted me and asked how I was doing, although at this point I only knew a few of their names. When Heather arrived, she kissed me on the cheek, said "Good morning, love!," and sat down next to me cheerfully.

"You're going to see Michael Stevens today!" she announced. "You know who he is, right?" she asked, grinning. She was referring to our talk from last week, when I didn't know the name of another star photographer, nor could I pronounce Miu Miu ("me-you, me-you").

But today I did know whom I was going to see. Anyone with minimal exposure to pop culture knew the name Michael Stevens. He was legendary, one of the most powerful photographers in fashion. Heather prepped me on how to handle this appointment.

"Just a little tip about who you're going to see today," she started. "The woman you're going to see is Laurie. She's a very *strong* woman. What she'll do is usually sit at the reception desk, so when you come in to say, 'I'm here for Laurie,' she'll be the one you'll say that to, and she'll watch you to see what you're like. Sometimes. Not all the time, but usually. So don't like, sit there and say anything bad on the phone, or like pick your teeth or anything—not that you would anyway, but just so you know, be aware. Because you can't get to him without her liking you."

With this she patted my thigh and left me sitting again by myself in the lobby, feeling deflated. I had envisioned chatting with the great Michael Stevens; maybe I could ask him for an interview. Maybe he would turn me into a "huge star" instantaneously. In any case, it was unlikely that meeting with his assistant, the sharp-eyed Laurie, would be very exciting.

My booker Ronnie came in, kissing me on the cheek and handing me a list of eight appointments for the day. Ronnie is a hyper, small British man who wears worn T-shirts and jeans, and he is always really *nice*, even when he says unkind words.

This morning he was his usual perky self. We went over the list of appointments, and he told me I looked good, and almost as an afterthought, he added, "Oh, and you're eighteen. So when were you born, like 1980 . . . 5? Okay, 1985." Ronnie dashed back to his desk, but I paused in the lobby before collecting my coat. In our five-second exchange, I had just lost five years. As a student of feminist theory, I recognize the symbolic power that women accrue with age and the patriarchal implications of my new birth date. But now is not the time for the feminist stuff, I told myself. After all, I'm going to meet Michael Stevens. Or, more accurately, Michael Stevens's assistant.

Then I heard my named being called from the bookers' table. I ducked my head around the corner of the lobby to see Ronnie and four other bookers seated at the long conference table. It seemed as if they had been talking about me; all heads were turned to me. "Ash, come closer," Ronnie said. "Let us have a look at you."

All eyes in the office landed on me. Don, the head booker, slowly crossing his arms, looked me up and down and said, "What shoes are you in?"

All eyes landed on my feet. "I'm just in these, err, sneakers," I said, shuffling my black Adidas walking shoes as though I could hide one behind the other.

"We need to get her in heels," said Don, looking around as the others nodded in agreement. He called out to Bre, a booker with the Showroom board, seated at the other end of the room: "Do you have a pair of heels Ashley can borrow to see Michael Stevens?"

Bre sighed. She took the three-inch-heel boots off of her feet and slipped on a pair of old sneakers—"Good thing today's workout day"—and told me to bring the boots back before the end of the day. "And watch out for the right heel," she said. "It's a bit wobbly."

As I changed, another booker commented that when going to see Michael Stevens, "You have to be *dressed*." Now clad in heels, standing before the board, there was a moment's pause to study the new outfit.

"Now that's rock and roll," said Don.

"And it's great on her legs," said Ronnie.

Standing three inches taller, I slowly backed away from the bookers' table, receiving final good luck wishes and one last tip from Don: "And how old are you?" he asked.

"Eighteen."

"Very good," he nodded, smiling, and I teetered out of the agency.

Not more than ten steps outside, the right heel on Bre's boot snapped from the sole. It dangled wildly as I hopped across the street and into a shoe store.

. . .

I spent my teenage years tearing Michael Stevens's fashion images out of *Vogue* magazine—glamorous images of Kate and Linda wearing

Chanel and Gucci—and taping them up on my bedroom walls. Never did I imagine that before they became flawless muses of legendary photographers, they might have first been hobbling on borrowed high heels toward a casting with assistants scrutinizing them. This is precisely how fashion and the glamour industries work. If consumers are to be enticed to purchase fashion and beauty products, then it is imperative that they do not see the kind of work that goes into the production of fashion and beauty images. Those picture-perfect images of models once on my bedroom walls obscure the work—emotional and physical—and the craft and the precariousness that I would come to know well.

My experience of (almost) going to meet a superstar photographer was instructive with many lessons: be *dressed*; defer to your bookers; expect to be watched; embody rock and roll; be young; be your best self. Such lessons are part of the repertoire of bodily and emotional habits that models pick up and incorporate into their work routines. Some lessons are harder to learn than others. Some are pleasurable, others quite painful. The look is a social status that models work hard to achieve, though ultimately they are doomed to failure: no model can ever be the "right" look forever. How, then, in the course of this brief career, do people become "looks"?

THE LABOR OF BEING AESTHETIC

Sociologists can learn much by studying models' work. Models are paradigmatic of a shift in labor markets toward both freelance employment forms and the aestheticization of labor. "Aesthetic labor" characterizes the expanding "style labor markets" of the interactive service sector, including retail, restaurants and bars, tourism, and entertainment. In these industries, employees are recruited and trained to project both pleasant personas and handsome appearances.[1]

Since Arlie Hochschild's (1983) groundbreaking study of flight attendants in the 1980s, sociologists have theorized at length about the place of "personality" and the importance of emotions in the service economy. Aesthetic labor scholars, largely working out of the research program of sociologists in the UK, have since shifted the emphasis from emotions to embodiment, theorizing the "body work" that comes with feeling work. Companies today want their employees not only to act the part but to look it too. The modern business organization demands not only emotional management but also corporeal control. This *aes-*

thetic labor demands transformation of the "whole person" for corporate ends.

The concept of aesthetic labor is probably familiar, at least tacitly, to most of us—everyone knows the value of good looks. A sizable literature in social psychology, sociology, and economics has documented the advantages of being perceived as attractive in terms of employment, pay, and life outcomes.[2] The importance of being aesthetic on the job has been well documented for quite some time. C. Wright Mills, in his classic 1951 book *White Collar: The American Middle Classes*, details the sales floor successes of "the charmer," that clever shopgirl who plays up her "streamlined torso" and "brilliant smile" to increase her commission.

While laboring to be aesthetic is not new, what *is* new, according to labor scholars, is the explicit management, recruitment, and training of workers' appearances in an expanding range of jobs. Whether through the proliferation of job advertisements that seek candidates who have a "smart look," or by street scouting practices that recruit young men and women to work at retail chains such as Abercrombie & Fitch, landing a job in the new economy is a matter of both "looking good and sounding right." And not just any good looks will do. Increasingly, companies are seeking employees who embody the *right* look. You may have noticed, for instance, that salespeople at The Gap look like they belong in The Gap; they have a special "Gap-ness" about them. This is hardly coincidence. By screening and molding a particular set of aesthetics and attitudes of their employees, management strives for the right "fit" between corporate brand identity and employee identity. Companies use their employees as "material signifiers" and "brand enhancers," also known as "walking billboards," to exude brands and lifestyles, literally putting their best faces forward in the marketplace through labor on the retail floor. The worker, in turn, becomes an integral part of the product. If some workers are hired because they "look right," then this means, inevitably, that others are deemed to look wrong. Cases of lookism, explicit employment discrimination based on appearance, are on the rise, rewriting protected categories of race, age, and class in the code of aesthetics.[3]

The rise of these soft social and aesthetic skills comes on the heels of a broader shift in the organization of work. The aestheticization of labor is part of the post-Fordist transition from a manufacturing base to information and knowledge-intensive industries. In a post-Fordist economy, not only should labor look good, it should feel good too.

Increasingly, new discourses are stressing that work should be pleasurable and fun, full of choice, self-affirmation, and flexibility, a positive part of self-identity, in addition to an economic necessity.[4] To return to The Gap, folding sweaters offers the feeling of being special. It's flattering to be able to embody The Gap image.

What work in this newly aestheticized economy does *not* offer, however, is security. The charmer in Mills's *White Collar* is now likely to have the freelance, per-project job structure that Andrew Ross documents among information technology (IT) workers in his 2003 book *No Collar: The Humane Workplace and Its Hidden Costs*. As once relatively stable positions in the services and even in the professions are now being contracted out to freelancers, these workers increasingly face a volatile job market marked by nonstandard and interrupted employment. Like many other cultural production workers, modeling is contract based; it is project-based employment in a succession of one-time collaborative jobs.[5] Such labor vulnerability has traditionally been gendered. In fact, the vast majority of modeling careers resemble women's historically contingent relationship to the labor market, as goods themselves exchanged in marriage, as dependent housewives, and as temps, part-time workers, and stopgaps in labor shortages. Yet in the face of feminized and disempowering positions, the ethos of the freelance cultural producer is to embrace risk, revere chance, and, with ever more attention, promote and manage one's own career opportunities and hazards. Freelancers work for themselves, under their own self-management. Workers in such precarious positions tend to be risk-embracing rather than risk-averse, prompting sociologists to call them "entrepreneurial labor."[6]

Freelancing can be wonderfully liberating. For those who do not want to work full time, for instance, it provides the time to pursue other activities. It can also be an exploitative working relationship, diverting market risks away from companies and onto workers' unprotected shoulders. Not all casual workers suffer as a result of their contractor status; after all, high-priced freelancers, such as programmers and other IT workers in the computer business, enjoy quite favorable effort-reward ratios. Given the tightness of the labor market, models face a greater degree of unpredictability and rejection than most freelancers. As independent contractors, models work without managerial oversight and must learn the ropes and navigate an industry largely on their own. As freelance aesthetic labor, modeling poses new challenges to individuals who manage their bodies and personalities while coping with uncertainty—and models do this largely on their own.

These two trends, aesthetic labor and entrepreneurial labor, are on the rise, but sociologists have yet to link them. Under freelance conditions, aesthetic labor goes "freestyle," and this raises the question: How do workers both "look good" and "sound right" when there are no rules or definitions to do so?

While sociologists have noted managements' shifting attention toward worker corporeality, we still know very little about how aesthetic labor is accomplished without management supervision—the exceptions being Deborah Dean's interview study of female actors and Joanne Entwistle and Elizabeth Wissinger's interview study of fashion models.[7] These studies argue that in the absence of top-down regulation and grooming guidelines, aesthetic labor entails the ongoing production of the body and the self, demanding that workers are "always on" and unable to walk away from their product—which is the entire self. It remains unclear, however, just *how* employees come to embody something so unstable as "looking good and sounding right" on their own.

Here we have an opportunity to expand an analysis of labor in the new economy by asking this question: How does aesthetic labor get accomplished in the absence of corporate oversight? For workers in the new cultural economy, professional success hinges on control of the body and the careful crafting of an imagined ideal personality. But for the model, above all, it hinges on the acceptance of chance.

CHANCE

The first time it happened to Clare was when she was fifteen years old. Having just returned from a family vacation and waiting for her luggage at Heathrow Airport, a young man approached her, gave her flattering compliments, and offered to represent her as a model. It was a bit of a shock to the self-described "punk," and to her whole family:

> And I thought it was really funny because I had braces, I looked horrendous because I was just on a flight. Both of my sisters looked much better than me. I think my parents were really like, "Are you sure? How about these other two?"

Most models liken their adolescent selves to ugly ducklings. They complain of being teased and taunted during their childhood years because of their gawky and unattractive physiques. Such stories of miserable physical transformations seem more plausible for some models than others, but in Clare's case, there was no doubt. She has a thin pale face with a slight overbite, a long nose, and ghostly, deep-set eyes, framed by wispy blonde eyebrows. Her long orange hair parts down the middle and drapes down her back, covering an entire third of her lanky body. She is, in her own estimation, "funny looking."

So she brushed the scout off at first, but more scouting incidences started happening. In clubs, while shopping, and even just walking down the street in London, scouts stopped Clare, told her she had a "great look," and implored her to work with their agencies. So finally she did.

Like dozens of the models I met and interviewed, Clare did not choose modeling; it chose her. Of the forty models in this study, only six actively sought out a career by approaching agents, while the majority entered the field through scouts. In fact, very rarely does a model need to invest her own money out of pocket to enter the market. Therefore, the usual suspect of class has a weak hold over who can and who can't enter this labor market. Among the forty men and women I interviewed, the majority came from middle-class households, with five from working-class backgrounds, and six from upper-middle-class and higher backgrounds (see Table 3.1). The financial barriers for working-class men and women to model are minimal; anyone can be scouted, and no one needs expensive credentials or training.[8] Young people from supportive middle-class families can more likely afford to pursue their luck in the modeling market, but given the intensity of international scouting in the Global South, models are a diverse labor force in terms of their class backgrounds.

Herein lies one of the distinctive properties of modeling work: entry into and success in the field are beyond workers' control. Once they are admitted to sell their looks on the market, by invitation or through personal will, or both, they concede a portion of their careers into the hands of fate—variously stated as luck, karma, timing, and "the universe." One woman used the cultural production literature cliché of a "crap game" to describe her career trajectory, echoing the words of a successful Hollywood screenwriter.[9] Models face unpredictability from several sources: at castings, with options for jobs, and in everyday interactions with their bookers. Theirs is a line of work that exemplifies freedom of the new economy, with all of the entrapments of both body and mind that necessitate bearing rejection and risk onto individual shoulders.

TABLE 3.I OVERVIEW OF MODEL SAMPLE

New York

Women	Age	Years Modeling	Ethnicity and Origins	Sexuality	SES Origins	Years of Education	Income ($)
Alia	22	4	Black, Los Angeles	Straight	Middle	6	400,000
Anna	25	4	White, Russia	Straight, Divorced	Middle	4	200,000
Daniella	23	8	White, Brisbane, Australia	Straight, Mother	Middle	4	35,000
Dawn	25	9	Asian, Florida	Straight	Working	4	100,000
Jen	23	4	Asian, New York City	Lesbian	Working	4	35,000
Liz	21	4	White, New Jersey	Bisexual	Middle-Upper	5	25,000
Lydia	32	11	White, Michigan	Straight, Married	Middle	6	200,000
Marie	28	11	Latina, Chile	Straight, Married	Middle-Upper	8	125,000
Michelle	20	5	White, Texas	Straight	Upper	5	5,000
Trish	23	5	White, Arizona	Straight	Working	5	15,000

Men

Andre	22	4	White, New Jersey	Straight	Middle	4	45,000
Cooper	28	3	White, Florida	Straight	Middle	8	30,000
Ethan	22	1	White, Tennessee	Straight	Middle	8	-1,000
Joey	19	1	White, Boston	Straight	Middle	3	0
John	21	3	White, Oklahoma	Straight	Middle	5	50,000
Michel	44	17	White, rural France	Straight, Married	Working	3	70,000
Milo	26	5	White, Chicago	Gay	Middle	8	55,000
Noah	21	2	White, New Jersey	Straight	Working	5	<1,000
Parker	24	7	White, Wisconsin	Straight	Middle	8	25,000
Ryan	25	4	White, Michigan	Straight	Middle	8	30,000

TABLE 3.1 (continued)

London

Women	Age	Years Modeling	Ethnicity and Origins	Sexuality Status	SES Origins	Years of Education	Income ($)
Addison	19	3	White, London	Straight	Middle	4	10,000
Avery	22	4	White, Manchester	Straight	Working	8	2,000
Clare	24	8	White, London	Straight	Middle	5	100,000
Emma	19	3	White, Germany	Straight	Working	4	30,000
Eva	22	3	White, Utah	Straight	Middle	5	20,000
Kiera	22	3	White, Toronto	Straight	Upper-Middle	4	60,000
Lucy	21	1	White, Paris	Straight	Middle	5	4,000
Mia	28	1	White, New York City	Straight, Divorced	Working	5	4,000
Sasha	22	7	White, East Russia	Straight	Working	5	100,000
Sofia	21	3	Black, Jamaica	Straight	Working	8	40,000

Men

	Age	Years Modeling	Ethnicity and Origins	Sexuality Status	SES Origins	Years of Education	Income ($)
Ben	29	10	White, London	Straight	Upper Middle	4	200,000
Brody	28	5	White, London	Straight, Divorced	Working	4	60,000
Edward	22	2	White, London	Straight	Middle	8	20,000
Ian	25	3	White, France	Straight	Middle	8	36,000
Jack	22	7	White, Manchester	Straight	Upper Middle	8	2,000
JD	22	2	Arabic, Manchester	Straight	Working	8	48,000
Lucas	26	8	White, London	Straight	Middle	10	20,000
Oliver	25	2	White, London	Straight	Middle	8	10,000
Owen	26	7	White, East London	Straight	Working	4	10,000
Preston	21	3	White, Bristol, England	Straight	Middle	8	110,000

At the Casting, You're All Beautiful

In the spring of 2004, three months into the field, I attended a casting in an uptown designer boutique for a fashion show. When eight models arrived in the shop, a woman introduced herself as the show's producer and pulled us to the side. Standing in a semicircle and holding our portfolios, we listened to her deliberate. She did not look through our portfolios; instead, she looked us over, slowly, with care. "This is the hardest part of my job," she said, as she explained that she would have to "choose" two among us for an upcoming fashion show. "You're all beautiful!" As she spoke, an assistant, an older gentleman, took one each of our composite cards, and he scanned our bodies intensely, even craning his neck to see some of our backsides. He shuffled the cards in his hands, ordering them in a way we could not see.

After the casting, I walked with two models to the subway, and they laughed about how the casting felt "so weird." One model exclaimed, "That guy was looking, I was like, covering my ass!" She gestured with her hand covering her behind. Her friend laughed and added, "We all were. . . . And that guy was shuffling the cards. I was like, 'Am I on top or bottom?' "

Such a casting arrangement is not "weird" in the sense of being unusual. Castings and go-sees are part of a lengthy process of matching models to jobs. Castings typically involve models lined up against each other; models are chosen for employment based on criteria unknown to them. Models sometimes do not know what the casting is for, who will make the final hiring decision, or on what criteria they will be chosen or dismissed for the job.

The casting itself is a predictable procedure. There is a greeting with a handshake, some chitchat, and a review of the model's portfolio. Then the client glances over the model's face and body, perhaps asking to take her picture (once habitually with a Polaroid camera, now with the digital kind). The client then asks the model to try on a sample outfit and watches her walk the length of the room and back. The procedure closes with a pleasant valediction and a "Thank-you for coming."

So while not unusual in modeling work, such a casting arrangement is "weird" in the sense that it feels strange, even repeatedly, because it violates tacit social norms of politeness. For instance, it is rude to stare at women's behinds, or to flatly dismiss job candidates to their faces. Castings are, in Goffman's terms, problematic encounters.[10] Standing before clients for inspection, models must suspend such ordinary social norms and accept, at least for the duration of the casting, that they are display objects for sale in a silent auction. Clients, for their part, generally make their assessments with as much tact as possible, careful not to identify the losers from the winners or their logic in choosing one model over another.

This is one of the hardest parts of the model's job—walking out of a casting and being unable to assess how the meeting with the client went. Certainly, there are recognizable signs of the client's interest and disinterest, as models explained. If "they like you," clients are likely to spend time with you. They will carefully look through your portfolio, they will laugh with you, they will ask you questions about your life, your interests, and perhaps your future availability. They will compliment you and your pictures; they will smile. In short, they recognize and validate the model's presence. If they do not like you, they may exude the obvious signs: flipping through your portfolio quickly, or not at all, not making eye contact, and perhaps even looking at *other* models in the room (this happens with surprising frequency).

Such signs, however, are just that, mere signals that suggest but do not solidify. I have walked out of many castings with a huge smile on my face thinking, "I nailed that one!" At a casting for a T-shirt designer, the client said to me, "You're perfect." He even introduced me to the company's owner, and then both of them showered me with praise. But I never got the job, never again heard anything about it. Clare explained the letdown of the positive casting experience that leads to nothing:

> That's one of the biggest enigmas of the biz, if you can tell or not if they like you. Because the thing is, sometimes you can do a casting, and they're so positive, and they're like "Yeah yeah, you're great, we'll see you tomorrow!" They're *that* definite. You walk out, you call your agency, and they haven't even optioned you, let alone booked you. You're like, why did you bullshit me?!

Alternately, a casting may ruin your day but still land you the job:

> But then I've gone to castings where I just went "Oh what a fucking load of shit! I just won't even *think* about that one ever again." Then I get the job. So I think you could define it like a funny fish. You really don't know, like, you just don't know, what it is about castings. (Jack, 22, London)

The "weird" mystery of a casting assessment is the model's first encounter with precariousness to get work. It is the precursor to a series of career gambles.

Options Are Like Air

If the casting is the first tenuous step, then the option is the next blind leap toward securing work. After a casting, the client calls bookers to place models on hold, on "option," for upcoming jobs. They option models in rank order of interest, from first (strong) to third and even fourth (weak) option. While a strong option is an indicator of the client's interest, it is, like the pleasantries at the casting, still just an indicator. As Anna, a twenty-five-year-old Russian émigré put it, "Options are like air. They come off."

Options may appear suddenly and for reasons unknown. In London, a model named Oliver one morning received the news from New York that he was on option for the Dolce & Gabbana campaign. "I was like, just going about my daily activities, you know, waking up, going to the loo in the morning, everything. And meanwhile [as] I was doing those things, there was like Steven Klein or whoever picking out my photo off a website!" To Oliver this meant that somewhere across the Atlantic important decisions were being made that could change his life, and all without his knowledge.

But just as suddenly as they appear, options can be dropped for no reason, often at the very last minute. Edward, a twenty-two-year-old Londoner, learned this the hard way early in his career. Within weeks of signing with a select agency, he was optioned by one of Europe's most powerful casting directors for a prominent Milan show:

> My booker's like, we definitely got that, because [that casting director] really likes you. And then they cancelled everyone else's options and left mine up until ten o'clock at night, and then they cancelled my options. I hate [that casting director]. You can put that on tape!

The opposite is also true; models can be called on to attend bookings at only a moment's notice. The result is a schedule that is not of the model's own making, nor understanding. Most models I spoke with tried not to dwell on their options, and a few preferred not to know them at all. Explained Daniella, age twenty-three, in New York, "I would rather not get my hopes up for something that's not cemented."

Try as models might to ignore them, options leave behind an anxiety-producing trail; in fact, they are written at the top of a model's daily schedule and often include gut-wrenching details, such as the name of a famous photographer shooting the job that could have been theirs, or perhaps a lucrative sum that will be going to someone else. For instance, on my schedule with a list of unpaid castings for the day, the following was written at the top of the sheet:

CANCELLED: Option 1: Job: HOTEL ADVERTISING
TRAVEL LA, SHOOT LA, TRAVEL BACK TO NY
$3,750+20% P/DAY×2 DAYS – NEW YORK
$3,750+20% P/DAY×1 DAY – LA
$250 P/DAY TRAVEL (LA)×2 DAYS
TOTAL FOR JOB: $14,200+20%

When questioning why I did not book a job, or why an option "fell off," the bookers could rarely produce an answer. During my first Fashion Week, before I was broken of the habit of requesting feedback, I asked Don, a booker, why a major designer had cancelled my option. He answered sweetly, "Just that you're a little fresh, they wanted more seasoned girls for the show." Don did not offer advice for how to overcome the problem of being too "fresh" for future work, and after a few weeks I gave up asking.

Precariousness with Bookers

As self-employed workers, models are freelancers. They work for themselves, and in contractual terms, bookers technically work for models and receive commission for arranging jobs that models secure on their own. This working relationship is more complicated than it might appear, however, because it *feels* quite different than what it formally is. It feels like models are at their bookers' tenuous mercy.

Models need their agents to be their "biggest fans," said Clare, "or else you're not gonna get anywhere." She explained:

> Their attitude about you, their enthusiasm about you, is a huge key to making it big, or at least making regular great jobs. . . . They need to be the one who calls up clients and says you have to see this girl, or, like "Since the last time you booked this girl, she looks even better."

Almost every model explained to me the importance of "getting on" with his or her booker. Agents are gatekeepers who restrict the flow of models to castings and, indeed, to entire segments of the fashion field. A booker's perception is everything. How an agent sees a model determines her range of possible career outcomes. As Addison, an eighteen-year-old woman from London, said, bookers are "really, really important. If you've got a good relationship with them, they'll put you in for jobs [she snapped her fingers], and you're set."

Though bookers play a key role in establishing their models' careers, they distance themselves from such responsibility. In their everyday talk with models in the agencies, bookers frame their models' success in purely individualized terms. On several occasions I received tips from bookers on the specific importance of a casting or job, but at most these are accompanied with rather vague suggestions for how to secure them.

Failure has its consequences. Models can be "dropped" by their agencies with no warning. This happened to sixteen-year-old Louisa, who quit the tenth grade to model, to "see how it goes." Not having seen her in a few weeks, I asked Heather, on staff at Metro, how Louisa was doing. Heather sighed and said to me, "We dropped her." Heather went on to explain that Louisa did not get a very "strong" response from the clients. But she could not tell me why; she herself did not know. When asked about the typical chances a model has of booking jobs from her castings, several bookers replied, "It depends."

Even more insidious is the slow fade of bookers' excitement. Bookers' enthusiasm blows up or winds down according to their clients' fickle tastes. Models' egos are similarly inflated and deflated, and just as unexpectedly. Models explained that at the start of their careers, bookers would exude a kind of enthusiasm; however, this does not, indeed, cannot, last forever. Addison, a young woman modeling in London, began her career at a top agency amid much fanfare: "Well, yeah, you know, it's always, 'Wow, you're gonna be *amazing*! We're so excited, you're great!'" But after two years of steady work and rejection, she had no more illusions of being the "It Girl." She explained, "Then it, like, doesn't actually materialize." It's not Addison's fault—it's just that her bookers simply cannot give every model their fullest attention, nor can they sustain excitement about each model each day. By Addison's estimate, bookers' enthusiasm wanes within six months, at which point new models have arrived to the tune of new buzz.

A constant stream of new faces enters an agency, while old ones are filtered out: twenty-five in and out at Metro and ten in and out at Scene each year. A sense of substitutability is inescapable, because models are in fact substitutable. Though each model's look is highly idiosyncratic, models are replaceable with an enormous pool of competitors eager to join the ranks. This hit home when a booker in London sent me an e-mail explaining that I had been requested by a big stylist to shoot for a British magazine. I was in New York at the time and unable to fly back for the job. So the stylist replied to my booker, "I don't suppose you could send along some Ashley Mears look-alikes?"

One Thing Is for Certain

While models face ambiguity daily with their schedules and at castings, with options, and through interactions with their bookers, they can be guaranteed of one thing: rejection. Rejection is common to a number of occupations, particularly those in which workers try to persuade others to purchase a product or service. Studies of sales work have confirmed that the attempt to sell something to someone fails far more often than it succeeds.[11] Because there are far too many people chasing too few jobs in modeling, rejection is inevitable and ubiquitous.

Not even successful models are immune from it. This was a particularly tough lesson for Lucas, a twenty-six-year-old model in London. He is now a graduate student of philosophy and religion, having discovered Buddhism after his career crashed in New York following a good two years during which he was, in his own words, "hot shit" in the modeling world. His picture was featured in the Versus campaign billboard on West Houston Street, just opposite a Guess billboard that featured a female model whom he "really fancied." He happily recalled the days when he had strutted through the streets of Manhattan and looked up at his own billboard. He was on top of the world, he said, and then:

> I remember going into the agency and hearing that one by one all of these options had come off, and so I realized the next season I wasn't gonna have any campaigns, and that was like, oh shit.

As it turned out, a major photographer declined to re-book him for the Versus campaign. Other clients followed suit, his billboard came down, and he was sent back to London as old news in a matter of months.

Rejection comes in sweeping waves, as in Lucas's case, but also in daily interactions at castings, as in the exceptionally slighting experience that Liz, the twenty-one-year-old from New Jersey, shared with me. She attended a casting for a big department store, and when she arrived at the casting office, she fell in line with about eighty other models in a long hallway. A casting director then scanned each girl in the line and told her one of two words: "Stay" or "Leave." Liz, being told to leave, just laughed it off. But the other dismissed models, she said, were

demanding that the director at least look at their books or pa¹
cab ride home. Another model told me about the time she foun(
posite card in the trash can upon returning to a casting to r(
sweater. Another saw scribbling on cards: "No way," and "too cutesy."
Someone had even taken the time to write and underline "<u>No Thank-
You</u>!" on a model's card. Rejection really stings with the additional sense
of being ignored or not taken seriously.

Models may have traveled across the city and waited in line for hours
to meet the client (in my fieldwork, my longest waiting time was five
hours on a Sunday night), all to be unceremoniously dismissed because,
for whatever reason, they are deemed not "right" for the job. The reasons
are endless: one may be too commercial, too edgy, too fresh, or too old,
or perhaps one is all of these in a single day. Sofia, a twenty-one-year-old
Jamaican woman modeling in London, was once quickly dismissed at a
casting for being 5'10", a height most bookers would see as ideal. "So,
yeah, so it makes you, it just makes you wonder what they are looking
for in a girl," she said. "What do they want?" She elaborated on the emotional toll of not knowing the source of her failures:

> 'Cause if you go on a casting and they don't like you, you're like, why? And
> if it's a show casting, you don't like my walk. What should I do? And you
> have nobody to encourage you and tell you what went wrong. So you're
> there, blaming yourself, "I'm too fat," you know.

Most often no reason for the rejection is given, and the model is left
to guess what he or she did wrong. This is a lonely endeavor, and it
wears down one's self-image with a slow, growing sense of doubt, as
Ben, a twenty-nine-year-old London model, describes:

> There's a *vast* majority of castings that you go to, where there isn't a re-
> sponse and then the *vast* majority of options you do get don't confirm. . . .
> At the end of the day there's just not enough work around for the amount of
> people competing for it, so I think it's very hard to tell what people really
> want or what they really like.

Models are playing odds at each casting that are repeatedly demonstrated to be long shots. They are reminded of this by a career in which
a normal series of work proportions is reversed. Most people spend a
rather long time preparing for their jobs with schooling and training, a
short time trying to get them via the interview process, and then a long
time doing them.[12] Models, conversely, are almost permanently engaged
in trying to find work, a growing precarious predicament for workers in
the new economy.

LOOKING GOOD, LOOKING RIGHT

However elusive the project of becoming a look may seem, models are not fatalists. They work to increase their odds. Having accepted the arbitrariness of their career successes or failures, models next turn their attention to what they *can* control: their bodies and their personalities.

The look is first and foremost located in the body. Like athletes, dancers, and sex workers, models use their corporeality as a form of capital. They are entrepreneurs in what Loïc Wacquant calls "bodily capital," his term to describe the raw materials of flesh, fist, and physical force that the pugilist converts into prize monies in the boxing ring.[13]

Like boxers, models devote meticulous attention to their bodies as they work to convert their bodily capital into sellable "looks." This includes training, conditioning, dieting, and shedding weight before crucial events: the monthly bout for the pug; the daily casting for the model. Managing bodily capital is, of course, a major concern for all athletes, although few are required to be as obsessed with weight—with some exceptions such as wrestlers, jockeys, gymnasts, and lightweight rowers—as boxers are.[14]

Models are also akin to display workers such as strippers and exotic dancers, though modeling involves wearing rather than removing clothes, in that the bodies of both are observed and publicly evaluated. Strippers similarly take up "body projects" to keep patrons drawn to their physical wares, but the striptease physique varies widely in age and appearance, reflecting in part the diverse tastes of the strippers' broad audience.[15] Models who deviate more than slightly from the ideal height, physical dimensions, and age will have considerable difficulty obtaining employment; strippers do not have to meet equivalent norms of bodily perfection.

Like athletes, dancers, and other workers in the style labor markets, models do "body work," meaning they spend considerable time and effort to maintain a particular state of embodiment. But unlike these types of workers, models work as independent contractors, not members of organizations; they do not perform aesthetic labor under the direction of supervisors or employers. This has important implications for how models mold and monitor their bodily capital. Models are first mobilized into looks through routine objectification, *floating norms* of bodily perfection, infantilization, surveillance, and the threat of embarrassing reprimands. Models must have standard perfect bodies yet simultaneously project a unique, special kind of self. This self—both physical and emotional—must manage to fit within a proscribed general framework, and it must be distinctive. Both requirements take considerable work and manipulation to achieve.

Being a Body

Before any fashion show, the backstage of the catwalk is a chaotic swirl of stylists and producers yelling for models to line up for dress rehearsal. At the hectic formation of one such line backstage at a show in New York, producers who could not find their models made do with college interns subbing places in queues, shouting, "Where's Carla?! Carla?! Okay, we need another body in here!" At this, the model behind me scoffed and said, "Did you hear that? I love how they talk about you, 'a body!'"

In the market for looks, women and men become commodified bodies for sale. As display objects, models' bodies are contorted, touched, and exposed. The model is oftentimes treated as an inanimate object on the job, touched and molded into poses like a malleable doll, and talked to in the third person. At my first photo shoot, a test to build my portfolio, a team of two photographers took turns taking my picture and assisting with the shoot. When one of them instructed me to pose by putting my arms tightly by my side, the other interjected, "Umm, no, wait, her arms look thick."

Showroom and fitting work is the most physically objectifying work because models are hired for the sole purpose of trying on garments while designers make alterations. While a team of designers, stylists, consultants, and interns frets over the hem of a skirt, the model is likely to be standing naked, waiting patiently to be given a shirt. Other times the model is asked to hold awkward poses while designers pin, stitch, and adjust garments onto the body and is sometimes poked with pins or yanked about forcefully by rough designer hands; as one very successful runway model told me, she is often "pinned like a scarecrow" in the showroom.

To an outsider, such situations appear rude or inappropriate, but models are complicit in maintaining their normalcy, and they grant passes to achieve what Erving Goffman called a "working consensus."[16] In this sense, objectification is quickly incorporated into the work routine. As one male model put it, "It's a business where you're paid to like take clothes off, put clothes on, you know, you can't be really [a] prude with that stuff."

FIGURE 3.1. Becoming body
perfect: A makeup artist
applies lotion to a model
moments before the show

Experiencing one's body as an object puts the model in a shared corner with the athlete. Consider the boxer. Both the model and the boxer
see their bodies as things to be worked on, things that require constant
and meticulous attention. And yet the boxer wants not just to look
good, which is the model's aim, he wants to *be* good; his body becomes
a tool of force and mighty intervention. The difference is between being
an instrument, that which does work, and an object, that which is
worked upon. The boxer transforms his body for an active means toward
a self-controlled end. The model's body is more of a passive object, waiting to be chosen and put to use for other people's ends in advertising and
fashion displays. The boxing ring and the catwalk are both corporeal
and competitive, but the champion boxer has a more tangible value
than the fashion model: he is either knocked out or does the knocking.
Models, however, have little sense of what will make for a "knockout"
in the market for looks. That's because, unlike the boxer, the model is
not primarily in control of her wins and losses.

Looking over oneself, this process of self-reflection requires individuals to internalize standards of a "good self" and to exercise restraint toward the achievement of this "good self."[17] So what happens when that notion of "good" is never obvious and always changing?

The Best Taste Is Skinny

All of the models I interviewed were keenly aware of the physical demands of their job, and they framed these demands as job requirements. They were not mere lucky winners in some genetic lottery; they were fighters in an ongoing struggle against their bodies. Kiera, who followed a grueling liquid diet, explained:

> No, it's incredible, our job is to be body conscious, that is our job, you know. A computer programmer has to learn software programs. Our job is to keep our measurements to a certain number, you know, so it's our business. It's funny. (Kiera, 22, London)

Without ever being told, I understood right away the bodily criteria required to be a Metro model. Before I signed the contract with Metro, I was first led into the back of the chic office and wrapped with a measuring tape, first around my bust, then my waist, and finally my hips. Heather did this in the middle of her agency while her office mate Anton sat and watched, arms folded. She wrote down three numbers on the Post-it on her desk without telling them to me. I caught a glimpse of them over her shoulder: 31"–25"–35.5".

Two days later, when I got my first composite card, the measurements read 32"–24.5"–34.5". No one ever mentioned that these were not my real measurements, or that I should strive to attain this size. When I mentioned this to another model, she said the numbers on her card were doctored too.

Throughout the interviews, men and women alike explained to me that their true bodies were "off" from their represented model bodies. For women, they deviated mostly in their hip measurement, and many spent a good deal of their interviews discussing problematic hips. Male models were most likely to have erroneous measurements reported concerning their height, giving or taking an extra inch.

Numbers and "stats" that allegedly speak to physical facts are in fact manipulable parts of the look's packaging. The discrepancy of inches on composite cards serves several purposes. First, it aligns the body to fit within a range of expected sizes. Based on the measurements presented on Metro's website, the average Metro woman's body measures 33.3" in the bust, 24.1" in the waist, and 34.5" in the hips, with an average height of 5'9".[18] These numbers refer less to the actual physical properties of bodies than to the conventionally "normal" size of the ideal model body. For male models, waist measurements of 30"–32" are not as important as being "cut" and "fit," meaning muscular and toned, or, in the case of editorial men, skinny and free from all body fat. Men are not measured nearly as often as women are, but instead they routinely must take off their shirts to show their bodies at castings and at their agencies.

These general measurements and requirements of a "cut" stomach or 34" hips loosely constitute the floor of qualifications, below which candidates are unacceptable. Such criteria are not set in stone, however. They are fuzzy. They float. Given the subjective worth of any model's look, the physical criteria for a model do not adhere to any definite, objectively quantifiable standards. Models are instead measured against ambiguous *floating norms*. Floating norms are elusive benchmarks of fleeting, aesthetic visions of femininity and masculinity.[19] They must be reproduced and normalized through practice to gain substance, hence a second function of so-called "measurements" on composite cards: they stabilize a set of bodily requirements and enroll clients and models alike into the belief that (1) concrete standards exist; and (2) these standards have been met.

There is a third, more insidious function of the erroneous inch. It signals to the model that her body has deviated from this norm; she is in noncompliance. Mia, a twenty-eight-year-old American model in London fretted about her misleading measurements after having to be, in her words, "poured" into the dresses at her last job:

> I think it said I was a 35 hip and I'm 36, okay, which is not really a big deal, but at the same time, I *squeezed* into these dresses and I felt really fat. And I felt like, I wished I would have just told them the truth because then I felt embarrassed. . . . I had to like basically be *poured* into these dresses, you know?

Mia's body has become a walking lie, and a liability that will betray her. Here we have two twin uncertainties: on the one hand, how to know if the body will adhere to floating norms, and, on the other, how to make it adhere. Unlike boxers, who have the support and close management of a coach, models must engage in "body projects," such as losing weight and toning limbs, largely on their own. These are ongoing commitments that spill over into outside working or casting hours.[20]

Anna, for instance, adheres to a strict diet of raw vegetables and fish during the week, and on the weekends she binges on cakes and pizza. She's been eating like this since she started modeling four years ago, though more recently she supplements her weekday grind with a steady dose of Adderall, a prescription drug used to treat attention deficit hyperactivity disorder (ADHD), which has the side effects of an appetite suppressant. When I first met Anna between castings, she was snacking on a large stalk of celery and extolling the virtues of drinking "green juice," a concoction of cold-pressed raw vegetables such as kale, beets, and carrots.

"But does it taste alright?" I asked her, to which Anna replied, between mouthfuls of green, "The best taste is skinny," a prelude to the now-infamous remark made by supermodel Kate Moss in 2009, speaking about her personal motto, "Nothing tastes as good as skinny feels."[21]

Men become similarly committed to their body projects. Ethan is a twenty-two-year-old male model from Nashville who lost thirty pounds in the quest for a more fashionable, lean body. After a six-month, 700-calorie diet of Hydroxycut protein shakes and daily five-mile runs, his friends back in Tennessee barely recognized him with his new chiseled jawline. On his last visit home, intended as a vacation from the modeling world, his girlfriend finally told him to stop talking about his body: "Because every time we would eat, I would talk about it, like, 'Oh I have to go run now,' or I would like look at myself in the mirror and like feel out where I had fat."

As the raw material, models' bodily capital requires processing and packaging it into a look. As one stylist put it, "Models are palettes," or "chameleons," ready to transform into the dreams and fantasies of photographers and designers. Bookers direct models in this transformation, suggesting to them cosmetic changes in their hair, weight, clothing, teeth, skin tone, and makeup regimes, as well as in their projection of upbeat personalities and fashionable selves. With effort, one's look can be dramatically altered, and stories of reinvention are aplenty. There is the model who cut her long dark hair into a platinum pixie look, and the model who changed her name to start over with a blank portfolio at a new agency. Surgical alternations such as nose jobs and breast implants are not very common, in part because agents only take on models who adhere already to physically specific standards.

While bookers act as gatekeepers, controlling the access between models and clients, they do not explicitly control the model's bodily assets. Working to achieve floating norms requires models' constant adjustment to ideals that are at once rigidly specific yet impossibly vague and always changing, such that models are never entirely satisfied with their bodies.

And how could a model ever find satisfaction, asked Eva, a twenty-two-year-old model in London. "It is a standard of perfection that is impossible to achieve," she explained, exasperated, "and that you're constantly, I mean, [a] lot of times you try and achieve this constant level that's just impossible, and so you're never satisfied. Like it's just unfulfillment, constantly, every day, you know what I mean?"

I did know what she meant. I experienced it firsthand shortly before coming to London, when Heather and Rachel, both of whom handled my schedule at Metro, took me to lunch to discuss my summer travel options. We talked over plates of fajitas, and the mood was exciting: "I think you'll do well in London!" said Rachel. From London, Heather suggested I might easily head to Paris for a couple of weeks to meet with agencies and see clients.

"Especially if you go to Paris," added Rachel, almost as an afterthought, "I'd like to see you get in shape." Regarding my hip measurement, she said, "You should really get down, not a lot, but like to 34 and a half, or 34." Rachel explained that I would work better in New York if I "got in shape." I felt my face flush red, and Heather, who looked slightly uncomfortable, became quiet. She would confess to me two years later in our interview that she hates telling girls to lose weight; usually she asks someone else to do it.

For the record, I am in shape. At just over 5'9", I weighed about 125 pounds at the time; that's no size zero, but it is still thin. What Rachel really meant was for me to get into Paris runway shape, to get skinnier. Neither of them suggested a plan to do this, nor did they monitor my progress in any systematic way. In fact Rachel only brought it up one other time, three months later, when I called her from London and she asked in her usual peppy demeanor: "What are your hip measurements, what's the deal with that?" I told her the truth—that I hadn't lost much weight at all, but not for lack of trying. At this point I was partially following something like the Atkins diet, one of a number of feeble attempts to shrink my obstinate hips.

"Okay, so when you get back," she stated, "we'll sit down and talk about the shows, take the hip measurement, and see what's goin' on." I perceived her statement, vague as it was, as a threat, a reminder that my body soon would be held accountable. When I returned to New York, no such measurement was immediately taken; I was simply not given castings for the Fashion Week.

Ethan, the newly slim Nashville native, explained it best when he told me about the management of his body: "You always have to be *weary*." Even with his chiseled jawline and taut torso, he explained: "You always have to wonder, what can I do to either be better or to stay how I am. Because there's always something, there's always a little bit that you could do to—maybe book that job."

Floating norms keep models working on their bodies with only vague notions of how to do so, which leads some to a perverse occupational maxim: it's better to be skinny than to be sorry.

Against the Clock

There is a finite store of bodily capital; it will inevitably run out for everyone. The athlete knows and plays by this predicament. The boxer strategizes his fights to delay the collapse of his muscles, and the coach recruits young talent to extend the life of his trainee. For women in modeling, a career tends to run from the ages of thirteen to twenty-five, with editorial models "aging out" quicker than commercial ones. Beyond her mid-twenties, an editorial model finds difficulty obtaining work in fashion, at which point she quits or transitions into commercial or lifestyle modeling where she is no longer in the running for prestigious editorial or lucrative campaigns. Among women with editorial careers, entering the market at age eighteen was considered a "late start," and entering at age twenty-one was "really, really late." Thus the colloquial use of "girl" in fact does describe many female models. Aging is less of a concern for men because they can book fashion and catalog jobs well into their forties and even their fifties, though for editorial work, male models tend to be younger, between eighteen and thirty years old.

If youth is a physical criterion for modeling, then it is just as manipulable as size. A model can extend her "shelf life" by lying about her age, but she cannot escape the sense that growing up means falling out of fashion which, after all, is predicated on newness.

Metro advises wannabe models on its web page: "Please note that we ask women candidates to be between the ages of 13–22." Yet no one at the agency turned me away when I disclosed my true age as twenty-three. Bookers instructed me to edit my birth date without an explanation.

When I asked my booker Ronnie in private if I was going to be eighteen indefinitely, he casually explained that the "white lie" was common and necessary:

> There is the idea that if you haven't shot Italian *Vogue* by 23, then you're not going to. And it's not true. And if you believe in that then it's my view that you deserve not to know the truth. If you're not going to look at how a girl looks, and if she's right for you, then, you know, you're being ageist.

Ronnie was right about my experience being common. At one runway casting, I began talking with a woman whom I learned was a twenty-three-year-old college graduate. When I asked her if she had ever been instructed by her agents to lie about her age, she explained:

> Well, yeah, because I am 23 and they initially wanted me to say I'm 19. . . . The agency, when they were explaining it to me, they said it's like when you go to the grocery store to buy milk, which milk carton would you want, one that is going to expire tomorrow or one that will expire next week?

Based on this logic, Sasha, from Vladivostok, Russia, was "sour milk" at the age of twenty-two by the time I met her in London. But in "model years," she was still a fresh nineteen, which masks the impression that she is a *stale* product, one that has been rejected over and over.

> "You are not a top model, you are not a new face," she said. "That means *everyone* saw you, or a lot of people saw you. You became nothing spectacular. Why would [a client] want you? He's gonna book somebody who might become top model one day, or somebody new who nobody else has seen. . . . So when I say to them I'm 22 it's obvious I didn't start modeling yesterday, you know what I mean?

An older model, then, exudes failure.

The bluff is a common response to a woman's depleting shelf life. Some women even bemoaned how they felt "so old" at the ages of twenty-two and twenty-three. But the "expiration date" for a model is hardly fixed; the window of opportunity, while short, is also flexible. For instance, twenty-three-year-old Jen, an Asian American New Yorker who has modeled for four years, believes her looks matter more than her age:

> I don't lie about my age at all. When they ask how old I am, I say I'm 23, and all the clients or photographers or whatever are shocked because they're like, "wow, you look like you're like 12!"

Models are also aware that a younger age does not guarantee success, and that older models can be just as successful as younger ones.

Though they recognize the flexibility of age, they usually lie nonetheless, to be "on the safe side," which is to be on the young side. Anna, at age twenty-five, has routinely lied about her age throughout her four-year-long career—to agents, clients, and other models, myself included, when we first met at a photo shoot. She easily passes for the nineteen-year-old she claims to be, and despite feeling "lucky" to have "good genes," she carefully guards her true age.

> So you're around all these young girls, and everybody's always asking you how old you are and you don't want to say you're like 24, you know or 25, because then it puts you in a different category . . . like, "What can we do with a 24-old?!"

If norms for the look are floating, then models' identities can float too. This can mean living a false biography to match one's fictitious body. For faux-nineteen-year-old Anna, it means pretending to be an ingénue who finished high school at the age of sixteen, who was never married at twenty and divorced at twenty-three. It means convincing would-be employers that she has seen and knows less of the world than she truly has. It means, basically, playing dumb.

It is not necessarily enough for the model to *look* young. The model must *be* young, or she enters the competition from a disadvantage, real or perceived. This lesson applies more to women than to men. Eighteen of the twenty women in this study reported lying about their age, compared to just seven of the male models. After all, women have historically traded their youth and beauty for economic security on the marriage market.[22] Youth is a worry for women, who lose their looks and their marriage prospects with age, whereas men accumulate more power as time goes on.

The age-body relationship is especially damning for women, many of whom enter the field with prepubescent bodies, such as twenty-two-year-old Kiera, who began modeling as a rail-thin eighteen-year-old. That didn't last long, she explained: "Going back to my child-bearing hips, you know, I knew that would be a problem. My mom's just as skinny as me, you know, ribs and skinny waist, but she has got some booty. So I knew it was bound to happen at some point, it's just a ticking bomb, you know. My ass got bigger overnight, oh my God!"

If women's looks, like milk, "sour" with age, then men's looks are like a fine wine. The owner of Metro bluntly stated: "Men toughen up over time, but no one wants a tough woman." Most of the male models to whom I spoke did not fret about becoming sour milk, because they saw catalogs and even campaigns as likely opportunities well into their distant futures. Several male models looked forward to getting older so they could "cash out" in commercial and catalog work. One forty-four-year-old man I interviewed quips on his personal web page: "He has been in the modeling business over 15 years. And the older he gets, the better he looks!"

A few editorial men, having once basked in the limelight of prestigious catwalks and magazine work, remarked, to their own surprise, that they felt the curious sensation of embarrassment about being "old":

> It is strange how quick it goes and suddenly, because I was used to being the new guy and now I'm 21 and doing it three years [and] now there's all these like 16 or 17-year-old boys, it's just like, wow. It's scary fast. I feel old in that respect, but not that I feel I'm too old. (Preston, 21, London)

Men, especially in the editorial circuit of the market, are not exempt from the plain reality that fashion is an industry predicated on change and novelty. No look will be in demand forever, not even for very long. As one male model remarked, after first calmly noting that catalogs would be available for him until he reaches age thirty, "I understand that we are produce. We are meat, and it gets bad as it gets old, you cannot sell it at the same price." While there are no hard-and-fast age limits for modeling, there is a premium on "freshness" that necessarily puts all modeling careers in the precarious position of becoming too ripe.

Being Visible

Age and size, then, are manipulable parts of a look's packaging. What type of manipulation to apply, however, and in which direction, models discover through trial and error as they enter the field and its daily routines of assessment, the casting. Models turn their bodies into ideal objects subjected to relentless inspection and scrutiny. In this, they are again like the boxer whose body is scrutinized and fine-tuned into a prize machine. But if Loïc Wacquant's (2004) pugs see their bodies as weapons and machines, then models are more likely to see their bodies as problems.

The problem begins with the gaze. From the moment the model walks into the casting studio or her agency, she is under intense surveillance. All eyes are on her, sizing her up, searching, judging. At a routine casting, for instance:

> I'm in the chic lobby of an art direction company, here to see Ariel about an upcoming look book.

She asks the usual questions: Where are you from? How long have you been modeling? How old are you?

"19." *A lie!*

She nods and flips a page of my portfolio. "Stand up for me there," she says.

I stand up and she looks me over, then looks back to my book. "Okay turn around." I turn around and face the wall for what feels like ten seconds. I glance toward the receptionist and see that he is not paying attention.

"Okay great," she says, and I turn back around and face her. She takes a composite card from the back of my book and closes it, then studies the back of the card that has my stats printed on it. "What are your hips?"

"35." *Again, a lie!*

She looks up and says she'll see me soon, thanks for coming.

A sharp pair of eyes can do a lot of work on the body, whether the outcome is praise, critique, or silence. Michel Foucault has suggested that a gaze can be a more powerful mechanism of control than direct force. The anticipation of being watched, he argued, could render anyone a self-policing subject, a self-monitoring docile body, one that willingly surrenders to be improved, worked on, and used. The gaze is a superb formula for controlling bodies: "There is no need for arms, physical violence, material constraints. Just a gaze."[23]

Sociologists and feminists have extended Foucault's conception of the gaze to the production of women as visual subjects. Studies of flight attendants, strippers, and some athletes, such as lightweight rowers and ballet dancers, show that when people are constantly on display, they end up constantly *thinking* about their bodies being on display, internalizing the gaze and remaining body conscious even off the clock.[24] But fashion's gaze is less forgiving than the strip club patron's, and floating norms of bodily perfection demand more individual attention in the absence of coaches and managers. Stripped down, exposed as objects for inspection against anonymous criteria, models work under constant surveillance. Exposure is a key disciplinary mechanism through which models mold their bodily capital.

At castings, at jobs, and among bookers, a constant gaze breaks down the model's body, ruthlessly, carefully, searching for its faults. At one casting for designer jeans, I tried on a pair of size 28 jeans and stood against a wall with ten models to be seen by two women. We were asked to turn around and face the wall so they could see our backsides, chuckling apologetically as they made the request. One of the models joked aloud, "I feel like I'm in a criminal lineup!"

FIGURE 3.2. A model at a
fitting session

Like the criminal body, the fashion body is carefully monitored. Sample clothes are frequently and effectively deployed to inspect the body's shape. Like the defeated customer in a retail fitting room, a fashion fitting is loaded with potential symbolic violence. I felt this acutely at one photo shoot when my legs would not fit into a pair of leather pants. The designer had to cut open the back of the pants and tape the leather to my calf. He explained to me that the model whose body was used to design the fit of the pants was "really skinny." The floating norm of "really skinny" bends and gives way to the needs of each client, catching models off guard at any moment.

Bodies are further made to confess their flaws in pictures, as in the common practice of clients photographing models at castings. Backstage at any fashion show, Polaroids of the models will be on display to keep track of girls and clothes. At one job, I scanned the Polaroids tacked on a poster board and found faint pencil writing on one of them.

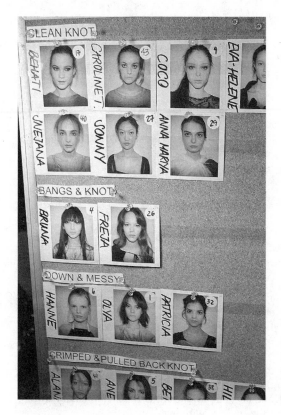

FIGURE 3.3. Rows of Polaroids help hairstylists categorize models into hair types, such as "clean knot," for the show

It read: "GORG–GREAT BODY–BUT NOT BEST LEGS–SEXY–19 YO–MILAN." On display for everyone to see, this bit of information betrayed the client's otherwise secret assessment. It affords us a glimpse of the expert gaze that breaks down the model, scans her body, and passes judgment: "This girl is gorgeous. She has a great body, but not the best legs. She's sexy and nineteen. She's been to Milan."

The gaze also works between models as they compare their bodies to one another, judging themselves and each other against an illusive ideal, constantly assessing their inadequacies. JD, from Manchester, explained seeing his physical flaws for the first time at an underwear job early in his career:

> You know I had thought I had quite a good body, but when I see these guys next to me they got eight-packs, I'm like yeah okay you bastards! It's only because you're at home and you're with normal people, and when you're around normal people you are quite good. And then when you become a

FIGURE 3.4. Poster boards are used to keep track of models, clothes, and accessories, backstage at a show

model, then obviously if you're used to being better lookin' outa your group, when you get to modeling, you start thinking, shit man, there's so many beautiful people in this world, and like, I'm not the center of attention in this room, not with these other nine boys in here with me!

Throughout the interviews women assessed their bodies in constant anticipation of being assessed, with a sense of anguish, of the perpetual worry that the clothes would be too tight, that their bookers would make a negative comment, and that they would be measured by the client. Deviance from floating norms is always a step away, and thus the model must be one step ahead. For many models, this is a new relationship they have with their bodies. After two years of modeling in London, Addison explained that she has never looked at her body with quite so much disdain. These days she can't look at it any other way, not since her bookers in London suggested that she slim her 37" hip measurement. She told me, quietly, in a café:

> And after I went to the agency, I was just, I've never stopped thinking about it. It's like everything I eat, I just wonder like, "oh God I shouldn't be doing this" and I never used to do that. It's just completely changed my image of myself, and everything, what I eat. Yeah, I find myself comparing, to other girls, like my body, and I just do it without thinking.

Male models also talked about and experienced the surveillance of their bodies, but not in terms of anguish and anxiety; they were more likely to confront the challenges of their bodily capital with straightforward acceptance, as in, "Well, time to hit the gym," or, "I must pay better attention to nutrition." For JD, it was expressed as a simple matter of eating fewer kebabs; for Owen, it was fewer Krispy Kreme donuts; for Ian, it was playing more sports. Several male models joked about their skinny bodies and bemoaned their inability to put on weight or to build muscle. But it seemed just that, a joke:

> You know, like at shows, you're taking your top off and stuff, and you look around and then suddenly some guy will take his top off and has this amazing six-pack, you know, and you'll be like "wow! Where did you get *that*?!" [laughs] No, I don't ever, like my booker said to me the other day, are you going to the gym? But I just take what he says with a pinch of salt really, I'm not concerned. (Edward, 22, London)

Women models and, to a lesser extent, male models related that they shared a heightened awareness of their bodies and a distinctively self-critical awareness of what they perceived to be physical flaws. Almost all of them were careful, or at least thoughtful, about what they ate, and most exercised regularly. They engaged in such body work at their own resolve, turning their bodies into personal projects under constant surveillance and a punitive gaze that normalizes the pursuit of the perfect body. Models learn to follow floating norms of bodily perfection through their daily routines of being watched, observed, scrutinized, and compared to one another. They internalize this gaze; in the absence of formal regulation, they regulate themselves and learn how to be aesthetic bodies through constant bodily exposure. Should models not discipline themselves, they will face biting, if tacit, criticism.

Taking Abuse

Given the instability of floating norms, then, much of the work of modeling involves detective work; models learn the look from social signals, clues, and, most damning, through subtle criticism in the form of gentle insults and humiliating situations. Being "too big" is perhaps the most common and least pleasant problem that models face on the job. But admonishments for size are anything but straightforward. For example, Heather and her colleague Anton photographed me in a bikini at the agency:

Standing in Metro's private meeting room in my bikini with Heather and Anton, who holds a Polaroid camera and is looking at me up and down.

"Do you have high heels?" he asks. When Heather has found a pair in the agency for me to wear, I again stand before Anton who looks through the camera lens at me and says, "That's so much better, makes her look so much longer," *click, click.* He asks Heather whom these pictures are for. They are for a big casting director in London.

"Oh, okay," he says. "I know what he's gonna want." To me he says, "Stand like straight again, okay," *click.* "This way, he's not gonna say you are fat," *click.*

The two of them sit back on the couch and allow for the Polaroids to develop on the table. Anton says, "This one's good. He can see nothing is falling down." Heather says to me with a smile, "Don't you just love the way we talk about you?" For one last shot, Anton asks me, "Can you like, make tight your butt and your legs? Yes! That's good," *click.*

Neither Heather nor Anton ever told me to shape up. After this ordeal, it was understood. Bookers are in a position to wield considerable power over models, but usually they exercise tact in the form of friendly advice. They don't *enforce* body projects, they *suggest* them, and with a smile.

Clients also use caution and politeness to cushion their criticisms. At one casting, a male designer asked me, "We were wondering if you did ballet? Because we were noticing that your legs are really . . . *defined.*" I used to play soccer, I explained, to which the designer nodded. He then said to his assistant, "So maybe we should put her in the pants?" Through indirect and implicit disparagements, models are subjected to insidious regulations that get read "between the lines."

Sometimes nothing needs to be said. The Ford Models agency explains on its web page: "If you can't fit into a designer's garments, you will face difficulty in finding work." If you cannot fit into the garments, you will also face considerable embarrassment. At the show casting for one prestigious line, I sat to the side of a room with about ten other young men and women models, waiting my turn to meet the client. I uneasily scanned the room: there was a sparse rack of clothes separating the models from the clients, and, if chosen, the model would be asked to try on a sample garment with hardly any privacy. That's not such an unusual setup; what bothered me was the extraordinarily slim cut of the sample jeans. When called to try on something, my excitement for being chosen quickly disappeared as I struggled and squirmed with the jeans for ten minutes before giving up, and I avoided looking up at what I could only imagine were a dozen eyes fixed on my misfortune.

While comp card stats can be fudged to present the model as slimmer than she really is, clients can and often do fact-check by measuring her or having her try on a sample garment at the casting. This technique works to dismember, dissect, and break down the subjected model body, to reduce it to parts that are then forced to speak the truth of their deviant owner. Unlike public weigh-ins before athletic competitions, or weigh-ins for flight attendants (which have now been eliminated), a public measuring can crop up anytime for a model, such as at this humiliating fitting:

> When I try on his dress, the designer, George, shouts, "Oh, it fits perfect!" The next outfit involves a pair of pants, and I can't manage to zip them up. George cries, "Oh no! What are you here?" he asks, patting my hips. I offer 35 and a half. He leaves the room, returns with a tape measure, and wraps it around my hips (damn!). He says, "You're a 37, girl!" and lightly smacks my thigh. "We need someone who's a true 35. . . . We call those child-bearing hips!"

Pointed and cruel language is used as a last resort, when a model's body becomes problematic. One model told me how Anton humiliated her in the middle of the agency by shouting, "Your hips have never been 38 [inches]. You can't go to Milan like that!"

Such criticism, while usually subtle, threatens the model at every turn, as bookers, stylists, and designers feel entitled to make pointed comments about models' appearances. Among the dozens of brutal comments I heard: one has thick ankles; one's head is asymmetrically shaped; one is too "street-looking"; one has a bad mustache; one's shoulders are too narrow; one's scar is too prominent; one's nose is "busted"; one has too many freckles; one's ass is too big. Comments that would otherwise be dismissed as sexual harassment in most workplaces are routinely deployed, propelling models to keep on their toes lest they stray too far from the floating norms of the look.

These daily confrontations with objectification, floating norms, infantilization, the gaze, and abuse form a set of work routines and expectations through which models learn to embody the "right" look or, at least, to stay beyond the parameters of the "wrong" look. Under relentless surveillance and the threat of embarrassing ordeals, freelance aesthetic labor requires an adherence to floating norms. Bookers and clients need not exert managerial force—the impromptu taking of measurements, an embarrassing comment, a pair of too-tight jeans. The rest is up to the workers' own devices. But work on the body involves considerable effort of the mind, and bodily capital can only be sold in the presence of another soft skill, the personality.

BE YOURSELF, BUT BETTER

In addition to having a standard perfect body, models try to project a unique, special self, which they define as "personality." Time and again models stressed the importance of personality when explaining why clients book them. Physical looks, of course, matter a great deal, but the look is one part physical appearance and another part persona. Both, with considerable effort and vigilance, can be controlled. Such is the flip side of selling bodily capital: one must engage in emotional labor.

Sociologists have recognized the importance of emotions at the workplace since Arlie Hochschild's initial conception of "emotional labor" in *The Managed Heart: Commercialization of Human Feeling*. Studying airline management and the training of flight cabin crews, Hochschild defined emotional labor as the "management of feeling to create a publicly observable facial and bodily display."[25] In her early formulation, Hochschild pessimistically theorized emotional labor as extending commodification into the laborer's heart and soul, even to the loss of an authentic self. Emotional labor has been the focus of much scholarship on service work, which theorizes the ways that employees variously work to resist management and commodification, enjoy and reproduce their commodification, and navigate the various emotional demands of their jobs.

But in all this theorizing of the emotional self, labor scholars retired the embodied self. Emotional labor involves the body; indeed, early work on emotional displays, most notably Goffman's presentation of self, implicated the body as a surface for the appropriate emotional controls.[26] Hochschild's work on the smile as embodied artifice also points to ways that emotions are connected to the body. Emotional labor requires the body and body work, and while this point has been argued, here I want to suggest also the opposite: that embodied labor likewise entails emotional work.

One can't speak of *either* emotions *or* bodies in labor, because emotional labor enlists the body, just as body work requires the mind. Here I want to bring the body and mind together to consider the ways that work with the body engages emotion, and how aesthetic laborers devise rules for feeling in the absence of official rules. Modeling enlists feelings through three primary means: through crafting the body, projecting personality to get jobs, and coping with rejection.

Crafting the Self

Within my first week of castings, Heather pulled me aside at Metro and asked if I needed or would be interested in "walking lessons," as Fashion Week was soon approaching. How does a model learn to walk? How does a body digest a new mode of embodiment? I signed up to find out.

At 6:30 p.m. on a Wednesday night, after a day of eight castings, I arrived at Metro to meet another new model, Beth, age twenty-two, and Felix, our runway coach for the evening.

Felix is a forty-something petite black man, dressed sharply in a black sweater. He is as gay, he says, as a "gay dollar bill." He has the air of a runway pro, and as I would later learn when reviewing my list of agency deductions, he charges handsomely for his services: $75 from each of us for two hours. The women in the agency adore him, calling him "Felie," and kissing him on the cheek. He shakes each of our hands and directs us to the back of the agency, where there is a long corridor opposite the booking table, hidden between shelves of portfolios. We change into our high heels, and begin our lessons.

First we line up next to the water cooler for "hip exercises," which Felix says are just to "isolate" our hips, and even though it may feel strange at first it will all come together in the end, he says.

Beth and I stand next to each other with our backs against the wall, and Felix stands in front of us, demonstrating how to shift weight from one leg to another, bending the knees and shoulders in sync. Beth and I try to copy his hip-shaking movements, and he's counting it out like "one-two-three-four, okay, that's right, uh-huh." The effect is to make the model aware of her hip; to listen to its movements and feel—perhaps for the first time—the connection between body weight, hip, and shoulder.

After a few minutes of this, Felix says we're done with the hip exercises. It is time now to start walking. We follow him out of the kitchen and into the corridor. You'll go first, he says, pointing to me, and he takes both of my hands and walks backwards, leading me around in a circle: "When I lead you, I want you to feel like Cleopatra."

Beth and I take turns doing other odd exercises, like walking and bumping into the wall, pushing off of the wall, flirting with the wall. These things are meant to test our confidence, he says. Each time we do something, he says encouragingly, "Okay, good," or "You girls are getting the hang of it."

For the next hour, Felix will have Beth and I walk toward him and back again, taking turns. Sometimes he'll walk first, and we try to copy it, or he'll just say where we need to modify. He keeps telling Beth she needs to take larger steps. He tells me my right shoulder is stiff. At one point he tells me after I walk: "Don't charge at a man. Come to him. Flirt." Walking toward me coyly, the way I should learn to walk, he adds, "*Can I take your order?*"

Felix pulls up a chair and sits at the end of our mini-runway, watching. A pizza is ordered. Heather and Felix are watching us walk while eating pizza, and Felix instructs us how to work it better between bites of his cheese slice. It is 8 p.m. and I'm starving and tired, and with each step the leather of my new stiletto digs into my Achilles. Each time I walk, Felix will say something, like "good," "there we go," "all right," or just "uh-huh." Finally, we form a circle to walk in, and we march in sync with each other, and it's a bizarre model military scene and my feet really hurt, but with each step I feel stronger, more sure of my footing, and there is Felix, nodding his head, "There you go girl, there you go, yes!"

Embodiment, a phenomenological term, is the experience of having and using a body; after all, the body is a vehicle for the self to know the world. As such, learning a new way to be in one's body changes one's access to the world. How we see and feel changes through new modes of inhabiting our flesh—this is the real lesson behind Felix's runway session. As he coaches Beth and me into new modes of inhabiting our bodies, he's really opening up the world for us to feel in new ways—confident, sexy, powerful—ways that will come to be felt and lived more naturally and instinctively than the initial discomforts of self-consciousness, resentment, and physical pain.

By working on the body, models are producing a new self, not just a physical surface. They are crafting sets of feelings and dispositions as well, what Pierre Bourdieu calls *habitus*.[27] Some models have an easier time than others enlisting this body/self project, but all explained in various terms that learning proper comportment, whether on the runway, at photo shoots, or at castings, comes through physical practice:

> Well, you kind of grow into it. Like your first couple of photo shoots are mostly like tests and you try new things and photographers, like, tell you and, and you kind of get into it. (Emma, 19, London)

Learning to be a model is like learning any craft. It requires immersion in practice before moving from a conscious series of steps to a tacit knowledge so deeply ingrained in the body that it feels like second nature. Men and women alike talked about their early stumbles and pitfalls during this process:

> When I first did it, they would tell me, like because I was concentrating too hard, like my right arm was not moving, and my head was cocked to the side, and my mouth was open, and I looked like an idiot. I was like oh, great. (Mia, 28, London)

But, with time, questions such as "How should I swing my arm?" or "Where should my eyes look?" disappear, because the answers are lived in the body. If emotional, mental, or physical obstacles surface, then they must be blocked from one's thoughts. Going with the flow is similar to the athlete's mantra to "play through the pain," an apt metaphor for the various discomforts that must be ignored for the sake of the next casting or the next job. Among models' many experiences of having to conceal their emotions on the job, including my own, a sample of obstacles includes: hunger; kneeling down on a hard surface covered with sand; a man wearing a thong down a catwalk for the first time in his modeling career; standing in 3″ stilettos for four hours on a stage for a fashion presentation; wearing hot shorts while eating an ice cream cone for a Japanese magazine; getting tugged on; watching a client yawn as she flips through your book; having hair pulled and teased; waiting thirty minutes for a casting director to finish her cigarette before she can see you; wearing a "fat suit" for a maternity wear catalog. ("I was shocked when I turned up to the job, like *what*? You want me to *what*?")

Similarly, style in dressing the body is a learned craft. The model's style is a key marker of her self, and like the body, it must be cultivated. Bookers take the initial steps to guide models toward incorporating stylist dispositions, by filtering their wardrobes, instructing them to look at *Vogue* magazine, and even taking them shopping to hip retailers such as H&M and Topshop. At Metro, bookers instruct new models to arrive early on the day of an important casting for an outfit "check." A spare Marc Jacobs dress hangs in the coat closet, waiting to adorn the model who has immature taste. During one Fashion Week, I met a Ukrainian teenager new to New York, who always wore a black tank top and skinny jeans, because, she explained, it was her booker's orders. Two years later, I passed by her on the sidewalk of Broadway in SoHo, initially mistaking her for a meticulously styled celebrity.

In addition to cultivating the dispositions of a fashionable body/self, models are further required to cultivate a changeable disposition, that is, the ability to switch modes of comportment for each particular client's tastes. Early on, my booker Ronnie asked if I had some dress boots for the Valentino casting. He explained over the phone:

> So we've just gotta get you out of the jeans this weekend. Look, I have to give this talk to all the girls. But, think about Valentino; you've gotta dress a little more sophisticated, not dolled-up like a hooker or anything, but like

wear a skirt. . . . Maybe tie the hair back, you know, feel it out for each casting.

Crafting this stylish aesthetic self is easier for some than others. Models from middle-class urban backgrounds, the majority of those I interviewed, are better suited to assess and switch between fashionable styles and demeanors, having already entered the field with an internalized set of class competences, just as there is a class gradient to the kinds of aesthetics that retail management seeks in labor. Hochschild noticed a middle-class assumption among managers who expect emotional labor from their employees. When I caught up with Ethan, two days before his final return to Nashville, he explained how fashion was just incompatible with his rural upbringing:

> I would go to castings and people would be like, "Oh, this is a *huge* designer," and I'd have *no idea* who it was. Like, if it's not in a mall, I don't know what it is. And so, you know, I'd just go wearing like my Old Navy pants and like my Walmart shirt and try and pull it off—it didn't work that well. (Ethan, 22, New York)

There is also, of course, a gender gradient to the aesthetic body/self. Because the overwhelming majority of men enter modeling through the encouragement of scouts, not self-initiative, they enter the field with a different relationship to their body, and they are not as likely to have looked at their bodies as projects to perfect, as women are socialized to do more generally.[28] There are exceptions. Several men (as well as women) explained that they are natural extroverts and performers, having trained as actors, dancers, or singers, so they learned easily how to move comfortably in front of the camera.

Working on the aesthetic surface requires mental and emotional engagement, and over time and through practice, the surface and the feeling begin to blend into one. By working on the body, the model produces a particular kind of self, which can be mobilized in the form of "personality" to increase the likelihood of success.

Be Yourself

Part of the models' work of crafting the aesthetic body/self is the strategic projection of a personable self. Their looks' new cadence helps them get in the door, but once inside, models understand that their chances for booking, and indeed rebooking, jobs will greatly increased with the right amount of "personality."

The concept of personality marks a broader shift in modern discourses of the self.[29] New understandings of the "individual" in late nineteenth-century Western thought placed a premium on appearances as a marker of the true, "authentic" self. A person's real character and potential action could now be determined by the person's outward projection—physical and emotional.

Models are keenly aware of the importance of personality. They recognize that it is a "soft skill" requirement for the job, and it's something they actively "work on" to improve and perfect. With a personable "self," models hope to make a good impression on their bookers, who are in charge of getting them work, and to appeal to clients at castings, who are unlikely to choose models they think will be unpleasant or difficult.

Models therefore engage in what Jennifer Pierce calls "strategic friendliness," a form of emotional manipulation of another person to achieve a desired outcome.[30] Models display deference and politeness toward their bookers, as Avery, a twenty-two-year-old woman in London, with four years' experience, explained: "I always speak to them on time, or am polite to them, and I'll always e-mail them and keep in touch." Beyond these basic courtesies, models further pursue a personal relationship with their bookers to secure professional success. Ben, one of the most well-paid male models I interviewed, explained that a successful model must always be "on the lips of the agent": his booker has to constantly drum up a buzz, that is, excitement, for his model. Such backing comes from a personal relationship, Ben says: "There has to be that spark."

The personal is professional between models and bookers, as was best expressed by Ian in London:

> I would say it's not professional. I would call it like a friendship, you know, like a friend that knows you very well that can recommend you to a girl for a date, for example.

Models sometimes do connect with their bookers and become genuine friends. Otherwise, models "fake it." In Mia's words, this means having to "kiss their ass." Models who can't act the part of strategic friendliness can pay for it: every Christmas, Metro managers invite models to contribute to the bookers' bonus fund, and the name of each donor is printed on a card made public around the office. One booker at the men's division at a rival New York agency, receives up to $5,000 cash as a Christmas gift from his top-earning men, who remain top earners throughout the next year.

Beyond the agency, models present an ideal version of themselves on castings in pursuit of bookings. Models talked about their personality as something they had to "sell," as in the frequently uttered phrase, "I try to sell my personality." Selling the self involves producing an energetic, upbeat version of oneself that can "connect" to bookers and clients. Avery, for instance, always firmly shakes the client's hand at each casting. Between castings, Daniella talks to herself ("Okay, good things are gonna happen!") to bring good "energy" into the casting. JD tries to be "cheeky." Brody channels his "charisma," and so on. Above all, models are mindful of the fact that they are replaceable, as Anna explained: "There are three girls behind you that are having a great day, and who'll get this job, you know what I mean? There are so many girls waiting to be in your position. So, like, you always have to know this."

Once on the job, models recognize the importance of maintaining this energetic, ideal self in order to secure even more jobs—the goal is not just to book a job but to rebook a job:

> I try to, like, give a little something of me, like not just because I look pretty, because of my personality. Like I want them to know me as *me* and not as some model. . . . And I've found that clients book me over and over again because they like working with me, so I want to make a client feel comfortable and have fun. (Jen, 23, New York)

Not just any personality or energy will do; it must be appropriate *and* authentic. Models speak about showing their "real" self for clients, however, such a self is strategically different for editorial or commercial clients. The catalog client wants a different body/self than the edgy magazine editor, and models know to game their strategies accordingly. This requires not only understanding the differences between edgy and catalog but also anticipating which client wants what, and how to become the right type of look for the right moment. The most successful models I interviewed were experts in circuit switching, tailoring their appearances and personalities for either editorial or commercial clients, often several times in one day. As Clare, the "funny-looking" redhead from London, put it: "You have to be able to change up your look, and to be what they want you to be. That's our job." Adopting the supplier attitude, models cater to whatever the client and booker wants. This can mean adopting different styles of dress and corporeal cues, for instance, like Clare, who plays up her self-described odd features for editorial castings with vintage outfits and wild-colored accessories (at our interview she arrived in silver leggings and a pink sweater). For commercial castings, however, she "makes herself commercial" by wearing mascara, blush, and an outfit that is not "too weird looking."

However, it was Sasha, with her bobbed hair and Russian accent, who embodied this flexibility to practiced perfection. We met while standing next to each other in line for a casting for a cosmetics campaign in London, and when the client, a good-looking young man, asked Sasha where she was from, she replied blithely, "From Russia, with love!" and winked at him. Later she explained to me that clients book her for her personally tailored charm. For instance, "if she's a conservative lady who's looking for a catalog girl, you've gotta be sweet and nice and tell her that she has a beautiful jacket and maybe say you love Chanel or whatever." But if the casting is run by "a cool dude, or a guy and you know that maybe he fancies you in the back of his head," she advised, "you might tell him something sweet, you know, be a little bit flirty." Over the past seven years she has learned how to feel out each client and to "read" the appropriate manner of comportment at each casting.

When pressed to be more specific about how to project personality, several models replied that it is always best to "just be yourself." Lydia, a thirty-two-year-old woman in New York, learned this years ago in Paris, when she turned up in her ripped jeans and Converse All Star sneakers for an important show casting. Not having had much success so far in Paris, she figured she wouldn't get the job anyway, so she relaxed and started chatting to the young man sitting next to her for some time before leaving:

> And then I got in the elevator and I recognized Alec Wek from the magazines, you know, and she's like, "So you're doing the show?" And I'm like, no, I don't think so, they really hate me here, that's why I'm in my jeans and blah, blah, like, dumb girl from Michigan. And she's like "No, no, I'm pretty sure you're doing the show, you were just sitting there talking to Alexander McQueen!" He was probably like, oh my God, that's the only model who like, didn't come here and get nervous because I'm Alexander McQueen, she just like, doesn't care and is complaining about the weather and swearing. So I learned from that, that—and it's not easy to do—to just be yourself is the best thing you can ever do.

Lydia's tale is common industry folklore. Models, bookers, and clients speak often about the likelihood of chance encounters with important people that could change the course of a modeling career—for better or for worse. Since models' employment is on a per-project basis, it is important to make a good impression on all people all of the time. Like other freelancers in the creative industries, models must project personality to build credibility among networks of producers and to secure a reputation of employability.[31] Bookers even advise them to be "nice" to everybody at every shoot, because crew members quickly spread the word about models' personalities, and one never knows if today's intern is tomorrow's most important client.

To cope with the constant potential assessment of the personality, models explain, you should just "be yourself." The models' advice hinges upon several conditions. A model should be herself only if that self is outgoing and emotionally perceptive, confident, and able to recruit and perform the right emotions at will; if that self is happy to work but does not want any job too badly; and if that self is, with extraordinary effort, perceived as natural and carefree. The real lesson, of course is to be better than yourself. Through it all, the practiced aesthetic self must be one who does not take things personally, even though the "whole person" has been put up for sale.

Coping with Rejection

If models spend what seems to be considerable effort crafting a desirable body/self, then how do they respond when their efforts meet with the inevitable sting of rejection? This is a third way that models perform emotional labor, to protect their sense of dignity in a job that is often demeaning and personally affronting.

As we've seen, models are constantly rejected, sometimes with outright spite. This feels unpleasant, naturally, as male model Lucas remarked: "Everybody wants to be liked." For the aesthetic laborer, the body/self has become an external object; the whole person is now a commodity. An affront on the body is an attack on the self, and since models spend substantial energy crafting a look that is both physical and "personal," they must also devise emotional tricks to distance their "true" self from their aesthetic body/self.

For Edwin, smoking pot was good "casting armor," he explained, "because you go in not really caring, and you come out not really caring." Others deflect rejection with the quip "clients either like me, or they don't." By that, they mean one cannot accept full responsibility for one's failure, nor should one ever try to control the uncontrollable. Ryan, a twenty-five-year-old model in New York, explained, "If you can't control, like, your future, you shouldn't count on it. I mean you can't just be a better model tomorrow. What can it take to be a better model tomorrow? You can't."

A commonly reported strategy was to deliberately disengage one's emotional involvement and to not take rejection of one's body personally. Men and women alike remarked that rejection must be taken with a "pinch of salt," because it has "nothing to do with me," or that the un-pleasant booker or critical client "doesn't even know me." It takes emotional labor and skill to produce and believe in this distance between the product and the person. It is also a contradictory process, since the look *is* personhood. On the one hand, models say, "Here is the real me," and, on the other, they say they don't take anything personally. It wears one down, explained Lydia, not being able to escape from the rejection:

> It's like you start obsessing about every little thing each time you get de-nied for that thing, you focus on that thing, you're like, okay, I have to work on that thing, okay, I have to work—well, I can't work on the fact that my nose has a bump in it unless I get it cut off, you know? Or, like, I can't change that my eyes are blue, or that I look too Lithuanian or that—there are things that I can't change, and when you are constantly focusing about things that you're not able to change, it sort of drives you insane. (Lydia, 28, New York)

The notion of a true self is a fairly recent construction in the modern imagination. What is the "real you," after all, but a performance of dif-ferent versions of yourself depending on the context? In place of a sin-gle authentic self, we might think of multiple context-specific selves. As freelance aesthetic laborers, models are enrolled in the multiple perfor-mances of personhood that are never ending and that require continual care and self-management. They are entrepreneurs of their whole selves, all that which is the look—body, body/self, personality, and emotional armor in the face of rejection.

THRILLS

So far I have depicted a fairly bleak world of work—unpredictability, floating norms, self-discipline, rejection, and emotional labor. Why, then, bother modeling at all? What keeps the aesthetic freelancer going?

To manage their longs odds, routine rejections, and daily demands on their bodies and personalities, models overwhelmingly embraced the entrepreneurial disposition of the "enterprising self," taking personal responsibility for their successes or failures in the market. They become entrepreneurs of the self, voluntarily and cheerily working on their own images, bodies, and emotions. For example, they spoke often and easily about shooting unpaid editorials and walking for free on catwalks with an optimistic air of self-investment. Editorial work, they explained, is "advertising for myself." Working "for free" is recast as working "for myself," and building a portfolio is likened to building one's self-representation, which models recognize as being vital to securing future work. Echoing management guru Tom Peters, models spoke of being their own boss and marketing that "brand called 'You,'" which requires personal commitment and individual responsibility to be the best "free agent in an economy of free agents."[32]

This is not mere self-delusion on the part of the exploited laborer but a tangible source of motivation to continue working. As individuals, models are relatively powerless to set the terms of their work and the production of their images. Even in this structural position of weakness, there are spaces for resistance, agency, and even, as I learned from modeling, a space for pleasure.

Consider again the gaze. At one photo shoot, a stylist joked, "I don't know how models do it. You girls are under the microscope!" To be sure, the model in the casting setting is looked upon with a ruthless gaze that scans his body to see if he has the right "look" for the job. But this way of being visible can also flatter and reward. It can be a compliment to be the object of the gaze, especially when accompanied by encouraging feedback. At one show fitting, a designer asked to see me walk an additional time, even after she approved the outfit, telling me breezily, "Once more, for the pleasure." *What a thrill*, I thought.

Onstage and in front of the camera, the model is celebrated. She is the center of attention. After a fashion show, there is an unmistakable feeling of euphoria backstage. Models cheer and clap, toast with champagne, hug their designers and their makeup and hair stylists, and share compliments. One twenty-year-old model from Russia explained to me what she liked about modeling, despite the stress of castings and fittings: "When you are walking on the runway, it's the best." Like other rocky careers in glamour industries, for instance, photography and new media industries, modeling blurs the boundaries between work and lei-

FIGURE 3.5. Models cheer backstage in line for the show's finale

sure. It is a productive type of consumption, what we might call work consumption.[33]

Women and men, far from being docile bodies, can experience pleasure and agency in settings rife with powerlessness and objectification. No body is ever docile, as even choosing to be an object necessitates one's position as a subject. This is the theoretical take in much post-structural feminist theory; feminist researchers have redefined previously "oppressive" experiences, from sex work to cosmetics, as sites of negotiation and potential empowerment.[34] I don't wish to reiterate this turn in theory with aesthetic labor but instead to consider how the pleasures work, and how they keep workers working on themselves.

For many of the women I interviewed, stories of rejection, pain, and resentment flowed back to back with excitement and pride. There is power in crafting an aesthetic body/self, as much of the commodification requires active performance. Such empowerment is gendered, of course, as men and women come to the modeling field with different expectations and experiences with the gaze. Many women spoke of the craft of acting and the pleasure of "winning over" clients and bookers through their emotional wits. This too is a point that sociologists have belabored to counter Hochschild's initial formulation of emotional labor as the demise of authentic feeling. Managing one's emotions for money is not necessarily dehumanizing; it can be a resource for strength, a counterpart to working in a precarious market that prizes bodily perfection.

The ability to enjoy work that is physically and emotionally demanding is also a learned skill, one that takes time to develop and realize through experience. Many of the more experienced models in my sample stressed this point and explicitly compared modeling to acting, a craft that demands the mature willingness to engage. Now, at the age of twenty-five, Clare from London has an understanding of her job that challenges any standard view that her job is one of dehumanization.

"I think modeling, it's more like acting," she says. "And I think when you're brand new in the business you don't always feel confident enough. You feel stupid! As you get older, you just think, 'Okay, fuck it, I wanna get this job done, and that's it, *bam bam bam*, do what they want.' Or I push it as far—I mean one of the questions I always ask is, how far do you want me to go? Because I can take it far!"

In other words, Clare has figured out how to work "working it." There is pleasure and possibility in freelance aesthetic work, because, above all, it demands creativity with both body and mind.

HOW TO BE SPECIAL

As the new economy turns toward aesthetic labor and freelance work forms, previously "peripheral" labor markets such as fashion modeling can bring fresh insights to the sociology of work. But aesthetic labor, as presently conceived by sociologists, is lacking on two fronts.

First, as Entwistle and Wissinger point out in their research on fashion models, the management of body and soul becomes an individual responsibility for freelancers, a predicament that is pronounced in the cultural production industries as well as in the new economy.[35] Whereas workers in interactive service industries are hired to present and embody management's vision of a particular decorative "organizational body," freelancers are hired to present a free-floating one. The ways in which workers produce this freestyle aesthetic self, however, have not been addressed. In fashion modeling, models experience a set of work routines organized around floating norms of bodily and emotional perfection, which models learn and "pick up" through practice. Through productive power relations, models decipher the signs and cues of the look on their own. Hochschild (1983) argued that the flight attendant in *The Managed*

Heart was paradigmatic of work in the service economy of the 1980s. Today, the self-managed heart and body of the aesthetic laborer represent the future of work in the cultural economy.

Second, aesthetic labor is a potential source of power for workers. It requires skill and performance to overcome self-consciousness and to manage the manipulated self. This is a craft and a source of personal pride to models. A standard view of dehumanization, like past warnings that emotional labor will crush the worker's spirit, misses the creativity and empowerment—if only subjectively experienced—of the actual work. Modeling also offers a particular thrill of success, a potential emotional high that effaces the small, daily grind of rejection. Though the probability is low, the possibility of achieving greatness is so emotionally enticing that models continue working against vague and punishing aesthetic ideals.

Bridging body work and emotional labor into analyses of precarious work is important as more workers face these kinds of physical and personality self-disciplining in the new economy. While working on the body and self is hardly new in labor markets, the degree of short-term and long-term ambiguity managed by models is striking. Such are the tensions inherent in the look. It has an *ambiguous specificity*, at once unique to an individual while also conforming to a set of expected standards. It is an inherent quality in a person and simultaneously a practiced, packaged product. Models lie routinely to both stay within the floor of physical and age criteria and to stand out from the rest as "special."

The look is thus an embodied tension between two standards of excellence: on the one hand, it conforms to general standards of perfection—a generically perfect body and personality; on the other, a look sets a model apart as special and different from the rest—a *distinctive* body and personality. The look embodies this contradictory twin imperative for sameness and difference, to simultaneously fit in and stand out. It's a key tension in all of modern social life, as classic sociologist Georg Simmel noted, something that we're all trying for all the time, though few of us face on a daily basis the sharp consequences of failing to both conform and excel.[36]

So far we have a picture of fashion models at work: hundreds of them pulsing through the global city on subway trains and in taxis, portfolios and high heels in tow, fumbling their way through the incomprehensible filter of the casting process, hoping the dice will fall just right so that their looks will be *the look*, in what they can only imagine is the luck of the draw. All the while, just beyond their scope of vision, an entire field of players is engaged in an organized contest to define the look. These are the bookers and the clients, who are permanently engaged in the struggle to tame chance through the cultivation of their own careers as tastemakers.

CHAPTER 4

The Tastemakers

THE FEW FROM THE MANY

Walking into Metro's office, one first notices how *cool* it is. It is a sleek minimalist space, styled like a white cube of an art gallery: tall ceilings, bare white walls, black Herman Miller chairs. A pretty receptionist at the entrance of the office greets you from behind a marble table adorned with a tall vase of exotic fresh-cut flowers. Adjacent to her is a long pane of mirrored glass that hides a busy scene: the booking room, which fits two tables, a long one, which seats eleven agents, and a smaller table at the other end, which seats four agents. Through gaps in the mirror pane I used to watch and listen to them work: cradling the phones to their ears and scribbling onto notepads, searching their computer screens, sometimes shouting, laughing, passing a gift box of Parisian chocolates, talking to models, suddenly jumping from their chairs to check the printer outputs or to consult a colleague.

On the wall above the seated bookers are the cards, 4" × 6" composite cards of all the models Metro represents. There are four rows of cards running the length of the room, mostly images of models' head shots or profiles, some full-length body shots, and some women in bikinis and shirtless men staring seductively out into the booking room—hundreds of little images running across the wall.

Sometimes I would stand back and wonder at it, in awe of so many cards, so many models, and I would try to scan all of them, absorbing the looks, face after body after face, two hundred women and one hundred and fifty men. Many of these photos will hover there for a few years before being taken down without notice. Some models will make a decent living. Some will leave owing the agency thousands of dollars. And a few—maybe one this year—will become millionaires. What separates the few from the many? Why does one look rise from the pack into fame and fortune?

"That's a trick question!" declared Don, a booker, when I asked him this during our interview. He laughed and glanced out the window at the buzzing Manhattan street below, and, after a pause, said: "Well, it's not a trick question. But it's like asking the meaning of life."

Several blocks uptown, beneath the neon glare of Times Square, an editor named Joss sits in a small office, also busy at work on the "trick question." Her office wall is also plastered in pictures—over one hundred Polaroid head shots of young women and men stare out blankly at her desk. The models' names, ages, and heights are penciled into the margins. The Polaroids are recent shots that Joss has taken of models who come to see her for consideration for upcoming photo shoots in *Girl Chic* magazine, the "kid sister" of *Chic* magazine, where Joss works as the resident editor in charge of booking models.[1] She keeps track of models around the world through these Polaroids and explains: "I usually put up girls that I feel are right for us on the wall."

When I met with her, I wanted to know what it was that she was looking for in all of those castings, how a Polaroid makes its way around the world into her office, and how a client such as herself makes the decision to choose any given model. Though we talked for almost an hour, she could never quite find the words to explain it. Echoing the words of the thirty-nine other clients I interviewed, Joss explained that she "just knows" what she's looking for. She just gets a sense if a model she meets is *right* or not. She explained:

> They've got to be girls that we really believe have potential to go on. . . . So it's just a matter of, you know, developing your eye and seeing who you like and who you think is gonna be right. So you throw it to the wall and see what sticks.

What makes Joss pluck one Polaroid from among the hundreds on her wall? What does any client look for in such a vast editing process, and how do bookers know which models to supply to them?

These questions are central to unlocking the bigger puzzle of how something as ambiguous as a look attains value. Bookers and clients,

FIGURE 4.1. The office wall in Jennifer Venditti's JV8INC casting studio, downtown New York (photo by author)

those putative arbiters of taste, validate the look by converging on incipient taste. As amorphous notions of beauty and fashionableness swirl about the scene, tastemakers collectively converge onto similar ideas of good taste. In so doing, they make fashion trends happen. But their convergence is no egalitarian process. It is born of a struggle over artistic authority and a fight for the ability to consecrate fashionable taste. It takes social work for intermediaries to recognize and negotiate the value of a look, and though such work remains invisible in the pages of a magazine or on the catwalk, it is immensely consequential to any modeling career.

THE TASTEMAKER'S DILEMMA

Unlike the model, who rides the tides of luck, bookers are constantly engaged in churning those tides. Their job is to ensure that luck is not equally distributed among all contestants. Their key task is to keep track of the field of fashion producers, to predict and produce the tastes of their clients, and to fit the right kind of bodily capital into the right opening at just the right moment. They are gatekeepers, screening and pruning bodies into cultural products. They are also matchmakers, teaming looks to buyers to produce status and profit, usually in disproportionate amounts. Bookers face an especially tough predicament, given the inherent uncertainty involved in selling something as ephemeral as a look. Bookers, especially in the editorial circuit, cannot state in advance what they are looking for, nor can they calculate the probability of any model's chances, nor his or her own monthly booking record.

"You know, I can't see into the future, it's impossible," said Carl, a London booker for the past five years. "If you can sell a girl really well, then that betters her chances. But to know if she's actually gonna make it big, you can't tell."

Likewise, a senior booker at Metro explained a model's chances this way: "It's the luck of the draw. It's either you have it or you don't."

"And what is *it*?" I asked.

"Whatever *it* is at the moment," she promptly replied.

All hits are flukes, and all failures are a surprise. Alas, bookers too invoke the model's common saying: "You never know." All the same, actors in such markets have to do business somehow. Bookers have to sell models.

And clients have to buy.

It would seem that clients, as the final decision makers, are holding all the cards. Clients also feel the weight of market volatility, which for them stems from three sources: the oversupply of looks, unknown consumer demand, and the homogeneity of candidates.

First, faced with more models today than ever before due to digital technology and global expansion, clients sort through an ever-expanding pool of wannabe models. The sheer volume of models with whom clients shake hands seems overwhelming. At a casting for a department store advertisement, standing amid piles of Polaroids and composite cards, I talked with the casting director, who described a hectic three days of casting: "Yesterday was two hours, today is five, and already it's been three hours and I've seen 200 girls!" I asked if this was an "open call" casting, in which every model at every agency in town gets an invite: "Oh, *God* no!" he replied, indicating he had already sorted through hundreds of candidates before the casting began.

Second, clients face uncertainty because of changing consumer desires. Producers in creative markets can never know with accuracy which models will be most successful in selling their products, a quandary that market researchers continually attempt to control.[2] As cultural intermediaries who filter the look on its way to wider dissemination in fashion and beauty markets, clients necessarily interpret and construct consumer desires. These increasingly popular and powerful cultural intermediaries shape taste and inculcate new consumerist dispositions rather than respond passively to consumer demands "out there" in the public, waiting to be filled.[3]

Third, and finally, clients must search for the "right model" among a rather homogenous pool of candidates—meaning that they have to recognize small and subtle differences that make one look a better choice than another. Bookers, as gatekeepers, usually restrict clients' access to preselected, prescreened, groomed, socialized, and otherwise "developed" models. For instance, bookers tend not to make casting appointments for models with weight gain, breakouts, or noticeable drug problems. Clients therefore receive a relatively elite and minimally heterogeneous pool of candidates from which to choose, such that deciding about the comparative merits of one model versus another is tough. It is so tough, in fact, that during one casting for Fashion Week, I watched as the creative team talked with a celebrated New York designer, presenting him with a selection of Polaroids of candidates to walk in his show. They asked his opinion on which models to choose. He thought for a moment, then pointed to each of the cards: "She's good, she's good, she's good, they're *all* good!" he said, throwing up his arms in exasperation.

Within this context—oversupply and homogenization of looks, plus unknown consumer demand—clients must make their selections. While bookers and models think that "nobody knows" what clients will want, clients themselves are just as troubled. From their perspective, "nobody knows" any better what makes a good choice. To echo the dilemma expressed by magazine publishers and Hollywood screenwriters, "nobody knows anything."[4]

And yet, *they know*! When asked how long it takes her to decide on a model in a casting, one major stylist in London summed it up: "An instant! You know, you know, *you just know*!" Most clients I interviewed spoke with this kind of self-assured ease when explaining the casting process. They claimed to know the moment the model walks through the door—though there was some variation if in fact one knows the *very second* or the *very minute* the model enters the room. Yet despite their professed certitude, they could not articulate what it was that they saw. They said that they may not be able to explain what it is about a model that makes her "really good" or "right;" simply, they are able to *feel* it. "It's really, it's just a very instinctive thing, and I don't know what else to say about it," explained Florence, a London stylist for eight years.

The very fact that clients cannot articulate the quality of a "really good model" suggests that it lies in their own roles and actions rather than in the masses of looks they see before them. Choosing a look is at once an act of reading—deciphering and decoding—that presupposes literacy of the look. It is also an act of speaking; clients' own judgment will itself be judged in the model's career trajectory. Consumption, Bourdieu reminds us, is one stage in a process of communication: "Taste classifies, and it classifies the classifier."[5]

Though clients think of their taste as personal preferences, they don't enact taste alone. There is remarkable convergence among clients on what they consider "really good" models. Every season new catwalk stars emerge from dozens of new faces, just as former top models disappear out of vogue. Consider the inequality of popularity on the catwalk during Fashion Week. Based on a count of the 2007 Spring/Summer collections showcased on Style.com, an online extension of *Vogue* magazine, 172 fashion houses displayed collections in New York, London, Milan, or Paris.[6] Despite the relatively unfettered access to thousands of fashion models worldwide, these 172 clients chose a total of just 677 different models to include in their fashion shows.[7] Seventy-five percent of the models were employed in fewer than five shows, while just sixty models (9 percent) were chosen for over twenty shows in the four cities.[8] The three most popular models were extremely busy during Fashion Week. Behati Prinsloo walked in sixty-four shows; Iekeliene Stange and Irina Lazareanu appeared in fifty-nine shows each (see Figure 4.2).

The presence of such spectacular winners raises a great sociological puzzle: If models are chosen according to personal taste, then how does this collective convergence happen? Decades ago, sociologist Herbert Blumer grappled with a similar problem as he observed fashion buyers in Paris. He found remarkable convergence of buyers' preferences for new designs, but when asked, buyers simply claimed to like the garments they personally found "stunning." Though they rely on personal feelings when making aesthetic choices, tastemakers all happen to feel similarly at the exact same moment. Blumer argued that his fashion buyers collectively "grope" in anticipation of *incipient taste*—"they are seeking to catch the proximate future," in the hope of naming, as he put it, "the direction of modernity."[9] He theorized that incipient taste in fashion does *not* follow imitation of the upper classes, as had been previously thought by theorists such as Georg Simmel and Thorsten Veblen. Rather,

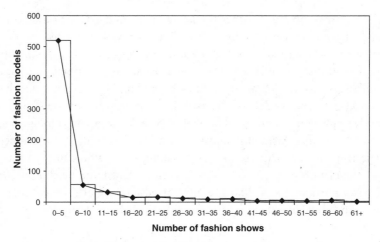

FIGURE 4.2. Inequality on the catwalk

incipient taste emerges from shared cultural space among the buyers, all of them chasing the future direction of fashionableness.

People often think they are exercising an individual choice, when in fact their decisions are bound up with other people's actions in subtle ways. Even in the seemingly all-personal decision to name a newborn baby, sociologist Stanley Lieberson has shown that parents are subtly guided by *other* parents naming their children such that popular names rise and fall year after year.[10] Like parents choosing a baby's name and buyers choosing garments in Paris, tastemakers who are trying to choose the next top model have an absolutely insoluble problem: there is no obvious "right" choice. There is no authority or rule-making body to organize the competition or declare the winner (the fact that Tyra Banks fails season after season to really launch America's next top model is further evidence). How do people choose between a lot of likely contenders whose suitability for being chosen isn't particularly obvious? And how do they end up choosing together? Blumer reasoned that if sociologists could unlock how this "collective taste" happens, we could come closer to understanding how cultural change works.

BEAUTY IS IN THE EYE OF THE BOOKER

Just as models frequently land in the industry by serendipitous encounters with scouts, bookers arrive to the booking table through similar chance events. One agency's senior bookers drove motor homes for a production company. Another booker worked in construction before a family friend needed help in a modeling agency. Though few realized that such a job existed until they occupied it, a majority shared a passion for art and fashion from a young age. They spoke of ripping out pages from older sisters' *Vogue* magazines or styling siblings' outfits. They idolized the supermodels of the 1980s and kept track of their careers. For example Paul, an editorial booker in New York, began ripping pages out of his sisters' fashion magazines as a kid. Gradually, he explained, "The ripping out pictures started becoming like, 'Who's the girl on p. 234, the girl on p. 237?' to 'Oh, that's Gilles Bensimon; he shoots *Elle*; he has a particular style.' So I really started looking at different magazines, and I felt like there was something there but I didn't know quite what."

On their way to the booking table, agents are likely to work in other culture or related media fields, for instance, as artists and stylists, though just two bookers I interviewed had modeled in their youth.[11] They are paid by experience rather than by commission, but their salaries vary widely, from $45,000 for junior bookers upward of $200,000 for senior bookers and managers in New York. In London, bookers start at about $18,000 and can earn upward of $80,000.

Socially, bookers are a mixed bag. They come from cities and suburbs from around the United States and UK and are predominantly from middle-class or lower-middle-class backgrounds, of the "petite bourgeoisie" that Bourdieu has claimed constitutes the "new cultural intermediary" occupational group. Since their expansion in the latter half of the twentieth century, cultural intermediaries have enjoyed greater and enhanced status; for example, stylists and casting directors have experienced an upsurge in pop cultural visibility and status since the 1980s with the boom in image-led advertising. There is no educational requirement to be a booker, but the majority of those I met and interviewed (twenty out of twenty-five) had attended college for at least one year, and about half had attended arts-related colleges or had arts-related majors. Half held college degrees (see Table 4.1).[12] Business or management backgrounds were unusual in either agency, except among the accountants, despite the agents' regularly negotiating contracts and managing lofty sums of money.

About half of the bookers and staff (fifteen) were male, and among them nine identified as gay men, while just one of the eighteen female bookers identified as lesbian. Six of the New York bookers were of nonwhite ethnicity (four Latinos, one Asian, one black); all of the eleven

TABLE 4.1   INTERVIEW SAMPLE OF BOOKERS AND STAFF IN NEW YORK
AND LONDON

New York Sample

Name	Job Title	Circuit	Books Men or Women	Years of Experience
Bre	Sr. Booker	Showroom	Women	11
Christoph	Booker	Editorial	Both	7
Don	Sr. Booker	Commercial	Women	18
Elle	Booker	Showroom	Women	10
Francis	Booker	Showroom	Women	10
Gil	Staff	~	~	26
Harel	Booker	Editorial	Women	9
Heather	Booker	All	~	11
Ivan	Booker	Commercial	Men	10
Jackson	Booker	Commercial	Both	28
Joe	Staff	~	~	5
Kath	Booker	Commercial	Women	10
Leonard	Staff	~	~	7
Lynne	Sr. Booker	All	Women	37
Missy	Booker	All	Men	8
Naz	Sr. Booker	All	Men	13
Olivia	Booker	Showroom	Both	9
Paul	Booker	Editorial	Women	12
Rachel	Booker	Editorial	Women	10
Rio	Booker	All	Women	8
Sal	Booker	Showroom	Both	6
Xander	Staff	~	~	1

London Sample

Name	Job Title	Circuit	Books Men or Women	Years of Experience
Amber	Assistant	All	~	1
Bella	Assistant	All	~	1
Carl	Booker	All	Both	5
Damien	Booker	Editorial	Women	12
Erica	Booker	All	Women	3.5
Fria	Sr. Booker	Editorial	Women	26
Gretta	Booker	Editorial	Both	5
Helen	Sr. Booker	All	Both	26
Isha	Staff	~	~	1
James	Staff	~	~	5
Kate	Booker	All	Both	5

TABLE 4.2   THE SOCIAL MAKEUP OF NEW YORK
AND LONDON BOOKERS AND STAFF

	Bookers and Staff		
	Total	NYC	London
Total	33	22	11
Female	18	10	8
Male	15	12	3
Gay	9	6	3
Lesbian	1	1	~
Non-White	6	6	~
Latino	4	4	~
Asian	1	1	~
Black	1	1	~
College	27	18	9
Art Background	15	9	6

bookers in London were white (see Table 4.2). These characteristics reflect the widespread belief that fashion is an industry with a high propor-
tion of white gay men and straight women. Straight men dominate business decision-making positions, for example, as accountants and business
managers—a pattern that exists among clients as well. Straights and gays
work on behalf of female and male models equally. The scarcity of
straight men elsewhere in the business probably reflects wider gender
tropes that men in fashion violate "hegemonic masculinity."[13]

All bookers—male or female, straight or gay—learn to view models'
looks with an eye on the field of fashion. Few among them claimed to
enter fashion with the ability to recognize looks. It is not a latent talent
in those art school students and college dropouts who arrive at the
booking table. In fact many of them talked about how radically different and "open" their sense of beauty had become since entering the job.
This is an ongoing process, forever changing in tune within the fashion
world, as bookers refashion their original sense of beauty with a specific set of conventions necessary to find and produce the look.

At the Booking Table

Once arriving to the booking table, bookers sit in a particular arrangement. At Metro, their seats correspond to the different looks of models

featured on the cards lining the wall behind them. When standing a few feet back from the wall, the cards blur into a jumble of good-looking women and men. Should an outsider unfamiliar with fashion come closer for a better look, she or he might see the same—a collage of pretty people placed seemingly at random next to each other.

To the bookers, the wall of cards makes obvious visual sense. Commercial looks to the left on the Money board, "edgy" looks in the middle on the Editorial board, and more commercial looks for the Showroom board further down the wall to the far right. At Scene, models and bookers are not physically separated, but informal differentiations are made between editorial and commercial bookers and models, and their cards on the agency wall shift from commercial on the left to editorial on the right. Someone taking a cursory glance at Scene's wall might see smiling, conventionally pretty faces to the left and stranger, less-welcoming faces to the right. A booker looking at this wall would see the transition from profit to prestige, the trade-off in fashion between high-risk editorial work and steadily paid commercial jobs.

Editorial jobs generate image and hype for an agency, which is vital to secure catalog clients and high-end advertising such as fragrance and cosmetic campaigns. Compared to the catalog and showroom boards, however, the Editorial board turns paltry profits. At Metro, for example, in just one sample month, the Showroom board was by far the agency's largest source of income, accounting for about 70 percent of the agency's total billings, almost three and a half times more than the Women and Editorial boards combined. Damien, an editorial booker in London, explained: "I would love to make more money, sure, everyone wants to make more money, but I bring in something else to the agency, I bring in the image, which is equally important."

Perhaps inevitably, a subtle sense of disregard sometimes creeps up on the commercial booker, whose reliable stream of showroom and catalog revenues is overshadowed by editorial prestige:

> Showroom, it's more body oriented, more about the height, you have to show the clothes. It's, I guess, less "*prestigious*" than the other boards. . . . But also of my division, the girls are more commercial looking. They might be more mainstream pretty, but less interesting perhaps, less *editorial*, whatever [rolls eyes]. (Bre, New York booker)

Metro's Showroom board is quietly referred to among other agents as the "B-level" models, because their portfolios feature tear sheets from the likes of *Parade* and *Redbook* magazines. But without their earnings, the agency would not survive. Commercial bookers are essentially the life vests of any agency, yet their work simultaneously sinks an agency's image. Bre's comments suggest that she both knows and resents this.

Commercial models resent it too, since their wages mortgage a prestige contest that excludes them. But commercial bookers like Bre have little patience for models who have made considerable wealth but persist in fighting for a higher place in the prestige hierarchy. An old office joke at Metro poked fun at one woman who made a good living as a showroom model but was continually pushing for castings to *Vogue* so she could get the editorial kudos she thought she deserved. She was known around the agency as "Supa-*star*." However much "Supa-*star*" wanted to be on the Editorial board, bookers explained that she just didn't have the right look. But how does a booker know what is "right"?

Training the Eye

Heather takes several scouting trips throughout the year, traveling to cities and towns across America, Eastern Europe, and Latin America, often with one or more of the bookers from Metro. She likens scouting events to a "traveling circus": fifty or so agents, primarily from New York, LA, Tokyo, and Europe, convene for two days in a hotel, where they merrily drink together by night and fight with each other by day over a select few candidates among hundreds in attendance. From each of these trips, Heather expects to return to Metro with Polaroids of one or two promising young women and men. Sometimes she returns empty-handed.

Patience and scrutiny, that's her job, Heather explains: "You really have to have the eye to be able to pick them apart . . . and I have to realize with a little bit of this and a little bit of that she can really be amazing." When it comes down to it, she can quickly sort through a line of wannabes: "I've done this for so long, that I can see a girl in two seconds and decide if she is right for me or not." But when asked what makes a girl "right" for the moment, Heather is at a loss for words.

Scouts like Heather have a difficult time explaining their work. A look either makes sense to them or it doesn't, and this they know because their "eye" tells them so. To a booker, having an eye is having the ability to spot models, envision their future career possibilities, and match them to clients. It is a learned skill, a form of cultivated knowledge similar to what journalists might call a "nose for news," or product designers refer to as "lateral awareness" as they create designs for things such as sofas and toaster ovens.[14]

Beyond loose physical criteria for the look (height, weight, and so on), there is considerable ambiguity about what makes a "good" look. Most bookers explained that when scouting, they first look for eliminations. Height, below 5'9" for adult women or 5'8" for growing teenage girls, cancels out a lot of people. So do "lazy eyes" and "problem" noses. Amber, an assistant for one year at Scene, learned to scout from a senior booker:

> The first thing you look for is the height. They have to be over 5'8". I remember the first time I went out scouting with Fria, she was just like "the next thing you have to look for is their nose." If they've got a dodgy nose, there's nothing you can do about it . . . frumpy noses, crooked noses, or something . . . and the third thing is, like, overall does it work?

Whether or not a look works "overall" is not immediately obvious to beginners. Bella, an assistant at Scene, is often rhetorically asked, "Are you *joking?*" by the bookers when she presents them with candidates that, to her developing eye, look like great models.

Depending on one's place in the fashion circuit, one look may be seen as beautiful or dull, weird or extraordinary. Bookers assess in different ways the raw talent that is presented to them by scouts and the mass of cards on their wall. Different and sometimes opposite ways of seeing emerge between editorial and commercial bookers. Commercial bookers tend to see commercial models as pretty and "all-American" looking. But when seen through the eyes of the editorial booker, this commercial look is rather dull:

> If all I can say is she's pretty, then that's boring. "Oh she's cute." That's boring. If I can say *wow*, not *only* is she pretty, there's something off about her, but she's still attractive, like she's really cool-looking. (Rio, New York booker)

Editorial bookers describe their "edgier" models as "inspiring" and even as potential game changers to definitions of "normal" beauty. As Gretta, an editorial booker in London, put it, editorial models are "not *just* pretty, they're just like—*wow*. Really incredible!" Meanwhile, commercial and showroom bookers used words like "slob," "borderline beautiful," "grungy," "dirty," "rodent," "hard," and "freaky looking" to describe Gretta's Editorial board. Leave it to an accountant to best explain the commercial way of seeing:

An editorial girl—you'll see her, she'll look awful, like my God, *what's that*? You know, your mother would say you could never guess what her job was. And a commercial girl is really beautiful, pretty, you know, a stunning girl. (James, London staff)

And so one agent's cast-off is another's treasure, and this very act of treasuring is circuit specific. Three looks match three circuits: The commercial booker wants something formulaic, classic, and safe. In addition to these specifications, the showroom booker wants reliably precise body measurements in sizes 4–8. The editorial booker, on the other hand, wants an edge—something special and new that cannot be put into words: "It's being beautiful and having something quite interesting about you as well. You know, I hate to say it, it's like the X-factor," said Carl in London.

Bookers spoke of a natural development in their careers into promoting models for editorial or commercial work, where it seemed their own personal creative sensibilities carried them into their seat at the booking table. Gretta, for example, has always just wanted to be a part of fashion; she loves flipping through magazines and admiring her behind-the-scenes handiwork:

All I wanted to do was book a girl in editorial and see it come out, and say, "I did this!" You know, I helped in some way to contribute to that, and also the importance of editorial to a girl's career is primary. (Gretta, London booker)

Bookers can also tire of a circuit, which tends to happen as they grow into their careers, typically in the direction away from editorial and toward commercial booking. It is a career arc that is similar to the models they represent:

I used to love fashion but nowadays I get more of a kick out of earning money than I do editorial. . . . You get quite, not cynical, but—as you get older, um, if you're 20 or 22, you get really excited about a call from a magazine saying "Oh we're doing a nautical theme this summer, this is the look we want, this is the girl we want," and now I'm 42, I've already seen everything revolve around. (Fria, London booker)

Every booker's eye is shaped by her or his circuit and fixed on a segment of the field and on clients' possible future tastes. Through experience, bookers learn to make sense of looks they might otherwise not comprehend. They also learn which type of "personality" resonates with each circuit.

The Potential of Personality

In spotting the look, bookers are also reading a model's personality. They study models' personalities—their attitudes, styles of engagement, and comportment—and try to "fit" them with clients' personalities. This is generally reflected in how bookers across the boards talk about desirable personalities. Most bookers like models to be "outgoing," "sweet," and skilled in emotional labor. For example, when sizing up the multimillion-dollar potential of one of his protégés, personality reigned supreme in Don's decision to promote a model to stardom:

> I just knew. She had the personality, first of all. She used not knowing English that well to her advantage. She would excuse herself and laugh at herself at the same time. And she made sure that she had the personality that made people remember her. And because they wanted to see her again, because they wanted more of her, she'd make them feel like "Okay, we are going to be on set together for eight hours, believe me, you are going to have a great time!" (Don, New York booker)

Showroom bookers in particular are concerned with their models being professional. Because showroom work is consistent and high volume, bookers value models who are responsible and pleasant to work with so that clients will book them again, sometimes for days or weeks at a time. Professionalism is also defined as being prompt and dependable—lateness and a bad attitude are not tolerated by showroom bookers, whose clients count on them daily for fit models.

Editorial bookers may prefer models with unusual or "offbeat" personalities to match their edgy appearances. They are particularly drawn to the "oddballs" and "characters," those young men and women whom they see as social underdogs, people who were probably unpopular in high school:

> I just spent time in London this last week and I met this girl at an agency—she had this little sweatshirt on, and she had like no makeup, she had her little hoodie pulled over her head. She was kind of like an interesting character from Argentina. I really found her really beautiful. (Paul, New York booker)

Bookers know that a showroom client probably has little patience for the quirky Argentine in the hoodie, just as a high-fashion photographer may be bored by the sweet and professional commercial model.

The least desirable among all bookers are models with "no personality," which includes shy and introverted personalities. Bookers try to coax models out of their putative shells by talking to them regularly, enrolling them in English language and drama classes, and taking them to agency-sponsored parties and dinners to develop their social skills. Elite Models in New York reportedly sends prospective models to a "movement coach" to learn catwalk composure and stylized poses.[15] To ensure that their models have *some* personality that will appeal to clients, bookers instruct them in the ways of basic casting strategies. In London, Fria sometimes observes models when the agency hosts a client's casting, and then she offers the models tips in basic communication skills, such as eye contact, a firm handshake, and simple talking-point suggestions, for example, giving a client a compliment: "It's silly really, but you know, 'Oh, I like your jacket, isn't that nice?' Everyone likes a bit of flattery, you know, everyone likes to hear that, even if it's a bloody lie!"

Because personality shows in the model's style of dress, bookers try to style their new models' fit with the particularities of the editorial or a commercial circuit. Commercial bookers encourage models to look well groomed, not "dirty" or otherwise unprofessional, and to not wear ripped jeans. When a model has "aged out" of the editorial circuit, bookers may try to redirect the model's career to the commercial circuit. They will usually advise the model to put on a little weight, especially the men, who may need to "bulk up" appropriately to fit sportswear catalog clothes, and they may change the model's hair, from an edgy style to something more "soft," which can be achieved perhaps with highlights and layers. Once the model embodies a mainstream "classically good-looking" appearance, he or she will be ready to "cash in," some of the models like to say.

Editorial bookers like models to look "cool": no chunky heels or platform shoes (too much of a "mall look"), and no excessively short skirts or overly sexy outfits ("too cheap"). Rachel, a booker in New York explained:

> Clients, especially editorial clients, are sort of snobby. They like models to dress a certain way, to be hip and be cool, so you kind of have to have that edge to you. And if you don't have it it's harder to get booked. Because they like cool girls. So we try to help the girls with their clothes, help them figure out kind of what style they're gonna land into.

To encourage "cool" models, bookers assign magazines for models to study, and then they take them shopping at hip retailers such as H&M, expensed to the model's account. They send models to world-renowned hair salons for complimentary cuts and colors. Bookers also tailor looks to their clients by fudging the model's stats, the height and body measurements listed on the back of the comp card. With an eye toward their clients' past working practices and preferences, bookers may report a model's age as a few years older or younger, her height as half an inch taller or shorter, and her hips, bust, and waist as typically within a half-inch margin of error, depending on what they think clients really want. There is disagreement among bookers about how much a model's look can be fundamentally altered or not, but most agree that they can "mold" a look by tweaking a model's dress, hair, and personality.

By training their "eyes" on the look, bookers absorb the specific logic of their fashion circuit. It is not an innate ability, somehow inherent in creative genius, but it is a learned skill, tailored to the editorial or commercial or showroom network in which bookers are immersed. They talk about it in the language available to them, as a "feeling" or as an extrasensory organ. Sociologically, the eye is a certain mentality developed from participation in the fashion world. It is a form of what sociologist Patrik Aspers calls "contextual knowledge" among producers, gleaned from shared social space and bits and pieces of colleagues' past experiences and values.[16] While crucial to their work, this knowledge only gets bookers so far; they must also be able to influence fashion clients if they are to convert this contextual knowledge into value.

AUTHORITY OF A FASHION CLIENT

Behind every model is a booker, pushing, promoting, and hyping her or him up on the phone. On the other end of the line there is a client. Clients are charged with the selection of models for designers and fashion companies. I interviewed forty such persons who held a variety of positions, including seven magazine editors, eleven photographers, ten art/casting directors, four clothing designers, two hair and makeup stylists, and six clothes stylists.

Some clients have more influence than others; stylists and casting directors wield considerable clout, makeup artists the least, and designers usually make the final verdict on which models to hire. Stylists don't just present clothes; since the 1980s, their role has been to create an innovative new "look," for which they have been rewarded tremendous cultural prestige, as evidenced by their names being featured in magazine spreads alongside the names of photographers, models, and, increasingly, even casting directors.[17] Casting directors frequently work for other clients, namely magazine editors, fashion advertisers, and designers. During

TABLE 4.3 · SUMMARY OF CLIENTS

New York Sample

Name	Job Title	Years of Experience
Ann	Magazine Editor	8
Billy	Photographer	6
Clive	Stylist	10
David	Casting Director	14
Donna	Designer	5
Frank	Casting Director	10
Gretchen	Magazine Editor	10
Hall	Photographer	17
Jay	Designer	5
Joss	Magazine Editor	10
Kelly	Magazine Editor	8
Lawrence	Stylist	16
Manni	Photographer	4
Nev	Magazine Editor	15
Oden	Casting Director	23
Peter	Casting Director	2
Rayna	Casting Director	17
Sarah	Stylist	5
Sheila	Photographer	11
Tomas	Art Director	20

London Sample

Name	Job Title	Years of Experience
Aspen	Photographer	8
Bruno	Stylist	12
Chloe	Photographer	2
Eddie	Photographer	15
Florence	Stylist	8
Gabe	Casting Director	1
Isabel	Magazine Editor	3
Jordan Bane	Casting Director	20
Kate	Magazine Editor	3
Lazarus	Photographer	12
Leah	Casting Director	15
Mishca	Art Director	5
Narcisco	Photographer	8
Peter Gray	Hairstylist	20
Tim	Photographer	5
Tim & Mike	Designer	20
Umberto	Photographer	10
Victor	Designer	5
Wes	Make-up Artist	11
Xavier	Stylist	8

TABLE 4.4   THE SOCIAL MAKEUP OF CLIENTS

	Clients		
	Total	NYC	London
Total	40	20	20
Female	16	9	7
Male	24	11	13
Gay	12	6	6
Lesbian	~	~	~
Non-White	9	7	2
Latino	5	4	1
Asian	2	1	1
Black	2	2	~
Some College	29	16	13
Art Background	34	15	19

Fashion Week, for example, a casting director can work for different designers and cast several shows.

Like bookers, clients are from mixed social backgrounds. Out of my sample of forty clients, about 60 percent were men (twenty-four), half identified as gay men, and none of the women identified as lesbian. Seven of the twenty clients in New York were of non-white ethnicity (two black, four Latinos, one Asian), and in London I spoke with two non-white clients (one Asian, one Latino). They came primarily from middle-class and lower-middle-class backgrounds, and they typically had some college experience, most commonly from art schools such as Saint Martin's in London or Parsons School of Design in New York. They were likely to have interned at the start of their careers, and they have held a variety of jobs within the creative economy, for example, as visual artists, fashion journalists, actors, and, in a few cases, models and modeling agents.

With the exception of magazine editors, clients are contingent workers on a freelance, per-project basis, without benefits. This is in contrast to the bookers, who enjoy an organizational safety net working as full-time employees. Clients face constant job insecurity, making them rather like the models whose careers they seem to dictate. Clients build careers along similar lines as models, building up editorial and commercial value and, unlike bookers, who tend to specialize in either the editorial or commercial circuits, clients overlap and navigate between the circuits.

For Art or Money

Clients want to do fashion—*editorial* fashion. Photographers dream of creating incredible images to rival Richard Avedon and Steven Meisel in *Vogue* and *Visionaire* magazines. Stylists want to dress top models, and casting directors want to produce famed catwalk shows in New York, London, Paris, and Milan. For most, this won't happen. Most clients will work sporadically or semipermanently on commercial advertising and catalogs. Like models, clients are stratified into a winner-take-all hierarchy: there are few superstars at the top—most work in mediocre jobs for mediocre wages.

Achieving success in the editorial circuit is a high-stakes gamble for clients. For one thing, prestigious magazine work can be quite costly; that is, it *costs* producers money to shoot an editorial. Expenses for a magazine photo shoot can run between $500 and several thousand dollars for items such as studio rental, equipment, assistants, post-production, and lunch. Photographers, stylists, casting directors, hair and makeup artists, and art directors are all willing to take a loss on magazine work in the hopes that a spread in *i-D* magazine will pay off in the form of symbolic capital and, eventually, in lucrative advertising jobs. As Hall, a New York photographer explained, "Editorial costs me a *lot* of money. Two to five thousand. Yeah, the idea is that you'll get one booking and it's paid for. But sometimes it doesn't work that way."

Photographers like Hall are taking a big risk on their editorial investments. Should something go wrong to wreck the shoot, for example, a grumpy model, bad lighting, or a wardrobe failure, Hall will lose out on his investment. For reasons beyond his control or foresight, Hall's pictures may not come out to the magazine's liking; the magazine might kill his story, and then he will be out the money. In the end, his pictures may run, they may look fabulous, but he will not land that big advertising job as he hopes, and he will still be out the money. However great the stakes might be, clients maintain that this is a necessary gamble. They talked about editorial work as an investment:

> It's almost like you need to work harder on the editorial than you do on the advertising, because the advertising is fruit, which comes from the editorial tree. (Peter, London hairstylist)

Because editorial work offers exposure and the potential to put great images into one's portfolio, the stakes are even higher for the portfolio to look great. Clients, like other freelancers, are only as good as their last project.[18] This is especially the case in the more visible editorial circuit, explained Billy, a photographer making his way up the prestige ladder:

> Your photographs travel fast. People are going to see them and whether or not you represent yourself well. . . . The bigger the client, the more pressure to pull something off. (Billy, New York photographer)

Creativity and editorial visibility thus demand a stressful imperative to be creative.

Most clients start with the aim of achieving artistic authority—the ability to set trends and name the look—and most give up the pursuit after a few years. Not all clients can fit atop the status hierarchy; there's just not enough room. While almost all clients paid verbal tribute to the editorial circuit, some simply could no longer afford to chase it. As the jackpot begins to look increasingly unattainable, it becomes practical, and even preferable, to trade artistic autonomy for financial stability and a predictable work life. Too much insecurity can turn one off from the game, as the makeup artist at a catalog house casually told me:

> I love fashion, don't get me wrong. But it doesn't pay. As you get older, your drive to be an artist goes out the window, because to do the things you want to do you need money, you have to make a living, so I say bring on the advertising jobs, get that money! (Roe, London makeup artist)

Money versus creativity, profit versus prestige—this is a tension that bookers and clients constantly must resolve in their work, as we will see by examining how they select models in two distinct cases: the catalog shoot and the catwalk.

PRODUCING THE CATALOG LOOK

Seated in a director's chair in front of a large vanity with lightbulbs, Roe, a hair and makeup stylist, dabbed a glob of shimmery gloss onto my lips, checked my reflection, and said: "You know it when you see it, that special *Vshop* factor, that *Vshop* look. I can always tell when they'll be back."

Any other day I might have been insulted, for Roe had just teased my hair to unimaginable heights and caked my face with thick powder, slightly orange in hue. I am now ready to start my second day of shooting for the UK-based online catalog *Vshop*, which caters to young consumers on a budget. I would rather not have a *Vshop* look, except that an eight-hour day here pays £1,250 ($2,500 in the 2006 exchange rate). The *Vshop* catalog is a commercial job par excellence: it is highly paid and consistent work, but it is low in status. It is therefore an ideal site to examine the catalog casting process.

Finding the Right Catalog Look

What is the *Vshop* look, and how do producers determine which models have it? *Vshop* resident photographer Chloe explained to me that casting models for a catalog is relatively "easy," in the sense that it is a straightforward process, but it can be quite challenging, because it requires strict adherence to a set of formulated guidelines. Like everyone else who produces the catalog, Chloe defers her creative decisions, including her selection of models, to a thick in-house reference book of suggested poses and styles provided by corporate headquarters. She calls it "The Bible":

> With this, it's very formulated, like the client knows exactly what they want. We've got a massive book, telling us exactly how things should be. The Bible. And it's like, you know, some girls just will not look right in the clothes, or not do the right posing. (Chloe, London photographer)

Casting criteria are fairly simple and predictable across the range of commercial jobs—models should be conventionally "pretty" or "good looking," with widespread appeal and agreeable personalities. Until recently, *Vshop* fell squarely within the parameters of the commercial look: "normal," "safe," and "classic," the same descriptions echoed by bookers and models. In the past few months, however, *Vshop* has taken an edgy turn in the hope of appealing to young, fashion-forward consumers. Their look is now described as "strong," and not your "everyday catalog look." *Vshop* producers have taken pains to clarify and control their new image; The Bible that rests near Chloe's tripod is a case in point. Another manifestation of *Vshop's* image control is a new "mood board," which an executive boss recently propped alongside the studio wall. (The mood board is a large piece of white poster board featuring pictures and pointers for all of the production crew, including models, to reference.) It read:

VSHOP WOMAN
Editorial not Catalog
Sexy, Good Eye Contact
= OR =
Naturally Looking Away, Feminine
Good Variance of Poses
Never Looking Sullen or Sad

Beside each line of the instructions were several photos of men and women in cool poses, mostly torn images from editorial spreads in high-end magazines—images that seemed unlikely to ever be replicated at *Vshop*. Part of the new vision of the *Vshop* catalog was that it should not look like a catalog, and yet the *Vshop* look was still directly tied to sales of products. This meant that Chloe and her crew of stylists were not in control of the look and feel of their own creative work. Nor did they necessarily want to be. One commercial art director explained:

> Oh, you can say a lot of things, but the client has a final say many times who you work with, giant clients have the say. I can persuade them, if I'm very intelligent and I'm really good with words. I can charm them and say this is exactly what we need. But many times, that didn't happen. (Tomas, New York art director)

On the whole, art directors like Tomas are not too concerned with exercising their creative potential on commercial jobs. They would rather just let the boss decide, even though this entails accepting arbitrary orders from corporate headquarters, as in the cliché among advertising producers that important aesthetic choices are ultimately decided by the CEO's spouse.

The commercial client's principal concern is pleasing the boss, and getting paid well for it. The casting process is not so much about taste-making as it is about following instructions. One photographer explained regarding advertising shoots: "It's just if you fill the shoes or not. That's it." The "shoes" in the commercial circuit are supplied by management.

Edge and taste take a backseat to the commercial world, where the principal concern when choosing models is money. *Victoria's Secret*, one of the most famous commercial catalogs, is known for hiring supermodels as brand spokespersons, but it also mines the data of its online catalog to find future campaign "Angels." Girls who "move merchandise" online and receive a high volume of mouse clicks are put in the running for *Victoria's Secret* stardom.[19]

The commercial producers I interviewed had less sophisticated but equally rigorous concerns for selling products. Back at *Vshop*, Alice the photographer is held accountable for online sales. At the end of a day of shooting, her boss and creative team review the catalog images. If their catalog suppliers deem the model too skinny, too young, or too big, or if her hair is seen to not sit well upon her head, then she is not invited back for future shoots. If the clothes she has modeled do not sell well in the catalog, she will be dismissed. In the end, a job well done at *Vshop* leads to management's satisfaction and, ultimately, sales of their line.

The Commercial Personality

While commercial castings like *Vshop* are "easy" in the sense that clear standards guide creative decisions, they can be quite challenging because of the potential difficulties in executing them. The biggest challenge, and the greatest source of uncertainty, to commercial clients is the model's personality. Personality, as we've seen, is central to the look, and it is a primary concern for bookers and clients; nobody wants to work with, variously stated, "wet lettuce," a "big, dead fish," or a "lame one that just lays there like a lump." For catalog and advertising jobs, which can last eight hours or more each day, sometimes several days, professional and agreeable models are mandatory to getting the job done. A model's ability to move and to take direction is crucial. Narcisco, a photographer, harshly explained that you don't want a model who "doesn't know her ass from her elbow," or you'll be stuck having to "push a dead donkey" on set.

To screen for personality, clients prefer to have an in-person casting, where they will chat with candidates, watch their movements in and out of the casting room, and get a sense of what it might be like to work with them. When New York-based photographer Hall casts for models to shoot department store catalogs, he sometimes watches security cameras as models ride the elevator up to meet him, observing them change from their sneakers into high heels. He says he looks for people "set apart" from the rest. He continues his observations during the audition as he chats with models, often asking them questions to see how they respond: "Where are you from?" or "Do you have any dogs?" It is a gauge of personality. He explains:

> Sometimes I don't even care what they're interested in, I just like the way they express what they're interested in. So I can see what kind of expression that they have, what kind of emotion that they have, it's something that they can give me. (Hall, New York photographer)

Castings help clients size up a model's personality, but these brief meetings may not be adequate predictors of a model's performance on the day of the shoot. Despite an intriguing demeanor during the audition, a model may in the end turn out to be "wet lettuce" after all. To minimize this possibility, clients talk.

Gossip

Fashion runs on gossip. Clients ubiquitously swap stories as a way to gather information about models' on-the-job performances. Within their social networks, clients pass tips to one another, and they expect to receive tips in return. These tightly knit circles are known as "production networks" in Hollywood, another volatile industry. As Hall explained to me, all producers share their "war stories" of working with uncooperative models:

> As a freelance photographer, I work with all the clients, you know what I mean? . . . Everybody's doing the same catalogs with the same models basically. It's a small little world. So when one of them says, "Hey have you ever worked with this girl?" I'll be like, "Oh yeah sure, she's great." Or I'll be like, "Oh no, not on a Monday, never on a Monday with her!"

Small and seemingly trivial tips, such as Hall's suggestion that a particular model works well except when she has her Monday morning hangover, are highly valued. Similarly, David, a casting director, is likely to share detailed tips about which models his colleagues should hire— and how to treat them on the job:

> "Oh my God it is so hard to get anything out of her!" Or, you know, like "She's really, really great, but don't feed her, because as soon as she eats, she gets tired and her energy changes." (David, New York casting director)

Thus before any model makes her way into the *Vshop* studio, she has likely been thoroughly discussed by a web of gossiping clients.

But before she is even considered for a catalog job, a model has been steered there by a booker. How did I come to find myself so far from the glamorous catwalks of New York, donning teased hair and discounted knitwear on behalf of sales for the small *Vshop* catalog?

Matchmaking in the Commercial Circuit

As they look out at the wall of composite cards spread before them, bookers see not only the faces of models but connections with clients, and they have basic assumptions about the fashion-buying public. At the commercial end, bookers imagine that the girl or boy next door will "make sense" to a mass middle market. Legible and relatable, this look sells by appealing to the everyday consumer. The editorial look, they reckon, will not make sense to the masses, and nearly every booker I interviewed spoke to this end, several invoking a tattooed young woman named Devan, who was at the time a highly successful and very "edgy" editorial model. For example:

> If you were a buyer from Neiman Marcus in Dallas, you would be scared by Devan! Therefore, you may not buy all the outfits she is wearing, which would really be damaging to the client. And they know that. Plus, some of my clients are really tame, like St. John's, for example. You cannot put Devan in a St. John's knit suit and expect somebody to buy it. (Bre, New York booker)

Bookers *imagine* catalog and showroom consumers to be conservative, middle-class people with mainstream tastes.[20] Based on their generalized interpretation of this unknown mass of people, bookers can imagine that an edgy look like Devan's will not go over well. Bookers operate with a tacit understanding of two classes of consumers: the middle-class masses and the creative field insiders.

More immediate to bookers' concerns are the actual clients to whom they try to appeal. Bookers develop notions about who clients are as individuals and what they like. For the commercial booker, this is a relatively straightforward process of tracking the client's history:

> Throughout the month, the year, in dealing with them, they tell you, "Okay this is the face that I like, I like a brunette who is kind of quirky." They explaine a person to you, that's in your head. You get a kind of mold. And then you find a model that fits that mold. . . . Sometimes you are wrong. But most the time, if you are any good at it, then you're right. Nine times out of ten, I am right. (Don, New York booker)

A model's "specs"—the details clients give to bookers when they are looking for a specific type of model—and a shared history of working together are general guides for the commercial booker as he matches the model to the client. Bookers don't want to merely *fill* orders; they strive to *create* them. To strengthen their influence over clients, bookers cultivate relationships among clients and try to charm them.

Just as models try to connect with clients at castings, bookers draw upon emotional labor to engage their clients. Bookers showcase their own personalities as they promote their looks. One Metro booker likes to speak in different voices and goofy accents when he's talking to clients on the phone. Some tell jokes or try to get a laugh on the other end of the line. They use dramatic fashion words such as "hot," "fierce," "brilliant," and "a-*maz*-ing" to generate interest. When one gay booker truly believes in his male model, he is apt to joke with clients over the phone, "Look, *I* want to sleep with this boy, so you know he's *gotta* be hot!"

Much can be accomplished over the phone, but most bookers prefer to meet clients in person to establish a more intimate connection. Forming personal ties is good for business:

> Because once you've got a face to a name, it's much easier to kind of call them up and ask them for cheeky favors and stuff like that. (Erica, London booker)

Meeting face-to-face, perhaps at a lunch expensed to the agency, makes it easier for bookers to ask for "cheeky" favors such as extra go-sees for new models in town and even, as we'll see, higher booking fees.

I Would Never Deal with Catalog

Commercial clients can make a good living. Catalog tends to be well-paid, predictable, and secure work. Yet nearly every client I interviewed snubbed the commercial circuit. One casting director scoffed: "No. I would never deal with catalog." A photographer described such work as "mind numbingly soul destroying, and it's not fashion!" It was consistently referred to as "cheesy," "boring," and "naff," British slang for tacky. The ease of catalog work is perhaps the number-one complaint among clients. One casting director likened choosing a model for a catalog to working as a concierge, in that he just has to find a generically good-looking model and make the travel arrangements:

> I did a couple of times production for catalog. It's very nice. Is easy money. Is not exciting. Is a job. Is really, a *job*. But I don't find anything artistic to make a production for a catalog when basically I'm a travel agent. . . . I mean, there's a bathing suit catalog, you need a beautiful girl with a great body, and you have to find a location. It's not about the girl, it's about mostly the location that is fabulous, and the girl can be also without a head, just so you still see the bathing suit! (Oden, New York casting director)

Clients don't want *jobs*—that is, they don't want mere employment in the fashion industry, they want to be influential within it. In fashion, status is not reducible to money; it derives from having authority as a tastemaker, to have one's taste recognized as good taste. The opposition between the two circuits isn't so much in wanting to making money—all clients have their eyes on the million-dollar campaign prize. Rather, the opposition is economic success in the short run (catalog work) versus the long run (editorial work). Those who pursue short-term money and power via the commercial circuit will lack authority as tastemakers. The catalog producer who works steadily toward great financial success might be rich in earnings but poor in status, as Lazarus, a London photographer, explained:

> You'd make steady money, but you might end up killing yourself, because you're a workhorse. And you're not looked upon as an artist anymore, you're looked upon as a technician, really. As a facilitator of the client's need to photograph 10 dresses a day. And it can get pretty boring.

Not only is the catalog producer a workhorse, he is, in fact, a *joke*, and so is his model:

> Some girls come in and all they do is kind of like naff catalogy kind of over-the-top pose number 38. And you just go, "Listen, I don't want you to look like that . . . this all comes from some really naff shoot you had done with some naff photographer." And it's very hard to work with those girls because they've got it, like muscle memory, you know? (Narcisco, London photographer)

Bookers know this, and to protect their models' work biographies, editorial bookers carefully consider which kinds of images will boost models' profiles, in an attempt to preserve the artistic integrity of the look from the commercial character of the trade. An editorial male model, for instance, explained that he booked catalog only once in his two-year career. It was a catalog for Halloween costumes and during the shoot his booker demanded that the model's face be partially hidden for all shots. (At $2,000 for the day, it was one of the best-paying jobs he had ever landed.)

Clients also expressed disregard, sometimes subtle, sometimes outright, for mass consumers of catalogs. "Cheesy" commercial images with "naff" catalog models appeal to the least appealing of audiences, the mass market. Clients, echoing the bookers, shun the middle-market consumers in their various incarnations as "middle America," "Nebraska," "Texas," "my mom," "suburbia," and so on.

Clients therefore tend to disparage the boredom and creativity constraints of commercial work. Working for *Vshop* was in fact very dull and routine. Every day I modeled about forty different outfits, each one for roughly twenty minutes, with a rigidly controlled schedule: clothes on, photograph, clothes off, repeat. Chloe, the photographer, would often sigh at the end of each shoot and say wearily "Got it!" or "Okay, next!" to indicate that it was time for me to change clothes yet again.

What kept it interesting was how the set crew frequently derided the quality of their own work and the low status of *Vshop* fashion. For one shot, the stylist fastened a plastic necklace around my neck and exclaimed, "That really is appalling, isn't it?!" to the laughter of Chloe and her assistants. During one jewelry shoot, the whole team was laughing hysterically when Chloe suggested that I put my *Vshop* pictures in my portfolio and show them to Tiffany & Co., the upscale jeweler, and ask them for a modeling job: "What do you think about me shooting your next campaign? I've loads of experience. I've shot some blue plastic necklaces, some *Vshop* silver. I can shoot about 120 in a day!"

Each day at *Vshop* was a daily microcosm of producers' rebellion against commercial concerns. A sure sign of the legitimacy of dominant culture is when people tend to disguise ignorance or indifference toward it, as when lower-class consumers feign appreciation of high-cultural objects.[21] Here, among these cultural producers, we see the opposite workings of legitimation in the form of witty self-deprecation. By belittling their own work, clients who produce catalogs such as *Vshop* draw a symbolic distance between themselves and middle-market consumer tastes. They rally against the mainstream commercial realm by making a public display of their distaste for it. Those who work in catalog and commercial jobs play it down as something they just do to pay the bills. Their *real* sensibilities and talents, so they imply, come from the prestigious editorial circuit of work, where authority, not money, can be earned. Enter the editorial circuit, the aspiration of all clients.

PRODUCING THE EDGY LOOK

If commercial castings have relatively clear and stable criteria, then editorial castings are opaque at best. The process of choosing models for the runway is especially murky. I observed one New York designer audition models for her upcoming show—out of one hundred candidates, she ended up with six whom she wanted to hire. The composite cards of these six models were neatly laid across the floor in the young designer's studio, and Post-it notes were stuck to them with hurriedly slanted handwritten notes: "Yay! Good walk," and "Pretty."

"Look at this girl," the designer said to me as she picked up one of the cards. "I cast her right away. Seriously, she looks like a freak! I mean, who looks like that? And this girl," she said, pointing to another, "she looks like a bird. I love her."

Whereas the commercial look is stable and predictable, the "edgy" look is always shifting. Photographers, directors, and stylists are always searching for it, just as bookers are scrambling to supply it:

> They're all monitoring tastes and they're kind of finding these girls and I mean they kind of—they're almost the coal feeder in a locomotive, because all they look for is the aesthetic. . . . And in that glut of aesthetics, you're hoping—it's like Russian roulette, hoping for a full chamber. (Peter, London hairstylist)

Just what kind of edgy look should clients load into the chamber? Recognizing edgy is no straightforward process; it does not come with a corporate style guide. Even at magazines, which would seem to be accountable to their readers, reader feedback is not the top priority.[22] Editorial producers imprint their own informal knowledge upon readers' tastes, with an eye to their advertisers.

While almost all of these producers religiously consumed *Vogue* magazine, none of them read advertising presses such as *AdWeek* or *Campaign,* and only a few clients claimed to read the fashion industry press *Women's Wear Daily.* They seldom conducted focus groups, and only occasionally invoked market research, usually to express the vague motivations behind things such as budgets, which are mandated by faraway corporate offices. One casting director in New York occasionally uses "Q Scores," which are marketing indexes designed to capture the likability of a person or product among target consumers.[23] But, in general, the people who choose models, style them, and photograph them have little interaction with the people who ultimately view their images and purchase apparel. Sociologist Ben Crewe has similarly found, in his 2003 book *Representing Men: Cultural Production and Producers in the Men's Magazine Market,* that magazine publishers routinely disregard marketing data and instead focus on images and ideas they find personally interesting. There is what sociologists call a "decoupling" between supply and demand in the fashion modeling market, such that bookers and clients make their decisions based not on customer preferences but on *other* producers' attempts to satisfy customer preferences.[24]

Editorial producers therefore mobilize their informal knowledge of fashion to forge tastes around "edginess" and "cool" by turning their attention to other field insiders. Editorial fashion is a case of what Bourdieu calls the field of restricted production.[25] In their quest for edginess, clients search the field to find looks that will impress other photographers, stylists, and fashion insiders who consume editorial magazines.

Figuring out the edgy look requires a good deal of social legwork—and it begins with the bookers.

Matchmaking in the Editorial Circuit

Editorial bookers are forever on the lookout for new trends. The look that excites them is one of difference, novelty, and the potential to change the face of fashion:

> A pretty girl is a pretty girl. To me it's finding someone who is different who doesn't look like anyone else, can't be compared to anyone else. Eyes might be super big, ears might be big, lips might be shaped differently . . . if it's still perfect, and symmetrical, there's something that can be very cool about that. And hey, if you can sell it, if you can sell that look that you like and think is cool, you might just be able to change fashion. (Rio, New York booker)

To do this, however, editorial bookers have to know their editorial clients intimately—they have to carefully watch and study the editorial circuit. They are avid magazine consumers—not readers necessarily, but visual consumers. They constantly flip through a wide range of magazines; when asked which ones, several exclaimed: "Loads of them," or "all of them." When asked which magazines they liked best, bookers consistently mentioned American, Italian, or French *Vogue*, and, in the UK, bookers frequently also mentioned famed avant-garde titles such as *i-D*, *Pop*, and *Dazed and Confused*.[26]

They hone in on clients' tastes by watching the choices of photographers, stylists, and magazine editors. Bookers keep up-to-date with fashion trends with industry websites Style.com and Models.com, and they read the industry newspaper *Women's Wear Daily*. These sources help bookers keep a general finger on the pulse of fashion:

> You know what people are asking for, you know what you see in the magazines, what you see on TV commercials, you know what you see on billboards, and you know what markets to send the girls to. You see what they're putting out there; you need to have models like that. (Elle, New York booker)

In addition to watching clients, bookers watch each other and keep tabs on what works for their competitors, who are likely to be friends, or at least friendly, with one another. Within an agency, bookers are intimately connected through many shared meals and drinks, trips abroad, and late nights at the agency. At Metro, two bookers lived together as roommates, one booker was dating another's brother, and one booker is married to a former scout. Beyond the agency, they are also personally connected as friends and former coworkers, since bookers switch agencies several times over the course of their careers.

Bookers' connectedness enables them to see what works at other agencies and to quickly adapt. Likewise, they watch designers and pay close attention to breakout "stars" during Fashion Week, making sure their own boards are stocked with look-alike looks of the moment.

One editorial booker described her job title as a "predictor"; she has to know the future trends of the look, and she has to know them before everyone else. While this can never be known, it can be sensed and *felt* from socialization in the editorial circuit. In addition to sharing social space with each other, bookers schmooze with their clients. Some of them know each other closely from working together for years. They speak on the phone constantly and build relationships at lunches, happy hours, and even, at one point in New York, weekly karaoke nights. They share a sense of fashionability, they know which trends are hot, and they know who is booking whom:

> You have relationships with clients. And you kind of know what they like and don't like. You've been dealing with them for so many years you see the kinds of people that they react to, and you sell that. (Missy, New York men's booker)

Even after developing interpersonal relationships with their clients, bookers approach them with care. They are cautious about which models they promote to which clients, realizing that they might only have a limited number of shots to get it right before a client permanently dismisses them as wrong. They don't want to ruin their credibility, so bookers strategize their relationships and deploy them with care:

> You might have a great girl—she's great, but you kind of think actually at heart, I don't think she is his type, so I wouldn't give it a hard sell then because she's not his type. So the next time around when she *is* his type, he'll trust me, and that affects my judgment. Because if you say that to a photographer, "Oh she's so you," and she's *not*, then you've lost the job the next time around. (Fria, London booker)

To minimize the chances of misreading their most valued clients, bookers test the waters initially by sending new models on their first go-sees to either lower status or new start-up clients—those whose trust they don't prioritize. They solicit feedback from clients after go-sees and request castings, especially pertaining to their new models. In one such trail run in New York, bookers were able to learn that a novice model said "ma'am" too much at her first casting ("Yes ma'am, thank-you ma'am"), a habit that casting directors were quick to report to her agency.

Bookers, then, protect their hard-earned social relationships with clients by sending them appropriate models whose appearances and personalities will likely be a good fit. They take risks sparingly only on models whom they believe have reasonably good chances to impress. Ultimately, too, they rank their ties with clients above models:

> I can't sell a drip to a client and expect that client to pay that much money for a bad personality. If I know the girl is just going to stand there and not say anything to the client, the client is going to call me immediately and say to me, "What are you doing?!" And I can't do that, because my relationship is going to be with the clients for a lot longer than the models. (Don, New York booker)

By building strategic ties among clients, bookers earn client loyalty. This too is a currency known as social capital, and it is convertible to both financial gain and upstart capital to launch new models' careers. In other words, by consistently supplying the right look to their clients, bookers win favors they can redeem in the form of getting new models in the door. As one booker put it, "Models trade on our relationships with our clients." Bookers are strategic social butterflies, cultivating and maintaining relationships with clients—relationships that will last much longer than those they develop with their models.

The Booker's Buzz

Bookers generate buzz around a model's prestige or *potential* for prestige that is likely to impress editorial clients. A model's prestige level depends on the social status positioning of the clients with whom she has worked, or with whom she has the *possibility* of working. Status is especially important in markets like fashion because it acts as a stand-in for quality in the absence of objective measures of quality differences.[27] Status is a means for bookers and clients to ascertain distinctions among a fairly homogeneous group of people; it tames uncertainty.

All of the bookers shared an understanding of which clients are high · status. Nearly every booker mentioned photographers Steven Meisel (who has shot every cover of *Vogue Italia* since 1988), Steven Klein, Nick Night, or Mario Testino, fashion houses Prada and Marc Jacobs, and some edition of *Vogue* magazine as examples of high-status clients. Ultimately, the booker is hoping to land his or her model on a job with one of these clients. One booking with a high-status client is expected to snowball into dozens more, catapulting the model's popularity. It is a small thrill when a new look catches on, and bookers are quick to exploit the excitement:

> "We have this amazing new guy, you have to see him, everyone is talking about him, everyone is calling us about him, e-mailing us about him!" And sometimes you're lying, you're creating a little buzz. . . . Nobody wants to be the one to miss out. They don't want their boss to say, "Well how come you didn't book this guy?" A little hype, a little mystery, we've found that it works well for us. (Missy, New York men's booker)

In hopes of generating a buzz, bookers try to generate excitement. One booker likes to whisper over the phone to his clients *"She's ready"* to denote that his model is on the cusp of enormous success. Keenly aware of the importance of status, bookers spread the buzz to build excitement and inflate prestige around their models. Just how the clients respond, however, is another matter.

Clients Buzz Back

"Bookers suck!" exclaimed Clive, a New York stylist whom I met on a shoot for a Japanese magazine. Clive books models for international avant-garde magazines and major campaigns alike, and one of his biggest challenges is deciphering bookers' buzz. "The majority of bookers always are pushing the buzz," he complained. "They are always telling you and elaborating on something that is really not true." Because bookers are professionally engaged in generating buzz, clients tend to take their enthusiasm with a grain of salt. As one top magazine casting director put it, bookers "spread a lot of bullshit." A better source of information, they note, are other clients.

Like bookers, clients are avid magazine consumers. As two of them put it, they are "fanatics" and "obsessed" with magazines.[28] They pay special attention to the latest luxury-brand campaigns, editorial pages, and bylines. They also religiously check industry resources Style.com and, to a lesser extent, Models.com to keep track of which models are booking what.

Beyond this, they talk. They hang out with each another, talk with each other, and share tips on upcoming "hot" new models. By the time each Fashion Week season rolls around, clients have likely heard a great deal about the models they are meeting at a show casting:

> Throughout the season we speak almost on a daily basis also with other casting directors. They are friends, they are competition, they are colleagues, but mostly they are also friends. So there is really a buzz that during the off season you will start to hear about, oh this girl did this, this, this, and this, so you check it out in the magazine, you see which photographer she is working with, you check it out with the designer . . . with the makeup artist, with the stylist she's working with, and this is building the buzz about the girl. . . . Most of the girls, we know already who they are. (Oden, New York casting director)

By spreading the buzz, clients expect to hear the buzz in return, which simplifies their work of finding editorial models. Furthermore, gossip strengthens clients' ties with other clients and bookers; it paves the way to receive favors, as Kelly's story of a karma-laden casting implies:

> There was this really handsome guy. An agent sent me a picture of him. And he was maybe a bit not right for us, but he was so amazing that I e-mailed my friend that works for [another casting director] and my friend that works for Patty Wilson, the stylist. And then two seconds later they called him in for a go-see and the booker from the agency e-mailed me, like, "Thank you so much for passing it on." (Kelley, New York magazine editor)

By building up the buzz, clients can become allies to bookers. They can then mortgage this capital for favors down the road, for instance, when they are in a pinch and need to book a model at the last minute.

Importantly, clients enjoy being a part of the buzz; they share a passion for fashion and a respect for edgy looks:

> I'll call a few key photographers that we work with, like, "You should see this kid!" Because it's exciting and it's also, you know, everyone is looking— our business is entertainment. We're essentially looking to get excited, and to be a part of something new. (Rayna, New York casting director)

Clients find excitement and pride in producing editorial fashion, and each season they relish the chance to take part in the collective redefinition of edginess.

When casting directors, stylists, and photographers find a look that excites them, they don't keep it to themselves but do their best to broadcast it. "There's no point in keeping her to yourself, because a girl's only worth as much as her career," said David, a New York casting director, in the business for fourteen years. First David gets on the phone to thank the model's booker for sending her, and he compliments the booker's eye: "What I do is I want to call the agent up and tell them, 'Oh my God, we love her. We know she's going to be a big star!' "

After this step, which David calls "pumping up the agent," clients next get on the phone to tell their friends and colleagues around the world. An extreme example is when David once booked a brand-new model for all seventeen shows he was working on, a remarkably high number for a new face, and a juicy bit of buzz that any booker will exploit with other clients:

> So we put her in 17 shows, and then [the booker] had ammunition. He was able to call up all the big designers and say, you know, "You've *got* to see this girl," or, "If you saw this girl, you have to see her again. She just booked 17 shows!"

Though David couldn't explain *why* he thought this particular young woman was superior, he acted on it in a way that attracted the attention of other clients, thus indicating that he must have known something that they didn't. This prompted other clients to follow his lead, and in turn induced others to follow them. Such a bold act of casting can have terrific rewards, as David explained: "Because then I'll be able to say—well it's good for me up until this day—I was the first person to book her in New York." By spreading the buzz in the editorial circuit, clients try to ensure that their chosen look *will* become a star. While editorial clients take credit and gain authority for recognizing stars, they work hard to ensure that their recognition is also recognized in the field. Being *in fashion* is to be ahead of the curve, which means having the authority to change the curve.

Options and Other Buzz Vehicles

A few years ago, when top casting director Jordan Bane "discovered" newcomer Tatiana, a skinny, unusual-looking teenager, he *just knew* she was the right model to open the Prada show. "I could tell the moment I saw Tatiana," he told me in his London studio. "When I found Tatiana, that's like [snapping his fingers] . . . it does something very physical. I mean, it really does, and I think it's really obvious when it's that kind of physical."

Jordan and his assistant sort through one hundred images of models each day, roughly three thousand faces each year, looking for, as he describes it, "a needle in a haystack." Like vintage shopping, he says, editorial casting is a matter of taste: "It's taste, it's purely taste. How else can you describe that? Why did I decide to buy this chair and sofa? You know, for me, it ticks the box. You know, it's an internal thing!"

But it's also a social process, and in fact Tatiana's value, like the dozens of women who have come before her and will surely come after her, results from herding behavior and status-driven imitation.

Like the dozens of fashion producers with whom I spoke, Jordan doesn't really know what it is about a young woman like Tatiana that excites him. He "just knows" if a model is right for him, and further, he "knows it when he sees it." Not everyone can see it, however. Depending on whom you talk to and crucially, *when*, Tatiana's look is either great or unappealing. She is very edgy: pale and thin, with long dark hair hanging over a small face with a sharp small mouth and big almond eyes. To the average American consumer, Tatiana isn't exactly good looking. David, the New York casting director of fourteen years, explained his initial reaction when he first saw her for show castings, back in 2005: "Like Tatiana, *urgh*! [making a sour face] . . . ooh, like she came in, and I was like, in my head I was like, 'What trailer park did *she* come from?' "

A year after this casting, Tatiana graced the cover of *Vogue Italia*, which was shot by powerhouse photographer Steven Meisel, and when the spring runway season concluded, she boasted a resume of over fifty shows, from Marc Jacobs to Chanel. By the time the next show season rolled around, when Tatiana made her way back to the initially skeptical casting director, he desperately wanted to book her.

"I can't just book any girl I want," David explained. "After I see all the girls, you know, I call the agents up and I say these are the girls that I would like for this show. And they don't normally give me girls right away. The first thing they ask you is, 'Well who else is in the show?' They want to know who else you've got. So I always have to get that one girl . . . I guess this season it was Tatiana." At this he rolled his eyes, and continued, "You know as soon as I got Tatiana in the show, it was like, okay, now I'll book *whoever* I want."

David's job is not as simple as just copying what established players are doing, however, because even the most powerful fashion clients also have to know what to imitate and, crucially, at the right moment. To do this, they rely on informal and formal mechanisms of information sharing. Informally, we've seen how clients gossip to spread the buzz about models. There is also a formal mechanism in place: the option mechanism.

Recall that options allow clients to put models "on hold" for a job before actually confirming the job. While the actual runway casting may take just minutes, the work of optioning models begins weeks before Fashion Week, when agencies send clients the show packages announcing every model available for hire. Each agency can promote twenty to fifty models, and, given that there are at least twelve high-fashion agencies in New York alone, they're dealing with a minimum of six hundred model cards competing for the clients' attention. It's a familiar sight in February and September to see stacks and stacks of composite cards lining the walls of casting directors' offices. During these months, clients begin to make preselections for the shows by putting models on "option" for their runways. This pre-Fashion Week ritual begins the important work of circulating the buzz. Options serve the symbolic purpose of "signaling" the model's popularity to all other clients. During castings, clients are likely to ask models, "Which shows are you optioned for?," thereby letting them know their competitors' tastes.

Bookers are quick to exploit the options mechanism to build the buzz, as in, "Jordan Bane just optioned Tatiana for Prada!" To most producers' ears, these are welcome words; they greatly reduce the difficulty of sorting Tatiana from 599 similarly qualified teenagers.

These formal and informal mechanisms of gossip result in a positive-feedback effect in the market, known as the "Matthew effect," where successful people accumulate more success ("the rich get richer").[29] A model with several show options is deemed to be in high demand, or "hot," compared to the model with no options. Thus small differences in quality snowball into large differences in popularity.

Today, David, the casting director, still cannot fully see what it is about Tatiana that makes her so popular. "I can *kind of* see it," he said. "But now, it doesn't matter. It doesn't matter what I think now. Like she is, you know, *It* right now." As in the fable of "The Emperor's New

FIGURE 4.3. Production crew unveils the catwalk before a show

Clothes," even if one does not believe in the legitimacy of a social order, one follows it on the belief that *other* people find it legitimate enough to follow, a classic condition of legitimacy noted by Max Weber.[30] Quite possibly, one may not be able to grasp why a model stands out as a winner, but the label legitimates itself as other tastemakers imitate their high-status peers.

Options enable investors to anticipate other investors' actions, which leads to herding behavior, where actors decide to disregard their own information and imitate instead the decisions made by others before them. The outcomes of these herding behaviors are what economists call information cascades, and we see them in speculative markets such as art, fashion, and finance (though the effects of inflating value on fashion models are rather benign compared to overvaluing stocks on Wall Street).

This is not to say that choosing a Tatiana is an irrational decision—hardly; as behavioral economists have found, it is quite rational for decision makers to take into account other people's actions, even at the expense of their own information or, in this case, their own aesthetic sensibilities.[31] The modeling market, like any marketplace, has a degree of arbitrariness. Superior products don't necessarily become best sellers; good products can win in the marketplace, but so can inferior ones. In place of Tatiana, the Fashion Week star of 2006 could just as well have been another model, such as Liz from Pleasantville, New Jersey or Sasha from Vladivostock, Russia.

As Sasha made her way through the London and New York modeling markets, she came to understand this well. When discussing how models rise to the top, she explained, "Your life would be, you came to a casting with Jordan Bane. For some reason he thought, 'Oh she looks like my mother when she was twenty-three. I love her!' And he books you for everything." It didn't work out this way for Sasha, who in the end was just another Polaroid moving in and out of Jordan Bane's studio.

Navigating the Hierarchy

"Bookers are the spawn of the devil!" the fashion editor at the commercial magazine *Modern* announced, slamming shut her cell phone to end a conversation with an agent. The booker on the other end of the line had delivered the unfortunate news that a confirmed model had to cancel shooting for *Modern* magazine that day, allegedly due to an upcoming school exam. The news was perceived as a lie, something bookers are commonly accused of doing to cover up cancellations with lower-status clients when a better job comes along. The importance of status, I learned that day at *Modern*, is often to the detriment of those on the lower rungs of the hierarchy.

When high-status clients work with lower-status models, they inflate the status of that model, bringing them up with a level of prestige that can be passed on to *other* clients. Models are, in this sense, vessels of status, and they can transfer prestige between clients, as quality differences in other uncertain markets have been shown to do.[32] Likewise, low-status models can bring down clients' position in the hierarchy. One casting director told me about having to field phone calls from irate bookers after one Fashion Week show in which top models shared the catwalk with low-status showroom models. The bookers demanded to know, "Who was that girl in the show?," and his trustworthiness was briefly called into question.

Employing the wrong models, those who are not recognized as "really good" by the right people, will detract from a client's status. Finally, low-status clients can damage or detract from a model's prestige. A "really good" model can lose some luster by shooting low-status catalogs or magazines. Bookers therefore carefully screen clients before confirming models.

This status hierarchy and the bookers who guard it can be trouble-some to lower-status clients hoping to book the "really good" models. Here is where clients' negotiation skills prove most useful, as Leah, who casts the shows for many of London's famous designers, explained:

> All form of creativity goes out the window. There's nothing creative about my job whatsoever. It's all negotiating. It all comes down to relationships. Where your best relationships lie, how you can work situations, and it can get very nasty.

Part of the client's job is therefore to navigate the prestige hierarchy with social networking. Explained Kelly, who works at a low-status teen magazine:

> There's like a hierarchy of models in magazines as far as who they'll let do what. . . . A lot of times since they are managing a girl's career, they'll sort of say, well you know what, she can't do your magazine. Or, she's already started to do this; she can't do yours. So they'll hold back sometimes. And either I'll have to beg or just sort of sweeten up the deal to try to get what I want. (Kelly, New York magazine editor)

To "sweeten the deal," Kelly gives agents incentives to accept her job, such as increasing the number of pages with which to feature the model, or guaranteeing that the model will be solo on a set number of pages rather than having to share the frame with anyone else. Navigating a lower-tier position in the fashion status hierarchy is a constant worry. Kelly told me, "It's so like high school." And just as in high school, a higher standing in the pecking order has real, tangible rewards.

PRICING BEAUTY

Bookers are ultimately salespeople. One booker described her job as a "glorified telemarketer," in the business of packaging and selling people, another as a "legal pimp." The job entails routine sales work: "It is basi-cally a very exciting but glamorized version of sales," a London booker remarked.

Bookers do not sell models at some predetermined market price, since, of course, none exists. The *New York Times* noted of Fashion Week, "It is an open secret in the business that there is no such thing as a fixed rate for a model's services."[33] Nor do wages emerge from a set of rules "out there" waiting to be followed, because a model's human capital is ambiguous, her productivity is unobservable, and her return on investment is fun-damentally unknowable. Though producers cannot measure models' productivity, they can produce a sense of following the market by adhering to pricing conventions. In the fashion modeling market, bookers and clients build social relationships and share habits, routines, and norms—in a word, *conventions*—that enable them to find agreement about what counts as a valuable look.[34]

Bookers and clients follow circuit-specific conventions to produce various notions of a "fair" price for their models. Once bookers have enticed any client to hire a model, they begin fee negotiations with the maximum sum they think they can "get away with," and they negotiate to keep the sum at a high level. Negotiations, considered an exciting sport to many bookers, are based on justifications that only make sense within the respective editorial and commercial circuits.

In the commercial circuit, bookers justify fees on the basis of a model's "name," that is, on prestige, as well as on experience, all of which will vary widely among models, sometimes double or triple the amount. A senior booker at Metro used my own record, albeit inflated by a good $13,000, as an example:

> It's the caliber of work you've been doing. In other words, if JCPenney wants to book Cindy Crawford and I'm gonna say she's $50,000 a day, and then they say, okay, we'll book Ashley Mears. Well, she's $15,000. Obviously Cindy's gonna get more money because of the fact of what she's accomplished and the fact that she's been doing it three times longer than Ashley has. (Lynne, New York booker)

Experience is a valuable selling point in the commercial circuit; it demonstrates that the model is both reliable and well liked by others. Furthermore, if she works repeatedly for a client, then bookers expect her fee to steadily rise, because she has proved herself valuable to the client. Experience is especially important to a model's showroom and fitting rate because it demonstrates competency in the showroom:

> Experience, if she has been modeling for a while and she has better experience, she has a better walk, she is more money. Whereas if you have new girls that are just starting out with the agency, they are fine with just getting a job. (Olivia, New York booker)

Though showroom rates are on a smaller scale, they also vary widely among models, from $500 to $1,200 for an eight-hour day, and from at least $150 to $300/hour. The showroom booker finally uses a model's popularity among other showroom clients as a means to jockey up the rate. With several designers on Seventh Avenue vying for a few hours to fit clothes onto a rare "perfect size 8" showroom model, Metro is able to charge up to $500/hour for its top fit model.

Similarly, in the editorial circuit, experience can be a good selling point, so bookers play up the buzz with appeals to what past clients have shown interest in their model:

> In fashion, a lot of people do pay attention to what the girl has done, and who she has shot with, and things like that. Just to be safe, they follow. . . . I would tell the client, "Well she did this, and she did that, she did that," you know, that would get a higher rate for her. (Christoph, New York booker)

Money isn't nearly as important to the editorial booker, who knows that a poorly paid job can be rich in status. This is almost always the case for magazine shoots by big-name photographers such as Steven Meisel, whose reputation is almost priceless:

> If it is a job that Steven Meisel's shooting, probably no matter what it was and what it was paying, they would have anybody do it. If it is a great photographer, they will get in who they can get in. (Heather, New York booker)

With an eye to the future, bookers forgo short-term earnings in the hope that prestige and buzz will have huge economic consequences further down the line. This is why some high-end advertising jobs, such as a print ad for a luxury fashion brand, may pay only a few thousand dollars. One male model reported being paid just $800 for the international D&G campaign, and although this amount could not be confirmed, a men's booker quipped, "You need D&G more than D&G needs you."

Likewise, most Fashion Week designers are unlikely to pay first-time models, or they pay them under $1,000 a show or in "trade" with leftover samples from past seasons. As models accumulate more prestige and become bigger names, their show rates increase, because (1) they have multiple bidders for their schedules, which bookers play off each other, and (2) top models attract press and increase the designer's publicity. Designers need top models as much as top models need designers, but they'll need deep pockets to bid for them, paying as much as $20,000 for a top model's catwalk appearance.

Sometimes, if the booker knows a client really wants a model, the booker will hold out and risk losing the model, playing for all or nothing. Central to such a bold play are the social connectedness and shared history that bookers have with clients:

You know how much they want the girl, not necessarily from what they've said, but from what they've done in the past, what they've said in the past and how they work and everything. That's when it's good to have relationships with people, because you know well how far you can go before they crumble and go, "Okay, fine, take all my money!" (Erica, London booker)

The individualistic negotiations for each job mean that wages will vary among models even as they perform equal work, an inequality that angers most models. To avoid conflicts, bookers try to keep their models from talking about wages with each other. During one Fashion Week, my job sheet had the following words printed at the bottom: *Do not discuss rate!!!* Presumably I was earning more than the other models, but, equally plausible, I may have been earning less.

Prices tell rich stories about the social relations between buyers and sellers.[35] A model's fee tells the narrative of her career and the skill of her booker's "eye." Bookers follow conventions to price models, meaning that they follow routines and norms that they learn and reproduce through shared history and mutual expectations. But conventions are just that, norms collectively produced through individual actions, and they can be broken, sometimes arbitrarily. Don, a booker in New York, recounted his early days in the business in the late 1980s when he naively requested an unconventionally high fee for a top model:

They said, what rate do you want? And I said $25,000. Of course, I was a junior booker, I didn't know a thing, and I was actually kidding! Now, of course, it's a norm, but then it wasn't to ask for $25,000 for catalog. . . . And so they said, "Okay, confirm her!" [laughs]

Thus a variety of payments—$25,000 for a top model, a bag of last season's clothing, pictures by Steven Meisel, $15,000 for Ashley Mears—corresponds to social categories and relationships specific to circuits within the market. Bookers, like models, have to learn these ropes, and even the most astute ones can, and frequently do, get it completely wrong.

When to Cut Your Losses

Conventions tame uncertainty, but they do not always work. Things can still go wrong, resulting in daily office dramas over flops and drops.

The flop does the most damage. This is an unforeseen failure of a once-touted star. Each flop is a menace to an agency's finances and to a booker's reputation. Flops hit agency accounts hard; bookers may have incurred considerable expenses to promote models whose careers never afford repayment. Beyond the basic expenses—comp cards, test shoots, and pictures—models may require visas, plane tickets, and apartment rentals. They may need pocket money to get through until their first check, and there may be a range of other unforeseen expenses such as health emergencies. Both agencies have dozens of indebted models. The most extreme amounts are over $15,000 at Metro and £3,500 at the more conservative Scene. The fact that both agencies are relatively small creates pressure for all of the bookers (and accountants) to get it right; neither agency has a money-making athlete or a celebrity endorsement division that can quickly recoup losses. Failed investments stand out.

The problem with debt is the lure of the gamble, an enticing game of chance to which accountants witness bookers succumbing all too often:

> What happens is once you've got a model in that much debt, the booker— sometimes you see it—well maybe the model's not gonna make the money. You don't want to cut your losses at $15,000, you want to get that model a couple of jobs that will recoup the agency that debt. You end up going deeper and deeper into the hole. It's like when do you cut the string, you know? (Joe, New York staff)

Editorial bookers, chasing the high-stakes prize of the winner-take-all contest, oftentimes continue to invest in a model despite her poor response from clients. At Metro, bookers told stories of a recent flop that cost the agency upward of $15,000, all because a persistent editorial booker had a hunch that a model's look was going to catch on and win the jackpot. It did not, for reasons no one could explain. Such stories are much to the chagrin of commercial and showroom bookers, who are far more market sensitive. With less at stake, they play it safe and simply drop the models clients don't "rent."

Because Scene is in London, a fashion capital rich with cutting-edge magazines, it faces the problem of editorial "brain drain"—models come to London from around the world to work for just a couple of months, long enough to shoot great magazines and rack up expenses, but not long enough to secure steady money jobs. And then they depart, their prestigious London editorials in hand, to make money in Paris or New York. They are unlikely to return to work off unsettled debts in London. "We didn't expect to see you again either," the accountant said to me as he was explaining this emigration problem during our interview.

He was referencing the £1,500 debt I left with Scene during my first year of modeling, before I returned, eventually clearing the red two and a half years later. Scene had recently resolved to refocus its scouting efforts within the UK, as foreign models were just too risky.

Bookers might do everything right, but the model does something wrong. Perhaps she parties too much, has developed a bad attitude, is homesick for family or friends, has developed drug or alcohol addictions, weight gain, bad skin, or simply cannot or "does not want to" project the ideal personality, that is, she is a "wet rag" after all, despite bookers' best efforts and warnings. Bookers see these problems, and other "personality conflicts," as models' annoying individual failures, and they result in a drop.

And yet agents can be quite reluctant to drop models. They have personal relationships and shared history; after all, many bookers oversee their models' progress from adolescence into adulthood. The "drop conversation" terminates the work relationship between agent and model, and while inevitable, it is always unpleasant for bookers, who even describe it as "horrible." Bookers typically stick to a standard line, such as, "We're not the right agency for you."

Finally, bookers and models may do everything right, and they still get it wrong—clients may simply not "bite." At this point, bookers feel helpless, as Carl explains: "If the client's not getting her, there's nothing else we can do. You can't make clients book a girl." Beyond Carl's field of vision, there are accidents, whimsies, and flippant coincidences that render the process rather arbitrary. For instance, when choosing a model for a fashion advertisement, Tomas remembered a past lover:

> I don't know what to tell you, you choose according to the concept but also sometimes you get carried away by looks, by faces, by what the face reminds you of. For example, one time I chose a woman because she reminded me of somebody that I used to have sex with, basically, and it's ridiculous that I say this but it's true, in that case. (Tomas, New York art director)

Likewise, accidents happen to exclude some models, especially in times of hectic schedules and large castings. During a fitting for one major New York designer's Fashion Week show, I observed two stylists in charge of the casting as they chatted happily about accessories and lighting, when suddenly one of them *gasped* and jumped up from her chair, "Ah, but we forgot Emily!" Pointing to a crumpled composite card in the seat of the chair next to her, she said, "But she is genius! Oh no!" In the rush of castings, fittings, and confirmations, Emily's composite card had fallen by the wayside. But the show must go on.

To bookers, unexplained failures are the most difficult flops to cope with, because they call into question the entire matchmaking process. Just as models feel rejection, at times so do their bookers—and neither has recourse to make sense of it.

THE ILLUSION OF CONSECRATION

What makes one model become a highly valued commodity? The answer to this "trick question" can be found in the social practice of brokering. Any model becomes a success by virtue of the booker and the client who have won in the struggle for visibility in the editorial field.

Bookers are the link in the chain of supply and demand in the fashion modeling market. They find, mold, and broker the bodies that will become fashionable looks circulated in pop media around the world. Behind every image you see of men and women on billboards, on the catwalks, and in magazines, there is a booker.

Bookers are plugged into a peculiar cultural world in which the winners lose. Editorial bookers play prestige for profit, while commercial bookers accumulate steady and predictable earnings that keep the agencies afloat. From this interplay of economic and symbolic values, bookers construct an objective market value from subjective knowledge; taste, feelings, and "buzz" translate into an hourly fee. Pricing a look is both an economic and a cultural exercise; it happens at the seams along which culture meets commerce in everyday practice. Economic value thus emerges from a *culture of production* that bookers make with each other and with clients.[36] Because they are plugged into a circuit, bookers can "see" distinctions among fuzzy categories of looks; their "eyes" enable them to discriminate between the "edgy" and the "soft."

This eye is a trick, a social illusion, beneath the optical kind. Bookers collectively misrecognize their own contextual knowledge and shared social and cultural space—at the pub and at the karaoke bar, at the countless lunches and dinners they spend with each other, with their competitors, and with their clients. The booker's eye is fundamentally a relational skill, and it sees not beauty or talent but a field of positions in a prestige contest.

The booker's eye is akin to the client's taste for edgy. The search for the edgy is a fight for field-specific authority, in which clients are trying to make their mark—to not just be different but to be different in the right direction; to be one step ahead; to be, as Herbert Blumer put it, "*in fashion.*"

Being *in fashion* necessitates knowledge not only of the look of the moment but also the state of the field and its high-status players. Clients *just know* which model is "right" or "really good" because they know much more than the plain sight of the model before them. They know the positions and statuses within the field, as well as their own capacities to maneuver within it.

Because they work in fashion, an art world premised on the belief of creative genius, clients perpetuate the popular heroic myth of the autonomous creator. The myth does casting directors such as Jordan Bane a lot of good; it lends him an air of magic, which he converts into a handsome consulting fee for each show he casts. Clients speak with utter certitude about matters of taste that are inherently ambiguous. They are quick and decisive about very vague and elusive ideas, especially compared to your academic here, for instance, as I belabor slowly to spell out my exact points. Cultural producers must make definitive judgments, feigning indifference to fears of market failure. To indulge doubt is to question the very nature of the undertaking, and to jeopardize its accomplishment. Clients believe in the rules of the game, the *illusio*, as this is the only way to get the job done.

But clients' rapid-fire recognition and rhetorics obscure the politics of recognition, that treacherous terrain of strategic alliances and battles over what the look will be, and over who has the authority to name it. Clients would seem to hold the most power in this market. They are, after all, the immediate patrons of models and agencies. Yet they too are in a precarious position, for even the highest-status player is invulnerable to the possibility of failure. Clients collectively grope for the new look. In the face of considerable ambiguity, clients turn to each other, networking, imitating, and constructing and spreading the buzz. From these processes there emerges a coalescence of belief in the choice of the top girl of the year, awarding a fabulous prize to someone not different from the others in any obvious way, except that now she carries the aura of having been chosen.

Thus creators self-consciously create themselves.[37] Their authority comes from following the field, because they have nothing else to stand on. In so doing, they collectively forget what they have created. In their discourses of uncertainty, bookers and clients misrecognize their arduous work, allowing it to become invisible even to themselves, so that when they "discover" the look, it appears to happen *as though by magic*. The tastemakers have "glamoured" themselves!

The ebb and flow of clients' collective taste will ultimately determine what the editorial market will offer. In the editorial market, an insular taste is driven by the invisible conventions of players who fail to see the look as their own making. The power of conventions, as we will see, holds hostage both bookers and clients in the face of public criticism on two polemic issues: thinness and whiteness.

CHAPTER 5

Size Zero High-End Ethnic

PROTEST

In the early spring of 2007, on a cloudy English afternoon, a group of protesters, mostly women, gathered outside the gates of London's Natural History Museum on Cromwell Road. They shouted and marched and braved the cold in the name of justice at a most unjust time of year in London: Fashion Week. Feminist activist Susie Orbach's brainchild for positive body image, any-body.org, organized its first protest with the aim of sending a message to British designers, magazine editors, and modeling agents. Their problem with Fashion Week—that month-long international showcase of designer collections passing through New York, London, and Paris and terminating in Milan—was not with fashion per se but with the fashion models. "WE WANT BODY DIVERSITY 'IN' FASHION," read one protest sign. "FREE WOMEN FROM BODY HATRED ... *strut body variety on the catwalk*," read another. The following show season, across the Atlantic, another type of diversity was being discussed as noticeably absent: "Where have all the black models gone?" Such was the opening question put to a sold-out panel discussion, held at the New York Public Library, titled "Out of Fashion: The Absence of Color," headed by industry leaders who were there to address their perceived decline of models of color on the catwalk.

Somewhere along the line, these critics claimed, fashion models went from idyllic to grossly unrealistic, from fantasy to nightmare, from playful icons to painful jabs at the rest of us. They are now so unrepresentative of the everyday woman that they are considered offensive.[1] They are far too young and slender, wearing a size zero and having dangerously low body mass indexes (BMIs), a problem that stirred international attention after the anorexia-related deaths of two Latin American models over the course of two show seasons. They are far too white, nearly exclusively Anglo looking, a complaint echoed by supermodel Naomi Campbell and designer Dame Vivienne Westwood, both of whom raised charges of industry-wide racism.[2]

The call for diversity on the catwalk has not accomplished much. The same lineup of models from spring 2006 were again seen on the catwalks in spring 2007, despite a flood of media coverage of the debates, a ban in Madrid on models with excessively low BMIs, and the threat of monthly rallies to pressure the Council for Fashion Designers of America to acknowledge and fight racial discrimination. In its highly publicized July 2008 issue, *Vogue Italia* featured only black models throughout its pages in conspicuous reaction to the media criticism, but, on the whole, fashion magazines continue to underrepresent minorities. Critics point to the persistence of excessively thin and exclusively white models as evidence of sexist and racist production practices in fashion.[3] As feminist and intersectionality theorists have long argued, gender and race are indeed powerful and connected social forces in cultural representation, shaping media as diverse as fashion ads to children's storybooks and political campaigns.[4] While sociologists recognize the salience of gender and race in fashion, less understood are those processes of cultural production through which producers' ideas of gender and race interact and take shape in the finished product, the look. To this end, we should ask, how do race and gender inform cultural producers' hiring practices in the fashion modeling market?

So far I have used the art world approach to peel back layers of labor and conventions that constitute the look. Immediately behind the image are the models and their corporeal and emotional craft. Behind the model is the matchmaking booker, wheeling and dealing in bodily capital. Behind the booker, finally, is the client, that precarious tastemaker scrambling for authority to recognize the look. Behind them all are social structural patterns of inequality that constrain individual action. Cultural ideals of feminine and masculine difference along race and class lines limit the field of possibilities of the look.

This chapter traces the role of social structural forces in fashioning the look. I explain how producers in the modeling industry weigh their decisions on two publicly polemical issues: slenderness and racial exclusion. When I interviewed industry insiders, I wanted to know how they talked about industry problems, what they saw as their own roles in creating those problems, and how they made potentially problematic decisions to hire—or overlook—certain models. What I found was a lot of empathy with any-body.org and Naomi Campbell, but also a lot of fear. As we saw in the last chapter, bookers and clients face intense uncertainty when selecting models. Under institutionalized constraints, producers rely on conventions, imitation, and stereotypes to guide their actions. Their everyday understandings of femininity, race, and class construct beauty ideals they think will resonate with imagined consumer audiences.

THE MEANINGS OF FASHION IMAGES

Models do much more than promote the sale of fashion. The model look promotes and disseminates ideas about how women and men *should* look. Models "do gender" professionally in ways that interlock with other social positions such as race, sexuality, and class,[5] and there are endless critiques of fashion models and their gendered and racial meanings.

The Shrinking Model

As prescriptions for gender performance, fashion models represent what feminist scholarship has critiqued as oppressive beauty standards, the objectification and exploitation of women's bodies for patriarchal and capitalist gain.[6] In feminist theory, patriarchy and its capitalist mode of production thrive on the disparagement of the female body and the gap between promoted beauty ideals and reality. As Dorothy Smith has noted, the ideality of feminine beauty (and the gap between body reality and image) is inextricably part of the perpetual desire-producing machine of capitalism: "there is always work to be done."[7]

But the real issue sounded in the media in the past three years has focused on the widening gap in high-end fashion—models are so incredibly thin, claim their critics, that we now have a catwalk aesthetic that is carnivalesque, even lethal. Research consistently suggests that the dominant ideal body for a woman has been slimming since the end of the 1950s, evidenced among *Playboy* playmates, Miss America contestants, and fashion magazine advertisements.[8] The National Organization for Women (NOW) frequently points out the large gap between the idealized body in fashion and the average body in reality, claiming the average weight of a model is 23 percent lower than that of the average woman, whereas twenty-five years ago, the differential was only 8 percent.[9] Today, the average American fashion model is 5'11" tall and weighs 117 pounds, while the average American woman is 5'4" tall and weighs about 163 pounds.[10] Naomi Wolf's feminist argument in her book *The Beauty Myth* is that the slimming of models goes hand in hand with women's rising social status. As women gain political and social ground, beauty ideals are held to higher extremes of slenderness and perfection. Thus in Wolf's reading, models are agents of backlash in a patriarchal political agenda.

Women's bodies are not the only sites for commercial redefinition; men, in recent decades, have joined women in the pursuit of more perfect bodies.[11] While the bulk of media attention highlights slim women in modeling, a few reports indicate a similar reduction in male models' sizes, with similarly unforgiving silhouettes on the catwalk.[12] In the men's editorial circuit, designer samples have shrunk from an Italian size 50 in the mid-1990s to the current size 46, roughly a size 38 in the United States. Editorial male models are expected to be within 145–160 pounds, with a minimum height of 6'. The average weight of an American man, meanwhile, rose from 166.3 pounds in 1960 to 191 pounds in 2002.[13]

The gap between the ideal and reality is a constant thorn in feminists' side, a reminder that in a patriarchal order, the female body is perpetually lacking, and in a capitalist economy, all bodies are game for self-improvement. However, these kinds of feminist analyses sidestep fashion as a cultural production process and, in so doing, cannot tackle the real puzzle of size zero: Why are the models so slim when the vast majority of the people who buy the fashions are not? What kind of gaze imagines the body at size zero, and to what end?

Where Have All the Black Models Gone?

Bodies are racially coded, and the size zero look comes in one color: white. Based on a count of the 2007 Spring/Summer collections showcased on Style.com, 172 fashion houses displayed collections, yielding a total of 677 models.[14] Of that 677, I counted 27 non-white models—those with dark skin ($n = 5$) or Asian features ($n = 12$). That's less than 4 percent minority representation on the catwalk. Similarly, on the popular industry website Models.com, there is a ranking of the "50 Top Women," a tally of models with the most prestigious editorials, runways, and campaigns. In November 2007, of the sixty featured models, there were two black models: Kinee (ranked no. 47) and Chanel Iman (no. 29); and two Asians: Du Juan (no. 40) and Hye (no. 16). Following the next Spring/Summer collections in 2008, the fashion press *Women's Wear Daily* took a similar count, finding that of 101 top shows and presentations posted on Style.com, 31 appeared to have no black models at all.[15] Why are there so few models of color?

Ever since modeling work formalized into an occupation in the late 1920s, non-whites have worked at the margins of the industry. With the rise of purchasing power of the black middle class in the post-World War II period, African American models, called "black diamonds," appeared in "duplicate advertising"—ads first pitched to white audiences were copied featuring light-skinned black models to target the affluent minority consumer.[16] Black models began appearing frequently in black publications such as *Ebony*, which was founded in 1945. Non-whites worked with separate agencies, such as Grace Del Marco Model Agency in New York, founded in 1946. In the 1960s, more non-white agencies cropped up, such as Black Beauties, which supplied its "black diamonds" to the African American market.[17]

Integration into mainstream fashion markets began in the 1960s, a time when black became both beautiful and good for business, and the prestigious Wilhelmina agency promoted black models to nonsegmented markets as a deliberate means to differentiate from its competitor, Ford Models. By the late 1960s, *Glamour, Mademoiselle,* and *Harper's Bazaar* had featured black cover models, and Beverly Johnson broke the last white barrier by shooting the cover for American *Vogue* in 1974. By 1969, Naomi Sims, considered the first black supermodel, appeared on the cover of *Life* magazine with the caption "Black Models Take Center Stage." The inside feature story began, "You see before you what may well be the most persuasive demonstration of successful black power ever assembled."[18]

Of course in 1969, as today, non-white models are still far from center, and modeling is far from a position of serious social power. Not only do non-white models find fewer employment opportunities in mainstream fashion markets, but darker-skinned women have been and continue to be posed and styled in exotic juxtapositions to the normative white body.[19] As fashion theorist Rebecca Arnold has argued, the 1970s saw an uptick in the numbers of black and Asian models in high fashion, though these models were used primarily for photo shoots and runways with "exotic" themes, chosen because they added an "extra frisson to the prevailing ideals of the time," ideals produced for whites, by whites.[20] Cultural theorists argue that representations of women cannot be understood without also studying race and class relations.[21] From medical and scientific texts dissecting the anatomical "anomalies" of native women, to present-day hip-hop videos glorifying "the booty," an imperial gaze fixes on the non-white woman's body. The West's cultural fascination with non-Western women's bodies, such as the fame generated around Josephine Baker's rear end or the published autopsy of Sarah Bartmann, the "Hottentot Venus" of 1810, serves as a means of controlling the Other. Representations of men frequently ascribe notions of danger, sexual threat, and pathology to non-white masculinity, thereby perpetuating the dominance of white, straight, middle-class masculinity in the social hierarchy. Sexual stereotypes are instrumental in marking racial differences; they construct "pure white womanhood" as something to be protected, and they legitimate the subordination of minorities.[22]

With this historical baggage, sexuality, gender, and race inequalities become mutually constitutive forces governing representations of women and men. In fashion, the model "look" is the embodied vision of imagined social differences. For intersectionality theorists, the look is a mirror for social inequalities, an expression of power. The look is a powerful symbolic representation of the intersections of gender, race, heterosexuality, and class; it is the embodied vision of our imagined social distinctions and fantasies.

Representation as Cultural Production

Representations do work. They arrange objects into sets of cultural meanings, they differentiate people into social categories, and they project scripts for personal behavior, morality, and desire.[23] But they also *take* work to get done. For all its cultural meanings, the look is fundamentally a cultural product; it is the outcome of an organized production process. As in other art worlds, the accomplishment of fashion looks requires conventions, shared ways of doing things. Conventions are especially important, I argued in the last chapter, for cultural intermediaries to navigate uncertainty and ambiguity in the production process. Conventions can also make the accomplishment of fashion difficult, should producers ignore them. Conventional ways of casting for models vary systematically across the spectrum of the modeling market; conventions for choosing a catalog look construct a set of legitimate selection criteria systematically different from those in the editorial market. How do these conventions perpetuate the skinny, racially exclusive look?

While models may represent entrenched systems of gender and racial inequality, models' bodies are themselves systematically screened for selection toward commercial and creative ends. The modeling market necessitates a mediation of social structural forces of gender and race through the organization and production processes of the market. Thus at issue is not the extent to which modeling serves gender and racial inequality but, rather, the question *how* do notions of gender and race inform the look? The fashion modeling industry is therefore a case to discover how social inequalities reproduce themselves in seemingly unlikely places, from the catalog house to the catwalk.

CLASSIFYING CLASS IN THE LOOK

The curious phenomenon of the white, size zero look does not pervade all segments of the fashion market. It is most likely to appear in editorial, not commercial, fashion. To get a handle on this type of editorial look, we must also examine its counterpoint, the commercial look, and the systematic differences among conventional understandings of both editorial and commercial fashion production.

The "classic" and "soft" commercial look, as we've seen, accrues reliably high, steady earnings. When trying to describe the appeal and purpose of commercial models, producers in both the UK and United States made frequent references to sexual attractiveness, the "layperson," and "middle America" several times mentioning "my mom," "Kansas," and "Ohio" by way of illustration. Putting these word combinations together gives us a working definition of a commercial model: (1) someone considered sexually attractive by the layperson in Kansas; or (2) someone "your mom" in middle America considers pretty. Or, as Isabel, a casting director in London, says, "To be perfectly blunt, it's the girls that do *Victoria's Secret*, and *Sports Illustrated*, and *JCPenney* and *Macy's*, you know, accessible to your kind of mass middle market where women want to look like, you know, women who are adored by men. You know that is bigger boobs, big hair, blonde, or at least some sort of like, you know, glamorous Giselle type."

In contrast to the "boring" commercial look, the "edgy" editorial model is "unique." Some producers spoke of editorial looks and bodies with words like "sticks," "abnormal," and "freaks." Only a particular type of audience will "get" the editorial type of model. In New York, Heather explained:

> Say you have . . . a painting that you think is so beautiful, and everyone else looks at you like "oh my God, she is crazy, that is so ugly!" But it doesn't matter, because it is a piece of art and you find it beautiful, and that is all that matters. Editorial works in the same way. . . . It is more of the photographers who are shooting the campaigns, and they look at that girl, and they think she's beautiful. She is their piece of art, and they are using her as an art form, not as a point of sale. . . . It's not for everybody. (Heather, New York booker)

Being "not for everybody," the scout explains, means not for the masses—not to entice them into consumption, nor to turn them on, nor even to make sense to them. That is because editorial looks are meant to appeal to the high-end fashion consumer and other elite producers; they are a wink and a nod to each other's cultural competences to appreciate coded avant-garde beauty. They are largely chosen to impress field insiders such as magazine editors, stylists, and industry buyers.

This is not to say that editorial fashion is indifferent to sales. Editorial fashion exists in the service of generating vast sums of profits, though by much different means than the commercial circuit. Whereas commercial models are hired to directly target and relate to consumers, editorial models are hired to communicate brand identities and to evoke ideas of luxury lifestyles. Only indirectly does this translate into profit through product licensing agreements and ready-to-wear sales further down the consumption line.

The editorial-commercial divide is therefore a proxy for how producers make sense of class distinctions among imagined consumers of looks. Editorial looks, as markers of elite taste, are more prestigious than commercial looks and their mass-market appeal. Visually we can picture fashion models as grouped along class hierarchies and their corresponding dress codes; there is the blue chip editorial in Prada and Gucci on one board and the commercial middle classes donned in Target knitwear on the other. The models in a Prada or a Target advertisement might have few concrete physical differences between them, but the labels featured in their respective advertisements do differ. In other words, the cannon largely determines the content. *Vogue Italia* says "edgy," while Target is a dead ringer for "commercial."

All of this is to say that within the high-fashion editorial market, anybody.org is rather far removed from the picture. Designers and directors selecting models for Fashion Week do not choose their editorial looks with the layperson or "your mom" in mind, regardless of how loudly she protests outside their gates.

The split between editorial and commercial modeling and the relative devaluation of commercial modeling are both key to understanding how bookers and clients look for appropriate looks, because class is a defining feature of the organization of the field of fashion modeling. Having mapped out their respective class connotations, I now trace how producers in each circuit of the market construct and navigate legitimate criteria for choosing their models, and how such criteria engage the two touchiest factors in their hiring decisions: size and race.

APPEALING TO EVERYBODY: THE COMMERCIAL LOOK

Consider first that which is "normal," the commercial circuit. In contrast to the editorial look, the "pretty" commercial look is slightly older, slightly more racially diverse, and ever so slightly fuller in figure.

The Body Next Door

Commercial women and men at both Metro and Scene are likely to be larger than editorial models, if only by a few inches. Editorial women wear sizes 0–4 and range in age from thirteen to twenty-two, while "money girls" range from sizes 2–6 and work from age eighteen to well into their mid-thirties and beyond. A hip measurement of 36" would be unacceptable on the editorial boards, but it is common on the commercial boards. Editorial men tend to be as slim as a 28" waist and a 36" chest and between ages sixteen and twenty-five, whereas commercial men are "hunks in trunks" who work from age eighteen to age fifty and beyond.

Returning to our protesters at London Fashion Week, note that anybody.org called for more diversity *on the catwalk*, not in the *JCPenney* or *Marks & Spencer* catalog. London casting director Lesley Goring frankly told the *London Times* that full-figured models "wouldn't sell collections at this level."[24] But they do sell at the commercial level, the home of the "accessible" and "classic" girl-next-door look. On the commercial end of the market, diversity in shape and color is more prevalent because commercial modeling is a deliberate attempt to reach a buying demographic. It is a straightforward marketing exercise, as a stylist explained:

If you look at an Old Navy commercial, for example, they have this big booty black girl, she's totally normal, looks like your best friend down the street that you have coffee with, dancing around, and there's three white girls in the background . . . that's more like, "Well our brand is targeting everybody. We don't want to be niche, because we want to sell the units, and selling the units means appealing to everybody." And that's commercial modeling. (Clive, New York stylist)

Notice the racial coding of the "booty" but also the dismissal of the Old Navy models: they're just *normal* and *ordinary* bodies, deliberately in step with the average shopper, as a casting director explains:

Well I think right now it's kind of controversial because models of catalog need to be fuller because the average consumer, you know, I can talk for America, I can talk for Europe, the average consumer is fuller, you know what I mean? (Rayna, New York casting director)

Commercial producers value and search for the down-market "big booty" as they will any look they think will resonate with their target audience. Commercial bookers are likely to dismiss size zero models in favor of practical bodies for catalog and showroom clients:

There is one who gained weight; she is now a size eight instead of a six. She has a big booty. Sometimes we might have a client that might want that big booty, like a jeans client, and we will be like, "Oh, so-and-so has gained all of this weight, she can fit these clothes!" (Francis, New York booker)

Commercial clients are directly accountable to their consumers' desires. For instance, when Peter Simons, president of La Maison Simons department stores in Quebec, recently received over three hundred e-mails complaining about the extreme thinness of the models in its back-to-school clothing catalog, he immediately cancelled distribution of the catalog, removed the images from the store's website, and issued an online apology.[25] By the end of the costly blunder, La Maison Simons pulled 450,000 catalogs, to the detriment of its back-to-school season sales but to its credit as a socially responsible (and responsive) retailer.

Faced with concerns to relate to the consumer, please the client, and, ultimately, sell products, commercial producers do not bother themselves with size zero models, because size zero is too "edgy." It is not compatible with commercial pragmatic undertakings, nor does it resonate to commercial producers' interpretations of mainstream beauty and sex appeal.

Pursuit of Ethnic Diversity

Commercial producers are also more likely to embrace ethnic diversity among models than editorial producers in conscious efforts to reach target consumers. Commercial bookers talked of having to "balance" their board and meet quotas for blondes, Asians, or brunettes to satisfy their clients. If the commercial client uses, or passes on, minority models, then it is understood as a response to a calculated cost-benefit analysis of the market. For instance, a men's booker at Metro makes sense of her commercial male models in terms of market research and target consumer tastes:

> A lot of it has to do with—they test out different things. They know who will appeal to their buyers. Like when you put the same shirt on the blond-haired blue-eyed guy, black guy, and Asian guy, I guess they can tell which sells more. (Missy, New York men's booker)

Similarly, one casting director explained why he pursues non-whites for some shows:

> But then I have, you know I've had designers say, "Listen, like all of my buyers, all the stores I sell to, are in Japan. So get me Asian girls!" (David, New York casting director)

One can visually discern a color divide between editorial and commercial modeling by flipping through a magazine and noticing on which pages models of color appear. Reporters for the popular fashion blog Jezebel.com did just this, counting the number of black models in advertising versus editorial in nine of the most popular women's fashion magazines.[26] Black women were well represented in the commercial world, appearing in the advertising pages of eight of the nine magazines. *Marie Claire*, for instance, showcased ten black models in advertising pages, selling nonfashion items, from deodorant to cosmetics. It featured just one black model in its editorial pages. This pattern emerged across the nine magazines, in which just two black models appeared in editorial spreads. Clients I interviewed acknowledged this pattern, but they didn't quite know what to make of it, as one freelance stylist who works with a number of top magazine publications tried to explain:

> I probably shoot ethnic or Asian girls more in advertising because they have to kind of get their demographic right, don't they? Editorial, I mean for me, it's never about, kind of, about a race issue, or whatever. It's just about what I've got, you know, who I'm thinking about in my mind. So it's never, "Oh let's shoot an Asian girl," you know, for me, that's never an issue for editorial—and

I don't know why, but I know I shoot more, kind of, more sort of, Asian or African girls in advertising, yeah. (Florence, London stylist)

This may strike some readers as counterintuitive, given the popular associations between artists and virtues of liberalism and cosmopolitanism, whereas the catalog shoppers of "middle America" are commonly accused of parochialism and intolerance.[27] Yet the catalog market is where fashion embraces ethnic representation. For instance, the casting director at one commercially oriented magazine explained how her team consistently hires an ethnically diverse range of models:

It's a conscious effort, but not to the point where we don't want it to seem like, "Oh there's the mold, or the template, for however a story should be; Asian girls, black girls, Latin girls." Like, you know, I try to mix it up and not make it so obvious. (Kelly, New York casting director)

Here, diversity is strategically sought—not to be too obvious or too closely aligned with an affirmative action agenda but just enough to increase market share by representing the demographic base. JD, the male model from Manchester, UK, is of Middle Eastern descent. He explained his own commercial appeal:

On the advertising side of it, if any client's actually trying to reach audiences, where they're trying to sell stuff to people of a wider market, to get more brown people or Arabs or this or that buying their clothes, then they go for someone like me.

Commercial clients need minorities to "fill in pieces of the story," explained Tomas:

Well it depends on the market, on the idea that they are selling. If the idea is they need a black guy to play this friendly character so people will think, "Oh my God that guy had the biggest smile! He's so friendly," whatever, he is really good for the demographic we are trying to reach. (Tomas, New York art director)

Commercial women are hired to embody a femininity that appeals to what producers *imagine* to be suburban, not-too-edgy, middle-class women and their imagined boyfriends. Similarly, commercial men embody heteronormative masculinity; they look like guys women will find attractive. This is not to say that catalog producers are the stewards of diversity and inclusion. Hardly, for though they cite "your mom" in the heartland as their target audience, whose mom, exactly, do they consider? Their imagined consumer upholds a restrictive and idealized vision of middle-class suburban attractiveness, but it is just that: an ideal with mass appeal, but nothing too surreal.

APPEALING TO OTHER PRODUCERS: THE EDITORIAL LOOK

If commercial producers are aiming to please, then editorial producers are looking to shock in a high-stakes game of distinction. In the last chapter we saw that clients working in the editorial circuit have more freedom to choose looks based on their personal taste, but greater freedom of course entails greater opportunities to make mistakes, with one's status in the field at stake. Given their limited possibilities for ascertaining sales effectiveness—and, indeed, their putative indifference to commercial endeavors—editorial producers create fashion for fashion's sake. To this end they need "edgy"-looking models. In contrast to the commercial look, the edgy look is younger and whiter, and it has been steadily slimming since the 1980s.

The Hanger Body

"*Too* skinny?!" said the incredulous Nev, a magazine editor, when I asked her for her thoughts on the recent media scrutiny of models' slim body sizes. "They're *models!*" she exclaimed. Nev is a former booker who now manages a popular modeling industry magazine. She's been around models' bodies for the last fifteen years of her life. Like dozens of producers I interviewed, she doesn't understand why slim models are a social issue. To Nev, as to many people in her industry, slender models are an obvious choice. They embody a naturalized vision of female beauty, one that all comes down to making clothes look good:

> Well it's only just clothing. Designers want them to look a certain way. Like the clothes that hang, like a hanger, as they say. You know, originally models were just hangers. (Nev, New York magazine editor)

Nev's idea that models are mere hangers for garments was a running theme among the bookers and clients I interviewed. Yet the idea does not speak to the original purpose of fashion models at all. The first models introduced a deliberate theatricality to fashion marketing, and they were a radical departure from previous displays on clothes hangers. Near the end of the nineteenth century, the English courtier Charles Frederic Worth was the first to show his designs on live "mannequins" in his Paris salon—an innovative way to show garments in action on live bodies rather than on dummies.[28] These young women were usually drawn from the workshop floor. They were not necessarily thin or taut; of chief concern was that they had good manners. French courtier Paul Poiret wrote of a favorite model in 1913: "With round arms and rounded shoulders, she was plump and elegantly rolled as a cigarette."[29] In the early 1920s, Cristobal Balenciaga showed his clothes on models with "short, stocky bodies," closer to his own physique.

Several decades later, Fashion Week catwalks are now strutting an American size 00 and a UK size 2; that's a waist measurement comparable to a typical seven-year-old girl's.[30] Almost all bookers I talked to explained that models are skinnier now than they have ever witnessed during their careers. A New York showroom booker, Bre, entered the business out of college in 1996, when supermodels Cindy Crawford and Linda Evangelista were still shooting *Vogue* covers. She explained: "The thin thing now is beyond anything I have ever seen. This is the thinnest time in modeling that I have ever seen. It's ridiculous!" When two models died of anorexia-related illnesses in 2006, it prompted a wave of headlines, conferences, and government inquiries into the potentially deadly fashion world.[31]

At the height of the media furor, I was observing backstage at fashion shows and castings in New York and London, where modeling was business as usual—skinny models, small sample-size clothes, and hectic schedules—except for one thing. Clients were openly discussing their unlucky position as anorexia endorsers. They even made jokes about it. In London, one casting director spoke before a crowd of slender models at his casting: "You know, it's really hard to find size 12 to 14 girls that are fierce, I mean they're all just . . . ," and here he puffed out his cheeks and raised his eyebrows. "It doesn't look good," he concluded, to the laughter of his model audience. Hidden in the joke is a serious quandary: Why are there no "fierce" size-12 models?

Throughout our interviews, bookers and clients unanimously agreed that the clothes determine the models. The overwhelming majority of respondents, when asked why catwalk models are a standard size US 0–4, deferred to the clothes. Standardized clothing sizes entered the fashion industry with the rise of mass-produced ready-to-wear clothing post-World War II. With the end of made-to-measure clothes, it was increasingly important for models to conform to ready-made patterns, to which models' bodies homogenized.[32] Clothing catalog samples tend to come in sizes 4–6, but high-fashion designers cut samples based on standardized measurements of sizes 0–4. When they're in a pinch days before showing a collection, alterations are the last thing they want to handle. Unlike the catalog studio, the catwalk does not lend itself to instant Photoshop or safety-pinning imperfections. A problematic fit cannot be sent down the catwalk; small clothes therefore necessitate small models:

> I don't want someone that looks emaciated or like they're actually about to die—there's nothing pleasant about that. But in general models have to be very, very skinny because the clothes hang better on skinny, tall people. You know an Alaïa dress is never gonna look as good on someone who's a size 12 as it is on [a] size 8. I have to deal with that every morning, you know, so you just have to be realistic about it. (Isabel, London casting director)

Many producers like Isabel relied on seemingly obvious aesthetics when explaining their taste for a size zero. Skinny bodies make clothes *look* better, they say, even if they admit that those bodies at times look unhealthy or "freakish":

> Because the shapes. Clothes hang off, they fall, they look better on a thinner model. (Xavier, London stylist)

Producers talked about slenderness as an aesthetic law for women and, to a lesser extent, for men as well. Considering the slim size 38 suit and "pencil-neck" bodies appearing on men's Fashion Week catwalks in Europe, one male model told reporters, "Designers like the skinny guy. . . . It looks good in clothes, and that's the main thing."[33]

Of course societal norms underlie aesthetic ones, and very few codes of physical attraction are timeless or universal. Universal aesthetics aside, sample-size clothes are not born out of thin air. They are measured, cut, and manufactured by deliberate hands. When you ask designers why they make their samples in those particular dimensions, many answer with an appeal to tradition. Sample size is what they learned in design school, the size of their trusted mannequin on the shop floor, and the size of the models they expect agencies to provide. Producers certainly don't like the thought that their clothes may terrorize women into eating disorders, but they don't know how to change an entire system of fashion design either. Like the QWERTY keyboard, we end up with a certain way of doing things because, over time, conventions get "locked in," and it becomes easier to *not* change them, even if we don't like them.[34] Bookers and clients don't utilize the language of economics when explaining their work, but instead they understand that it's just "the way things are done." Like any convention, sample sizes exert inertia. Once in place, conventions constrain the potentially limitless field of possible alternate ways of organizing an art world.[35]

Consider shoe size. A female model with size 11 feet poses an instant problem for any client. When Kelly, the bookings editor at a teen fashion magazine in New York, meets such a model, she makes a tough decision: A size 11 foot will not fit into the typical size 9 sample shoes that showrooms provide her for fashion shoots. To make the shoot happen, Kelly's company will have to buy the larger shoes, and they will probably end up in storage in the huge office closet (where the shoes will linger, along with racks of handbags and clothes, until they are used again or most likely distributed as office freebies). This means that Kelly has a bigger investment riding on the model with a size 11 foot than one with a size 9 foot.

Models who can't fit into sample clothing pose similar difficulties for those who hire them. Smaller models are not very problematic, as it is easier to pin baggy clothes in photo shoots than to add extra fabric to a tight fit. Clients foresee these problems all the time, even in their casual conversations. For example, at one photo shoot, I watched as two stylists flipped through a new edition of *Vogue*, pausing to praise and critique various images in typically flamboyant fashion terms:

S1: These hair ads are disgusting!

S2: It's very LA. [turns a page]

S1: Oh, I love this, everything, the light, the propping, it's amazing!

S2: I ripped that out and hung it up on my wall for inspiration. I love it too!

S1: It's sick, sick, *sickness*!

The conversation took a serious turn when the two stylists turned the page to find a plus-size model posing in a D&G fragrance ad shot by Steven Meisel. They admired the image and were enticed by the possibility of doing their own shoots with the full-figured model. But, they admitted, they were unlikely to ever choose her for a shoot:

S1: Good for her! I love that. She looks really good.

S2: I think so too.

S1: My friend [a photographer] likes it too and wants to shoot a plus-size model for an editorial story. But I can't do it. I can't get the clothes, not for high fashion, which is what I specialize in. I don't know where, do you know?

S2: No, I don't know.

S1: I don't know.

Without conventions like standardized sizes, art worlds like fashion would not happen. Finding the right look for an editorial job is a daunting task. Bookers estimated that anywhere between 3,000 and 5,000 models flock to New York during a show season, and over the course of about one week, runways with approximately twenty-five open slots must be filled. When looking for the right look, producers tend to look to each other, a normal fact of production markets noted by sociologist Harrison White, but even more apparent in a cultural production market like fashion, where uncertainty is the norm. Amid all the uncertainty, producers rely on imitation, especially in the high-risk editorial market, where fleeting aesthetic preferences can quickly snowball to make—or break—a model's career. The ironic result is an isomorphism of the look, frequently bemoaned in popular presses as the homogenization of beauty.[36]

Editorial producers are entangled in an institutionalized production system, where the goods produced—the models—are embedded in a historically shaped and commerce-driven network of agents, designers, and editors. Each actor in the system is trying to match as best she can what she thinks will complement the demands of cooperating actors and she must make these rapid decisions based on past records and experiences. Agents are trying to beat their competitors by supplying what they think will go over well with designers; designers produce shows they predict will appeal to magazine editors; and editors praise the kinds of looks they think their advertisers will appreciate. Bookers and clients alike are uncomfortably close to uncertainty. At one casting for a large fashion PR firm in London, I glimpsed a telling note scribbled on a dry-erase board hung on the office wall: "Look closely! She might be a Kate Moss."

. With everyone on the lookout for the next celebrated "waif," size zero may not be the intended outcome of any particular producer, but, under institutional constraints, it is locked in as a survival strategy. Magazine editors and stylists alike, those who seemed to have considerable power as influential tastemakers, appeared helpless against sample-size conventions:

> It depends on the stylist too and like what the story is. It's like if the clothes are tiny and you know, it's driven by samples, it's driven by the designers. It's not the magazine saying "we want skinny girls." That's what the designers are doing in the samples, and that's why we have to have these girls. (Joss, New York magazine casting)

Photographers similarly deferred to a higher authority; after all, they explained, they must produce appealing pictures for their advertisers and editors, and ultimately, designers determine the look:[37]

To the critics I say go out there and look at all the clothes that are made for people in fashion! It doesn't look flattering, like you're gonna put a bigger girl in Miss Sixty jeans? No, it doesn't work. And I think fashion houses direct the look of what kind of people they want to see wear their clothes. It's the result of them. (Billy, New York photographer)

Designers, for their part, appeared equally as helpless when faced with predicting an agency's supply of models. They expect models who audition for their castings to be the conventional sizes 0–4, and to prepare their sample sizes accordingly. They also anticipate that a well-received show will be one that meets an editorial audience's expectations for models.

For instance, London design duo Tim and Mike of the label *B-rude* were happy to have friends and nightclub regulars walk in their London Fashion Week show, including one woman in her sixties. "You know," said Mike, "we aren't just constantly worried about youth or anything. I'd like to show people that, people in their sixties and stuff. I mean she's a very elegant lady."

"Yeah, I mean we really want other people, we really want diversity in the show, you know, there's no fascism in our show!" Tim added.

However, both conceded that professional models are better at conveying their brand image, as models can walk with greater confidence and attract more favorable press coverage. Tim and Mike thus see themselves as rather limited by modeling agencies in their pursuit of body diversity:

Basically we take who the agencies give us—again, it's down to the agencies isn't it, and who they have on their books. You know, if they only choose that kind of waif, tall figure then that's what we've got to choose from.

Bookers, who control the supply of models and would therefore seem to direct the supply's shape and size, deny their own agency by claiming to merely cater to the wants and needs of clients:

I think it's about fitting the clothes. That's the bottom line. 34–24–34 is the ideal size. I have no idea where that came from. Of course I don't like that, I'm not that size. If you can't beat 'em, join 'em, honey! That's the way it is. We're not gonna change the majority here—then we'll all be outta the job! (Kath, New York booker)

Likewise, commenting on the increase in using more slender male models, a men's booker told reporters in New York, "It's client driven. That's just the size that blue-chip designers and high-end editorials want."[38]

Ask designers why they book skinny models and they'll reply that that's what the agents are providing. Ask agents why they promote skinny models and they'll reply that that's what the designers want. And around we go. As a structural organization system, the modeling market appears to be an external force to bookers and clients, though it is a product of their individually entangled actions.

Sex and the Unattainable Body

One may at this point be wondering what, after all, is the point of clothes if they look worse on actual bodies? This is precisely the point: editorial producers aim to depict identities, images, and feelings—not clothes—when they hire uniformly discreet bodies with field-specific distinctiveness.

> Runway especially, designers want them even thinner because they want their clothes hanging on them when they walk down the runway. They don't want people seeing the model—well they do, they want that face, but that's all they want is the face. And the rest of the body they don't want. (Hall, New York photographer)

It's not that producers *don't* want the body; they want a particular type of body for the catwalk, one that fits with the editorial convention of edginess, not sexiness. In the high-fashion world, models embody a version of femininity not intended to please the middle-market shopper or her imagined boyfriend. Sex doesn't do the selling in the editorial world. Instead there is a construction of unattainable fantasy femininities and masculinities, envisioned by multiple gazes—gay, straight, male, and female—with a self-referential audience of fellow elite producers in mind.

The gay gaze doesn't do all the work of fashioning the look. One booker boldly claimed that the size zero look is a result of the predominance of gay men in fashion:

> As the business has changed, more gay men have come into positions of power in the business, as casting directors, art directors, creative directors. Therefore, their ideal of beauty is a young guy, let's say a 15-year-old guy. So what comes closest to looking like that is a young girl who is almost prepubescent. She is really thin, has no breasts, no hips, no butt. . . . It has evolved into this young, thin, no-feminine aspect part of the body. It's because of gay men in the business, I know it! (Bre, New York booker)

Gay men indeed have an increased presence in the industry over the last decades, especially as fashion design has shifted from a formerly devalued and feminized trade occupation associated with manufacture and sewing toward a celebrated cultural occupation.[39] Since the 1980s, gay stylists, art directors, and designers have been at the forefront of changing fashion's body aesthetic, particularly concerning new representations of masculinity.[40] But this is too easy an explanation behind women's boyish fashion figures. First, masculine ideals vary widely within any community; from bears and bikers to metrosexuals, there is no single gay taste in physical appearance. Second, correlation does not imply causality, and a causal link between the presence of gay men and the slim look of women models would be impossible to prove when we analyze fashion as an art world. Through the art world perspective, it becomes clear that individual personal preferences alone—whether those of gay men or straight women—do not determine the look. Rather, the look results from a coordinated, collective process, constrained as much by convention and dominant cultural ideas as by personal taste and desire. At most, the presence of gay men in the industry indirectly influences the direction of the look, in tandem with producers' perceptions of consumer tastes.

These tastes circulate and transform within the circuit, sometimes getting picked up as the next hot look and other times being ignored altogether. The mediation of tastes and desire does not work in any linear or straightforward way. This became clear to me as I spoke with Victor, a gay American fashion designer based in London. Together with his design partner, also a gay man, Victor wanted to cast all voluptuous models for his Fashion Week show; as he put it, he had in mind a "hot tits-and-ass casting." But casting for a show, he explained, involves more than just his own taste:

> A great rack is great, you know what I mean? It's super hot, but it's like, not necessarily what you want to put in your clothes, you know. . . . When I'm sending clothes down the runway and you're trying to make everybody look different, but the same, and you're trying to present a really strong focused package, you know, you're just kind of; you're appealing to yourself but you're also appealing to the audience, you know, and what's popular. (Victor, London designer)

Also eager to distance themselves from ordinary visions of middle-class femininity, editorial clients actively look for the extraordinary body, one that so radically stretches mainstream slenderness that it borders on what they imagine "your mom" might register as the uncanny or the ugly. Curves and their accompanying suggestions of female sexual desire and availability are polluting images for high-end brands and high-end femininities. In other words, there's something kind of average, a little too attainable, and too cheap about curves. In constructing the editorial look, bookers and clients deliberately strip sex from the editorial body:

> I find boobs on the runway a little scary unless they're like in a corset or something or really like tamed and controlled. If you get a bit of boob action going on in a flimsy summer frock it's just all bubbling all the way down the catwalk, isn't it? It's just like everything wobbles. It doesn't look so good. (Leah, London casting director)

No, indeed, it is hardly appropriate for an elite symbol to flaunt her body, uncontrolled flesh wobbling cheaply for down-market consumption. Sexual unavailability is instrumental in producing high-end looks. It is a key marker for fashionable elite sensibility. As Victor, the fashion designer, put it, "You're displaying your clothes on this ageless unattainable beauty, really."

Laissez-Faire Racism

"In all of the high fashion that we are talking about, it is really super white," explained Clive, a New York stylist. By that he means that the high-end edgy look, with its youthful, skinny packaging, tends to come in pale shades of white. The white bias is evident on the boards of both agencies. At Metro, approximately 20 out of 200 women of color were on the books and 10 out of 125 men of color. At Scene, 8 out of 150 women were non-white[41]—proportions for which agents readily apologized, bemoaning the difficulties they faced trying to diversify:

> Yeah, we don't have many. It's very small, actually, it doesn't quite—it's shameful, actually. I just think more and more you just kind of like, I don't know, it's just so difficult to book the black girls and the Asian girls these days. . . . Because they don't work as much and it's all—at the end of the day, we're a business. (Erica, London booker)

It's not the case that women of color "opt out" of editorial high fashion. Agencies' supplies of models are relatively unlimited, as they constantly refresh their boards by tapping into global networks of scouts, taking international scouting trips, and even directly seeking out models to fill specific niches, for instance, Elite Model Management's notorious search for a dark-skinned model in remote villages of sub-Saharan Africa.[42] Self-selection effects, such as class or racial barriers that may limit the immediate availability of non-white models, most likely do not play a significant role in preventing agencies from supplying minorities. In an age of global scouting, non-white candidates are not difficult to find.

The shortage of models of color cannot be explained by prejudice alone. Bookers and clients, as I showed in the last chapter, come from a variety of social and class backgrounds. They are not a particularly bigoted bunch. On the contrary, they take great pains to distance themselves from traditional forms of racist rhetoric. Most producers I interviewed were frustrated by the absence of minorities in fashion—if it were it up to them, they hinted, ethnic diversity would always be "in." They laid blame in all directions: bookers blamed clients, clients blamed bookers, and bookers even blamed *other* bookers, as Rio, himself of Southeast Asian descent, did several times throughout our talk:

> People right away think that if you're ethnic then you're "urban." You're street style. You're ghetto. You're not higher class. Because you're white, you're more expensive, and because you're not white, your day rate is lower. I'm a person for color, and I feel that among agents I'm alone, totally. (Rio, New York booker)

Bookers said they could and would take on more models of color, and though they claimed to "love flavor" and diversity, they admitted that they have "bent" under the constraints to meet clients' demands. They shared a common understanding, that ethnic models have fewer job opportunities than their white counterparts, and said that clients and "the market" were largely to blame for any racial imbalance. As Rachel, a booker, put it, "It's literally what the market has. . . . It has nothing to do with us."

Like bookers, editorial clients defer their hiring practices to the whims of "the market," perceived as a formidable, though rational, force:

> Okay, let's say Prada. You don't have a huge amount of black people buying Prada. They can't afford it. Okay, so that's economics there. So why put a black face? They put a white face, because those are the ones that buy the clothes. (Lawrence, New York stylist)

But what is "the market," and how much of it is determined by economic forces? White consumers do in fact spend more total dollars on fashion and apparel. Black households spent $22 billion on clothing in 2005, when total US apparel sales reached $181 billion.[43] That's a black market share of 13 percent. Conventional wisdom and some marketing research suggest that consumers of fashion identify more with models of their own race, although other psychological studies have questioned the salience of race as a cue for social identification.[44] Therefore, advertisers may think they stand to gain more by using white models to appeal to majority white audiences.[45] This economic logic is certainly relevant at the commercial level of fashion, where in fact producers consider consumer demographics and choose representative models accordingly.

But in the editorial circuit, the relationship between models and units sold becomes blurred. It's not clear what a model on the Prada runway is selling, or to whom. We've already seen in the last chapter that editorial clients are not beholden to the mass buying public; they do not pay attention to things such as buyer demographics, focus groups, or market research. Rather, personal reactions to "edgy" and the buzz pulsing through the circuit are what drive them. Thus their economic decisions are fundamentally cultural considerations. When producers explain their actions using the logic of "the market," they are strategically pulling from neoclassical economic discourse to rationalize their choices. As an idea, the market does considerable discursive work: it naturalizes market outcomes, in effect reducing cultural products into some formulaic inevitability. It rationalizes the work of tastemaking into a set of neutral outcomes when supply meets demand. In so doing, it obscures cultural values and renders invisible sexism and racism.

At a time when most Americans are uncomfortable with racist arguments predicated on innate inferiority, a "kinder, gentler" anti-black racial ideology has emerged to perpetuate negative racial stereotypes while blaming non-whites for their own problems. Lawrence Bobo has called this "laissez-faire racism" because of the tendency to blame blacks themselves for black–white inequality.[46] Like "the market" discourse, laissez-faire racism naturalizes social processes so that they seem natural and unproblematic. This belief in the market's rationality permeates producers' aesthetic choices, making the racial inequalities of beauty seem normal, natural, and inevitable.

The orthodox economic concept of markets as neutral sites where supply meets demand does little to explain the racial imbalance in editorial fashion. Luckily this is a view of markets that most sociologists reject. We tend to see markets as economic, cultural, and structural formations. My aim isn't to reject market-based explanations but to respecify the analysis to ask what, really, is a market? And with regard to the race gap, what normative understandings of race do producers employ, and how do these shape their decisions?

Central to any cultural intermediaries' engagement with the fashion market are their conceptions of fashion consumers, particularly the differences they imagine between white and non-white shoppers. Drawing on entrenched stereotypes of Latinos, African Americans, and Asians, bookers and clients suggested that non-whites are unlikely ideal customers of luxury labels. A booker who runs the men's division at an agency in New York explained why his board of one hundred and forty male models includes just ten non-white men:

> Blacks and Latinos don't make a lot of money. What I'm in is marketing. I'm trying to sell products. I'm selling bodies that are going to be hired by the designers. People that are buying Calvin Klein, or RL, Gucci, Prada— they aren't black or Latino. Asian is kind of a grey area, because they're not entirely minority, nor are they entirely majority. Asians are kind of seen in the middle of being black and white. And they're extremely intelligent, talented, and they tend to be very successful in everything they do, but they're not Caucasian. They tend to, in a marketing sense—people assume they have money. Whereas blacks and Latinos are seen to have the money but aren't going to buy the brands. (Ivan, New York men's booker)

Rather than blaming consumers, several editorial clients laid blame squarely back onto the bookers for the racial imbalance:

> Me personally, in my opinion, there really is no good, good, black girl around. The really good, good black girl around [is] still the same, and [is] still the one that everybody wants. . . . It's very difficult to find one. The agency [doesn't] deliver enough choice to make happy the client. (Oden, New York casting director)

And around we go, yet again: bookers claim to be limited by consumer and client demand, and clients claim to be limited by bookers' supply.

What Makes a Really Good Ethnic Model?

Both the booker and the client can agree that it's very hard to find *good* ethnic models, presumably in comparison to their white counterparts, where good ones can be found aplenty:

> There's so very few that, so very few good ones. To be honest I think if there were more good ones here, they would be used. . . . I don't think . . . I'd definitely say that nobody here's opposed to using them. It's just that there are not enough good ones. (Leah, London casting director)

Agents are keenly aware of the alleged "shortage" and are under agency orders to scout for *really good* ethnic models. What makes a *really good* ethnic model? This makes for a tough interview question, one that producers could at best answer negatively, by describing those qualities that *do not* make a good ethnic model. Sheepishly, with a kind of awkward guilt, several bookers and clients drew from stereotypes of the "other" body and its cultural associations of ethnicity with urban roughness:

> We don't like using the same model too often, but it's harder to find ethnic girls. And . . . well, I don't want to sound racist, but—well for Asians, it's hard to find tall girls that will fit the clothes because most of them are very petite. For black girls, I guess—black girls have a harder-edge kind of look. Like if I'm shooting something really edgy, I'll use a black girl—it always just depends on the clothes. (Ann, New York magazine editor)

Many bookers and clients responded to the question of ethnic models by predominantly discussing their woes in booking black women, as though the problem of diversity is chiefly with blackness over other ethnicities. This makes sense, given the historical operation of racial categories, in particular the ways in which whiteness, over time, has expanded to include white ethnics and, increasingly, Asians and Hispanics. As long as blacks are present, a back door is open through which non-blacks can "pass," if not as white then as nonproblematic categories.[47] While fashion producers on the whole were seemingly wedded to the ideal of racial equality, their attention inadvertently turned to that troublesome race anchor, blackness, so disruptive to their liberal adherence to global anti-racist norms. A few bookers explained the issue of representing minority women as a problem of black physiognomy, for instance, a booker in London said:

> A lot of black girls have got very wide noses. . . . The rest of her face is flat, therefore, in a flat image, your nose, it broadens in a photograph. It's already wide, it looks humongous in the photograph. I think that's, there's an element of that, a lot of very beautiful black girls are moved out by their noses, some of them.

Likewise, an agent in New York said:

> But it's also really hard to scout a good black girl. Because they have to have the right nose and the right bottom. Most black girls have wide noses and big bottoms, so if you can find that right body and that right face, but it's hard.

Several other bookers saw the backside as particularly problematic when booking black models. The black backside has recently received plenty of attention in the press concerning First Lady Michelle Obama, whose entire body has been dismembered into arms, legs, butt, and hair, each part becoming a portal to read conflict, disorder, guile, and class.[48]

A black family in the White House has not eradicated bodily racial stereotypes but allowed for closer public inspection of them.

What matters is not the truth or falsehood of physical differences between white and non-white women but, rather, bookers' *presumption* that such differences are unattractive and problematic. The implicit frame of beauty is so firmly rooted in whiteness that any deviation from a white, bourgeois body is viewed with disdain:

> I think they have different body forms, so certain clothes don't fit that body type, and if they don't fit the body type, then they're not going to be able to sell the clothes. . . . Well, think about for a jeans ad—if you've got a black or Latina, are they gonna be able to fit the jeans, or are they gonna be able to wear that type? It's just, you know, specific clothes are made for specific people, and for high fashion usually you're trying to tell the story to a target audience. (Billy, New York photographer)

The fashion story, Billy implied, should resonate with a white elite audience, which is presumed to want an idealized svelte and asexual heroine. Such a story is incompatible with non-white women in the eyes of clients, who tended to equate black models with sexual availability. A stylist in London, who initially claimed he didn't like having to think about things like race in his work, proudly told me he had recently used a black model for an editorial shoot:

> Yeah, and I did that one project because I really wanted to do that project. And it was—yeah, in a way it was like a sexuality that I wanted. But I felt like I could only get it out of a black girl. (Bruno, London stylist)

Producers made associations between black looks and tawdriness, two corrupting elements they seek to avoid in editorial fashion. I spoke with one young New York designer in her downtown studio moments after she held her Fashion Week show casting. Out of sixty candidates, she decided on five models, and she stood, arms crossed, looking happily at their modeling cards spread out on the floor in front of her. While explaining her choices, she stopped to reflect: "I was thinking about what you asked about why do I choose the girls I do, and I realized sometimes I kind of feel a little racist, because look" [gestured to the pictures of models: all pale, blonde, young, and thin]. "I mean this girl has a really pretty face." She picked up a card from the stack of rejects, a head shot of a young African girl wearing an Afro, and said:

> I don't know, sometimes I feel like the black models aren't the same image that I want to show, like they're kind of [pause] err, not high fashion, or a

little cheesy in a sense. I want someone that looks really different or not ordinary. (Donna, New York designer)

Beauty is desired because it is idealized and unattainable, two criteria that are fundamentally incompatible with historical representations of non-white women.

High-End Ethnic Looks

A *really good* ethnic model, then, is one who embodies an attempt to reconcile contradictory social categories. One stylist calls the embodiment of this cultural contradiction the *high-end ethnic* look, which is a look of ethnic difference specific to the editorial fashion circuit:

> Basically, high-end ethnic means the only thing that is not white about you is that you are black. Everything else, you are totally white. You have the same body as a white girl. You have the same aura, you have the same, the old, aristocratic atmosphere about you, but your skin is dark. (Clive, New York stylist)

Because *ethnic* is automatically distanced from the *high end*, and thus relegated to the commercial realm, editorial producers must search for a model of color who embodies an air of upper-class exclusivity and rarity, no easy feat given the entrenched construction of non-white ethnicity as vulgar. The high-end ethnic look materializes in one of two ways, either with minimal or extreme markers of racial difference, which I call *ethnicity lite* and *exotic ethnicity* looks.

In the first instance, fashion producers create a look of *ethnicity lite*, an implicitly white look with a touch of otherness, what bell hooks has called a "sanitized ethnic image" and a variant of the "tragic mulatto" woman in nineteenth-century American literature and film.[49] This look is not confined to the editorial sphere but is visible across all advertising spheres, including television commercial advertisements, where studies show that black models tend to be light-skinned.[50]

Mixed-race models are the pinnacle of this type of look, and bookers and clients value their "crossover" appeal to wide consumer audiences. *Ethnicity lite* blends mainstream white beauty ideals with just a touch of otherness. For example, a booker, speaking about an Asian model, said:

> So, I mean we have a very successful Asian girl, but—do you know what—she has got a very approachable look. The structure of her face is not—her eyes aren't too wide set, she's got a very American version of the look, if you

see what I mean. She is very smiley, she's got such an American personality. (Paul, New York booker)

A few clients criticized this look as intentionally whitewashing ethnicity, though they scout for models who embody it all the same:

> "She's too black, she's too dark, her lips are too big. We want black but not too black." It's shocking! It's really, really shocking. . . . I've seen girls, and they'd say "no, no she's too Hispanic." The ethnic girl needs to represent everything that they're afraid of in a way that they're not gonna be afraid. (Frank, New York casting director)

Ethnicity lite combines high-class refinement with ethnic diversity. For instance, in a 2007 news article, one casting director made a racial and class-coded assessment of the success of a light-skinned black male model named T. J., who was one of three black men sought after by high-end designers such as Michael Kors: "For a young person, T. J. is a fine, elegant man. Michael Kors isn't cheap clothing, it's refined and elegant in a less urban way."[51]

In addition to upper-class suitability, producers see mixed looks as "interesting," a special and safe type of beauty they expect from mixing racial backgrounds, as one London casting director put it:

> To be honest with you, the most kind of unusual, the most kind of interesting girls on the planet are the girls that have got some kind of unusual mix. You know, they've got like parents that are from different kinds of backgrounds.

In these kinds of assessments of multiracial looks, producers invoke scientific racial discourses that presuppose essential, discreet racial lines. Whereas nineteenth- and twentieth-century science warned of the moral and natural hazards of miscegenation, present-day genetic science celebrates crossing racial boundaries. Some genetic scientists now say that "people with mixed-race faces appear healthier and more appealing" than people of just one race. The beauty bonus that mixed-race people supposedly enjoy signals their superior fitness to reproduce, according to some evolutionary psychologists who study attractiveness.[52]

Celebratory discourses of racial intermixing—and the triumph of cultural assimilation that they imply—have been cropping up in the last decade in media accounts of changing national demographics.[53] Yet praising the beauty of mixed-race people is fraught with essentialist tensions, even as journalists and scientists would seek to overcome them. As critics note, the glorified beauty of mixed-race women reifies the idea of biological "pure" and distinct racial categories as well as a belief in their distinct physical markers.

The heightened visibility of mixed-race bodies does not necessarily equate to social progress. Media tend to treat mixed-race people favorably as symbols of racial harmony, thereby obscuring social problems such as their systemic exclusion. Furthermore, cultural critics contend that the miscegenation taboo lurks in the background of what are oftentimes highly sexualized images of mixed-race women.[54] *Ethnicity lite* looks are loaded with cultural meanings: corruption, celebration, miscegenation, and evolutionary supremacy.

"What's your mix?" was a frequent question I heard at castings. When put to me time and again, I responded, "White and a quarter-Korean," as though my blood and identity could be parsed into quartiles of ethnic varieties. Sometimes I could tell clients wanted to hear more, so I'd tell them my story, part of Mears family folklore: a Korean grandmother born to a mail-order bride and a sugar plantation hand in Hawaii, a half-Korean father, and a third-generation Polish and Czech mother. I grew up white in the South and never thought much about my Korean ancestry until I learned it was a sellable part of my look.

Mixed racial identity, like any racial category, is fluid and context specific. Like everything else in modeling—age, size, and personality—ethnicity is a matter of passing, which I understood in the early days of fieldwork after this exchange at the agency:

> "Oh, one more thing," my booker stopped me on my way out the door to a day of castings. "You mentioned that you have a little Asian in you?"
>
> "Yeah, quarter-Korean," I replied.
>
> "Okay," she said. "When you go to see M. for his casting, don't mention that. Because he likes the all-American kind of girl, like not too much ethnicity. Not that there's anything wrong with it at all, but it's just what he likes. And you said you also have what, like some Eastern European, right?"
>
> "Yeah," I said, deflated. "Pole and Czeck."
>
> "Okay, that's what we said you were, like Czeck and Polish descent."

I was instructed, in other words, to pass, to feign membership across a different racial category. Passing as a different racial category has a long history in the United States, where the one-drop rule fixed into law otherwise fictitious race categories, prompting great numbers of mixed-race people to hide their black ancestry in order to access full American citizenship.[55] Passing in fashion is a modern inverse of this history, in which models tell seemingly inconsequential "white lies" to strategically blend in or stand out from the pack. Such is the story of JD, the London male model from Manchester we met in Chapter 2, who is now twenty-two years. Only "JD" is not his real name.

Jamal Daher is of mixed-ethnic heritage, from the Middle East and South America. After participating in a modeling contest—he claims to have entered on a fluke with friends while visiting London—Jamal came in second place. Scouts at the contest, ironically titled "Face of the Future," gave him a contract and a new name, JD.

"I'm like, fuck off, my name's not JD! It's Jamal Daher.

They're like, 'What's your name?'

Jamal Daher.

'Uhhh, okay, *JD*, anyway.' "

JD thought he was the only Middle Eastern fashion model, until he went to Paris and met Nasser, Asad, Nabil, and Samir, all cleverly nick-named Nate, Alex, Billy, and Sam. He quickly learned that ethnicity is a fashion accessory he could use to dress up his look. His new friends taught him how to pass between castings. He recalled:

> They were like, "Okay when you go to see this client, when they ask you where you originate from, make sure you say Arabic, North African, because he loves North Africans, don't try to hide you're an Arab. But when you go to see this woman, she's actually very racist, so make sure you're Spanish or Brazilian."

Brazilian, Moroccan, Italian—JD has worn all these labels. Conforming to the *ethnicity lite* look, JD might temper his ethnic identity to pass as *normal* and white, or *special* and ethnic. Bookers and clients generally praise the *ethnicity lite* look as a positive step toward racial inclusion, though it entails a rather limited definition of diversity:

> I will say that [a designer] is very open to ethnic models. They use one of my black girls. She's very small featured, almost like a white girl who is black. And then they use a half-Asian girl for me. So they are very open to ethnic models, which is good. (Bre, New York booker)

Ethnicity lite is one construction of the high-end ethnic look. In the second construction, producers can embrace racial markers to create striking exoticism. These *exotic ethnic* looks present a radical departure from the white frame and are best represented by Alec Wek, a famous once-bald Sudanese model with very dark skin. This is the sort of "funky" model that bookers and clients claim to really enjoy pushing, but they always acknowledge the difficulties in doing so:

FIGURE 5.1. A dark-skinned model, one construction of the high-end ethnic look, backstage during Fashion Week

> I want a great tall, great body, funky-looking black girl. Dark skin. Not *dark* dark, but could be. Depends. . . . But we have had black girls here that have not worked, that Leah Kabetty type of girl, you know a gorgeous girl, but a little bit lighter, or I would say, *whiter*. People want a white black girl. (Christoph, New York booker)

Exoticism too has a long history rooted in imperialism. Unlike racism, the fear and hate of otherness, exoticism views other cultures as "a series of beautiful fantasies to tease and enjoy."[56]

The Color-blind Grammar of Aesthetics

Because producers operate with tacit negative assumptions of the racialized body, they expect non-white bodies to be unruly and not fit for high-end display. "Ethnic looks" call attention to themselves in ways producers have trouble talking about. The trick in fashion, an industry of eccentric, liberal-minded artist types, is to create the cultural paradox of the high-end ethnic look without being culturally offensive. To do this, fashion producers must sometimes "talk nasty" about minority models without sounding racist, a PC (politically correct) trend noted by Eduardo Bonilla-Silva (2003). Sociologists have argued that since the achievement of formal legal equality in the 1960s, racism has taken the form of "color blindness."

Given the social unacceptability of bigotry, racial inequalities today are thought of as being about culture or individual choice—anything *but* race—and never structural in nature.[57] Throughout my interviews, race was the one question most likely to make people feel awkward and to stumble in their speech. In response to the question "Why do you think you tend to use few minorities?," clients frequently veered into long tangential stories before addressing the uncomfortable issue:

> Oh [sigh] that's a good question. We're always trying to get more ethnicity in the magazine. You know you have to work with what's available, you know, and for us we need the girls to be young, which often means that they can't be in school or they have to be able to miss school because we do advocate them being in school. School's a priority. They can always model on the weekend, they can model on vacation, they can miss a few days of school, but—they should be in school. But yeah, I just, I forget, why do I go off on tangents? (Joss, New York magazine editor)

Clients also tried to discuss their casting decisions entirely in terms of aesthetics and appearances, but rarely did their preferences for white models have anything to do with their own personal racial beliefs—witness "color-blind racism" to the extreme:

> I'm not into putting people in [my show] because they're this or they're that [race]. I'm into putting people in if they're cool looking. It's a feeling. (Jay, New York designer)

Another casting director in London had trouble trying to explain why the shows he casts have a reputation for being all white:

> I don't know, I think it's just an aesthetic, really, to be honest with you, it's not that we don't [use minorities]. . . . It's just that certain clients—It's a very PC thing, isn't it? . . . Well, it's not that they're not suggested, but it's about what's *appropriate*. And you know, I don't know, you know, I think, I hate to say it, but I still think we live in a very racist society, and that's just as a general comment.

Color-blind racism takes on an ironic meaning in the fashion industry, because it is here that color cannot *not* be noticed. The flip side of color-blind racism is deliberate racial awareness, which one client (out of forty clients) was eager to discuss. Tim and Mike, the design team behind a nightclub-inspired sportswear line in London, sent seven out of thirty-six men and women of color down their Fashion Week catwalk. They cast models with a deliberate eye for skin color:

Our clothes really suit black people, you know. Some of the guy's stuff, you know, we had this one, for example, where at the fitting we had this little baby-pink sort of tracksuit. We tried it on all the white boys and it just looked terrible, and we put it on [a black model] and it was like, straightaway, like *wow*, it was great. He could really wear it. (Tim and Mike, London designers)

Tim and Mike were the exception among clients who generally talked about non-whites as aesthetic disruptions. Non-white models are rarely deemed "appropriate" at the editorial level. Ostensibly this is not a racial issue but a mere aesthetic one. A similar line of reasoning kept the New York City Radio City Music Hall Rockettes exclusively white until 1987. Black dancers were excluded, explained directors, not due to racism but, rather, because of an "aesthetic of uniformity" and symmetry that would be disturbed by the introduction of a black pair of legs in the line.[58] Surely symmetry could be achieved in a myriad of ways, such as by hiring all black dancers, or anchoring the line with dark-skinned dancers, or placing them at even intervals throughout the line.[59] Of course at issue was not really the aesthetics of race but the cultural meanings of race, the hidden yet powerful historical baggage that hangs onto dark skin. It is analytically impossible to separate aesthetics from culture, but it is a savvy maneuver to avert political responsibility by speaking with a racial grammar of aesthetics.

Today producers frequently evoke this "aesthetic of uniformity" to account for white catwalks. The models are uniformly white, so producers claim, in an effort to highlight the clothes rather than the models:

I mean almost everyone has this very specific blank, blond look and I wish they cast it differently, we all do. . . . What's happened, I think, is that to keep the eye on fashion, on the clothes and not on the girls, they've taken all personality off the runway and off the girls. (Gretchen, New York magazine editor)

Color blindness reaches so far into the heart of the artist-type producer that she can barely stand to mention the term "race," preferring instead the ambiguous language of "personality." While "The Absence of Color" was the subject for debate at a New York Public Library (NYPL) event, "personality" was the word of choice for those reluctant to talk about race or racism. Echoing the editor's explanation earlier, the NYPL panel repeatedly decried a change in the industry, from girls with "character" in the 1970s to today's hoards of nameless, faceless "blank slates"—the code word for white models—who can presumably show clothes without distracting from them (as though alarmingly emaciated bodies don't draw the viewer's attention).

Editorial modeling is not only about showing clothes; it is about projecting an ideal brand world, one in which women of color and women of corpulence do not fit.

Tokenism

If this is the case, then maybe it's not so interesting to ask why there are so few ethnic models in editorial modeling but, rather, why are there any at all? The answer is born of producers' deliberate attempts to *not* seem racist:

> There always has to be at least one because they don't want to offend any group, you know. So I always try to get one Asian, one black, and also I think it does a service to a designer if we are trying, if we have *Essence* magazine, if we have *Trace* magazine. (David, New York casting director)

Producers hire tokens, non-white exceptions to their otherwise white lineups, as a way to signal their inclusiveness and to publicly embrace diversity.

Tokens, like any representations, do work in the field. They do the work of legitimizing exclusion. The token minority offers the false resolution of racial tension. If and when the token ethnic model hits the jackpot, her presence becomes a miracle on two counts: first to have triumphed in a seemingly magical contest, and second to have won as a racial minority. This sweet victory obscures bitter struggles, not just the field-specific fight for symbolic capital but also struggles over representation in the social world. The editorial wondergirl, the unconventional superstar who succeeds beyond all expectations, inadvertently naturalizes the slim chances for everyone else.

Tokenism may well now be incorporated as part of a set of aesthetic expectations, a sole outlier of difference that contributes to the appropriateness of the catwalk ensemble. The token minority gives sense to the whole visual apparatus; her singular presence is expected. Without her, fashionistas may notice something is missing, as one *New York Times* critic remarked of Calvin Klien's 2007 lineup of all-white models: "It seems out of touch."[60] In much the same way, an entire lineup of black models would also seem out of the ordinary, as was the July 2008 issue of *Vogue Italia* in its exclusive use of black models.

Tokenism is so entrenched in editorial production that several book-ers admitted it guided their scouting decisions:

> But with black girls, it always seems, as bad as it sounds but it's true and everybody sees it, there's like the token black girl. We're living in 2006 and there's one or two black girls in a show, in every show, and every maga-zine. . . . I don't know if it's so much a challenge as just luck in terms of the black girls. You wanna get that one black girl that all the designers will use in one season. (Paul, New York booker)

In a market that prizes token difference, one person becomes the symbolic stand-in for diversity, thereby limiting every other minority's chances. Rallying around the token means it's all or nothing for ethnic models, and hence for bookers it is a riskier endeavor than booking whites. Paul continued: "We have a black girl that's from Sudan that I really believe in. Very strong, very unusual looking. She's under that um-brella of interesting, but still you can tell she's a model and classic at the same time." He paused and said: "But with a black girl, it's such a hard risk, I hate to say, what's her direction and what's her longevity."

Two Tokens

The black models I interviewed, though few in number, spoke at length on this issue. Alia was twenty-two years old when I first met her, at which point she was consistently booking big commercial jobs in New York after a rocky two years spent hostessing in restaurants and looking for a break. When she arrived in the city from Chicago, she visited agency after agency in search of representation, toting her portfolio full of Midwestern catalog pictures, hearing time and time again the same line of rejection:

> "Oh, you are absolutely stunning, but we already have four black girls, we can't take on another one." Or, "Oh, you're beautiful, but we have this girl and you two look too much alike." And then they'll show me a girl that looks like Mariah Carey. And I'm like, in what way do we look alike, aside from the fact that I'm black and she's half black?

After months of following up with agents who had shown her the door, she finally landed a contract with a prestigious high-fashion agency, but on the commercial board. She was making almost $400,000 a year doing catalogs, shampoo commercials, and even parts modeling, for example, nail polish advertisements. Alia has dark skin and natu-rally curly long hair. She carries herself with poise and constantly flashes a brilliant smile, revealing a small gap between her two front teeth. It's easy to see why commercial clients like her, but as we spoke, it was clear that she was desperate to crack into the editorial circuit. To Alia, skin color is and always has been a salient factor constraining her opportunities. Race, she says, explains why her bookers do not push her as hard as white models for editorial campaigns:

> I don't think it's deliberate. . . . It's just how they don't *see* you. It's like they don't even think of me that way, and that's what's so sad.

Meanwhile, across the Atlantic, Sofia, a twenty-one-year-old Jamaican model, feels marginalized by both her race and her body. When I met her in London, she was struggling to lose an inch from her 36" hips, after being told by her agents that she had a "fat bum." Sofia has dark skin and short natural hair cropped into a flattop; at 5'10" it's hard to see any "fat" on her long and lean frame. She hopes to return to New York next season for the Fashion Week castings to try again to break in as the next star in the editorial circuit. Sofia is in the opposite position of Alia—she has some prestige without the paycheck. "I do editorials, catwalks," she explains. "So I'm like a *fashion* model girl," she explains. As for catalog, "I wish," she says. "They say that pays a lot. I've never—I guess they don't see me as that." As a black contender in the editorial circuit, success seems a slim chance, especially when Sofia imagines her chances compared to her white peers:

> It's never going to be the same. It's a thing in our culture that we always think black people have to try twice as hard as a white person. Twice as hard. . . . Yeah, if you look like at a show, there's like hardly any black girls. Or maybe there's this one black girl. So your chances are like, yeah.

As the marked category against the unmarked white hegemony, non-whiteness calls attention to itself. For the majority of white high-end cultural producers, it goes without saying that they want a *specific* type of non-white model that will fit an entrenched and subconscious valorization of whiteness. The presence of non-whites may alleviate liberal guilt, or make a statement, or reach out to a consumer, but it always does something that involves a conscious decision in a way that the hiring of white models does not.

THE INVISIBLE HAND

Fashion is an easy target of cultural criticism. The parade of size zero white girls down the catwalk affords fresh fodder for critiquing every six months, but charges of racism and sexism on the catwalk miss the larger sociological point. Fashion producers do not select models according to sexist or racist agendas; rather, looks materialize out of institutional arrangements and conventions that vary systematically across fashion's two spheres of production, the editorial and the commercial. Within these two spheres, models are chosen to embody market-specific visions of femininity and masculinity that relate to the class positioning of an imagined audience. The look thus articulates ideas of gender, sexuality, and race that are mediated by class.

The size zero high-end ethnic look exists primarily in the editorial fashion market, but it cannot be understood without also understanding that realm of fashion in which it is absent, the commercial. In the commercial market, a fuller-figured, more racially diverse look is normal; it is part of a standard, classic image that is understood to appeal to the middle-class "layperson." In a straightforward marketing game, producers identify their demographics and create a risk-free look that will be successful, defined as units sold.

To return to the NYPL event in New York, "The Absence of Color," panel moderator and former model Bethann Hardison praised advertisers for representing non-whites: "They know who they're talking to, they're talking to their consumers, and that's why commercial advertising is really on point."

To whom, then, are the editorial producers talking? Producers in the field of high-end fashion are attempting to awe and inspire each other. They choose models principally because they *do not* have anything in common with the average shopper. When it comes to the female body in modern Western thought, there has always been a premium on containment and control, and even more so in bourgeois society.[61] This aesthetic is visible in commercial work and advertising, where bodies are far from flabby or otherwise undisciplined. But in editorial work, producers push past Western norms of beauty in pursuit of edginess, rejecting sex appeal and mainstream heteronormative femininity. Whereas the commercial world is driven by a functional imperative to sell to mass consumers, the editorial circuit is driven by its own insular taste, picking up on the idiosyncrasies of elite producers who play off each other within tight social networks.

Within this *beauty world reversed*, editorial producers disengage mainstream reality in attempts to construct an imaginary world to which their brands belong. They prize distinction, which they narrowly define in elite terms. In this world, everyday bodies and their racial diversity have no place.

An invisible hand of racism guides the market, which producers understand as a rational, efficient force against which they have no power. Within our contemporary laissez-faire racial ethos, the seemingly natural force of the market ensures the invisibility of racism. As a discourse, "the market" is a powerful justification for producers to explain their preferences for models. Their idea of the market naturalizes their preference for white bodies, rendering the issue of race invisible in the process. By referencing the supposedly objective rules of supply and demand, producers ignore the sociality and cultural meanings so crucial to their aesthetic choices. Yet the economic realm is hardly distinct from the social world. The world of fashion, like any market, is a social entity governed as much by economic principles as by cultural values. Not only is the market embedded within social ties, as economic sociologists have long been arguing,[62] but markets *are social and cultural constructions*. The fashion market is composed of social ties entangled with cultural belief systems. Cultural meanings and stereotypes filter into organizational conventions, where they shape producers' informal knowledge, habits, and work routines. Any cultural product like fashion is the outcome of this kind of shared culture of production.

Fashion producers are not particularly racist or sexist people. Indeed, theirs is a well-intentioned liberal world, with self-proclaimed artists and urban bohemians. They are caught in the self-perpetuating cycle of production, struggling to make decisions under enormous ambiguity and basing their decisions on what has worked in the past, constrained by what they can only imagine will be successful in the future. The "look" of whiteness and size zero may not be the intended outcome for any one producer; it is institutionally reproduced and made durable by conventions. With their professional reputations on the line, producers believe there is little room to be political, or to second-guess collectively agreed-upon conventions to select the "appropriate" looks. Nor do they seem especially interested in trying. Indeed, they *allow* themselves to be guided by an invisible hand of racism. The irony is that in the editorial circuit, where producers have the most creative freedom to construct edgy looks free from consumer demographics or mainstream expectations, they are in a stronger grip of institutionalized racism.

Racism and sexism are not stable identities or categories of people; rather, they are tacit understandings, intertwined hegemonies that structure our vision and guide our actions without our full awareness. While bookers and clients are wedded to racial equality, they are skilled in expressing new, color-blind forms of intertwined racism and sexism with an air of liberalism and equality. Fashion producers are stumped to figure out why there aren't any *really good* models of color around, but the question is quite a generic one: Why aren't there any superlative [blank] of color around? The blank may be endlessly filled: Why aren't there any more CEOs of color, or school principals, or sociologists, or doormen? Fashion modeling is a telling arena to examine tacit biases, because here is a site that has no formal entry criteria based on credentials such as diplomas or certificates. There are very few informal barriers like cultural or social capital—all past and present blockades to minorities entering white-dominated positions. All the same, there just aren't enough *really good* models of color, just as there are no "fierce" size 12 girls, because with tacitly racist, sexist assumptions, they do not fit the bill—because it's a white, elite bill.

Bookers and clients cannot or, more likely, will not recognize this. Instead they diffuse blame and social responsibility to one another, imagining themselves helpless against the inevitable strength and rationality of "the market." But the market does not exist on its own. It too is structured by cultural beliefs. Cultural understandings of race, class, and gender are at the heart of how producers work in this industry. Like a fish in water, producers swim in whiteness. It is the air they breathe, the invisible yardstick against which they judge all bodies. In this culture, whiteness is at once everything and nothing.[63] Bookers and clients are cultural producers in the sense that they are creators of culture—they reproduce culture, invoking and reworking our shared social positions of class, sexuality, and race when looking for the right look.

CHAPTER 6

Runway to Gender

SOMETHING TO WATCH

I'm seated in a cramped lobby of a studio in Manhattan's West Side, with about ten other young women waiting to be called in for a casting for a designer fragrance campaign. My casting sheet for the day, filled with details for nine additional appointments, notes that at this audition, models are asked to bring their bathing suits. It's been about thirty minutes since the door last opened to admit the previous round of models to audition. In several short spurts, loud music thunders from the studio. It's a popular reggaeton club hit by Sean Paul, playing in thirty-second intervals: *Shake that thing, Miss Kana Kana, shake that thing.* When the door finally opens, spilling out candidates, a seated model asks, "What'd you have to do in there?"

The models explain, "You have to dance!"

"What do you mean we dance?" asks another.

"Just do your own thing, it's easy."

With that, the models leave, and a woman in charge ushers the next group of five candidates into the large studio. She directs us over to a man in a white dress shirt and black slacks, seated on a leather sofa in the corner of the large studio space. He is never introduced, nor is his title given, but he must be the boss, because he examines our books, one by one, takes a card, and looks at us briefly as we stand in a line before him. "Thank you," he says.

The woman then instructs us to change into our bathing suits behind a corner of the room that had been sectioned off with screens. There is a large mirror against the wall in our changing section, and I notice that each girl looks herself over and discreetly looks over the others.

One by one, we walk into the middle of the studio and dance to the music under a spotlight while being videotaped. While one girl dances, the rest of us stay in our dressing area, craning our necks to see, giggling in embarrassment and empathy.

I watch two girls go first, and then I walk to the spot marked with a piece of tape under the spotlight. The cameraman instructs me to say my name and agency, and then to dance.

"Just dance? Like however?"

"Yeah, however. Ready. . . . Okay, go."

"Ashley Mears. Metro Models."

Shake that thing, Miss . . . the bass booms into the room while I dance for twenty seconds (but feels more like twenty minutes). The music then stops abruptly, and the woman in charge politely says, "Thank-you."

I return to behind the screen with the other models, where they remark, "That was so weird, right?" and "Oh my *God!*" Some just shake their heads and roll their eyes. One model says incredulously, "And the guy model, he is just sitting there, watching us go. And that guy on the couch, he is just looking!" She has just identified the sensation of "weird" that I too am feeling—the eerie directness of a gaze fixed right on me—coming from the man on the sofa and indeed, I spot a male model sitting nearby watching the scene unfold. She continues, "Now the guy model should have to get naked and dance by himself in front of all of us watching. The guys never have to like that. It's not fair."

But just that second, the male model appears from the corner of the room in only his tight white briefs. To the shouts and whistles of the women, he moves into position under the spotlight. Peering out from our screen, we all crack up with laughter and catcalls as he dances. "At least now we have something to watch!" someone says.

On my way out, dressed and waiting for the elevator outside of the studio, I see the male model, who introduces himself as Dylan, from Dallas.

"So how about that casting?" I ask.

"It wasn't what I was expecting," Dylan tells me. "'Dance in your underwear all by yourself.'" We share a laugh about it, and when the elevator doors open, we say good-bye and we part ways.

. . .

That's where the mutual experience as sexualized objects, shared between Dylan and myself, ends. Dylan can probably expect his objectification to stop at the studio door—stepping into the street, he'll resume being a man, no longer surveyed as a display object. As for me, moving between castings in the city feels just like standing under the harsh spotlight all over again as I receive a series of whistles and stares from men I pass on the street—gestures that, in one feminist reading, serve to make women feel uncomfortable in public.[1] The passerby's gaze can surely be welcome by pedestrians, but these days on the sidewalk as I hurry to the next casting deep in thought, uninvited attention keeps coming my way. Dressing for castings as my booker has asked me to do, in a skirt and high-heeled boots, has only aggravated my daily dose of street harassment. "*Hey mama!*" hollers a man, sticking his head out of a car window, and then, "*Ooh la la,*" a drive-by holler. Dylan, in his jeans and sneakers, probably doesn't get this.

So many times at castings I witnessed the curious sight of near-nude male bodies posing under the direction of a client—typically a woman or an outwardly gay man. These were men I would watch as they strutted into casting studios wearing sunglasses and bored expressions; they sat with their legs spread wide apart, nodding to the beat of their iPods. Minutes later, I might watch one of them obediently take off his shirt and pants as instructed so that the client could take a look at his body. I also knew, as the male model exposed in his briefs knew, that if we both booked the same job, I would earn about double his rate for an equal amount of work. Beyond the modeling arena, the gendered order resumes: male subject, female object, and a lingering wage gap to men's advantage of about twenty cents to the dollar.[2]

We've seen the emotional and physical labor that models do to mold themselves into looks and the social work it takes for bookers and clients to produce the look's value. This social production is structured along racial lines, with high-end editorial looks culturally incompatible with the social meanings assigned to non-white skin. This chapter works to uncover how the fashion world is structured along another construct: gender.

To understand how gender shapes the modeling market, I start with a puzzle: it is widely noted that in nearly every occupation, women earn less money than men, about eighty cents to the dollar for full-time work in the United States, a relatively stable average wage gap for the last two decades. The exception holds true for only a handful of occupations, such as sex work and fashion modeling. Researchers in the sociology of occupations and gender have explicated those social forces that confer men their wage gap advantage,[3] but far less is known about those cases in which men experience a wage gap disadvantage. In this chapter, I flip the question and investigate those processes that enable women to consistently command significant wage premiums—anywhere from 25 percent to 75 percent—in fashion modeling. Not only do men occupy fewer top positions in modeling, but holding all else constant, women's rates are higher than men's, job for job, and hour for hour, of equal work. How do bookers, clients, and models produce and sustain an inverted wage gap between men and women?

Because three key players comprise the fashion modeling market, I answer this pay gap puzzle in three parts: First, how do bookers sell male models? Second, how do clients make their purchases? Third, why do male models accept less money? While male modeling complicates the way social scientists typically think about gender, work, and sexuality, I argue that, ultimately, men's devaluation reproduces masculine privilege, even as it seems to celebrate women's progress. Modeling appears to be the anomalous case, in which women come out ahead, but the case actually highlights how gender and culture structure a general pattern of labor markets, through what I find is the cultural exaltation of women's bodies and their greater relative worth as display objects.

GENDER AT WORK

Fashion modeling complicates much of our conventional thinking on gender. Here is a site where men are display objects, when much research on aesthetic labor focuses on women as ornamental objects. It is a site where men emphasize their sexuality to "act gay" to increase their pay grade, though much research suggests that women and gay men downplay their sexuality at the workplace. Like other men, male models work in organizations structured around gender norms, but quite unusually, these organizations operate with an implicit understanding that women, not men, are the superlative workers.[4] And finally, through it all, male models earn drastically less pay than female models, a paradoxical labor market outcome that inverts typical remuneration patterns. These wrinkles in the traditional relations between gender, display, sexuality,

TABLE 6.1 MEN'S AND WOMEN'S EARNINGS BY MODELING JOB TYPE

	Women		Men	
Job Type	Minimum	Maximum	Minimum	Maximum
Fragrance Campaign	$100,000	$1,500,000	$30,000	$150,000
Luxury-Brand Campaign	40,000	1,000,000	20,000	200,000
Commercial Advertisement	15,000	50,000	5,000	30,000
Top-Level Catalog	7,500	20,000	5,000	15,000
Average Catalog	2,500	75,000	1,500	3,000
Low-Level Catalog	1,000	5,000	1,000	2,500
Showroom/Day	400	2,000	250	500
Showroom/Hour	150	500	50	200
Fashion Show	0	20,000	0	1,000
Editorial Shoot	0	225	0	150
Maximum Values, by Gender	$-20,000	2,000,000	-2,500	200,000

organizations, and work present a fascinating world in which women seem to triumph over men.

Modeling is disproportionately a "female job," with a greater concentration of women, according to the U.S. Department of Labor, and it is a nontraditional job for men.[5] Almost uniformly, women who do "women's work" suffer a pay penalty, and yet in the job of modeling, women earn between 25 percent and 75 percent more than men.

At every level of work, from catalogs to catwalks, men's rates are below women's, and stark examples of the pay difference are aplenty. In February 2006, I attended a showroom presentation for an American retail chain that sells both men's and women's clothing; female models earned $600, while their male colleagues earned $400 for the same four hours of work. At a New York Fashion Week show for a major American designer, women modeling in the show earned about $2,000 for roughly six hours of work. Male models of comparable experience earned $2,000 worth of the designer's clothing.[6] For a worldwide luxury brand campaign like Prada, for example, a male model named Lucas in London earned $30,000 for a day's work—"fantastic" money, in his words. The woman in the ad next to him earned $1 million. Bookers, models, clients, and accountants provided estimated minimum, maximum, and average values for modeling fees per job, as listed in Table 6.1.

At Scene in London, the top male model earned £30,000 ($60,000) a year, and at Metro, the top man earned $150,000–$200,000 a year—not bad, but a paltry sum compared to the highest-paid women at both agencies: over $1 million at Metro and a million pounds (about $2 million) at Scene. Even in the major high-fashion and fragrance campaigns, a man may earn one tenth—$100,000–$150,000—of what a woman would earn for a similar job. Success breeds success in the fashion world, but only to a point for men; just as cumulative advantage widens the gap *within* individual models' salaries, so too does cumulative disadvantage widen the differences *between* men's and women's earnings.

The wage gap is not just a compositional effect, in which the inflated earnings of a handful of female stars raise women's overall average. Men's and women's earnings distributions are grossly unequal at every level for equal work across almost types of jobs. If modeling is "women's work," then why don't male models benefit from their masculine advantage as they do in other women-dominated jobs?

A Brief History of Men in Briefs

While a history of male modeling is yet to be written, the history of menswear clothing markets suggests that male models did not secure agency representation until the 1960s, four decades after John Powers's modeling agency for women opened in New York. Advertisements prior to the 1960s reflected a cultural discomfort with men in front of the camera's lens—illustrations of men were preferred to photographs. When men posed alone in a fashion image, they tended to look off into the distance, avoiding a direct, homoerotic gaze. Advertisers showed men in scenes with women and families to thwart implications of homosexuality.[7]

Male models appeared more sexualized in tandem with the rise of the men's lifestyle clothing market, which began in America with "California Casual" sportswear in the 1930s. As men's fashion became relaxed in an increasingly informal culture, out went the three-piece suit and in came men's bare legs in leisure poses for West Coast apparel. In 1942, the menswear industry produced the first fashion show featuring all men, the Palm Springs Sportswear Roundup, though it was cautiously called a "style show" rather than a fashion or catwalk show.

As menswear markets expanded, ready-to-wear designer labels turned their attention to men. In 1960, Pierre Cardin showed the first haute couture menswear collection in Paris, followed the next year by the first ready-to-wear collection for men. For both shows Cardin cast students, as professional male models in Paris did not exist at the time. The Cardin shows ushered in a new sense that fashion was no longer an exclusively feminine domain, and menswear lines and advertising boomed in the decade's "peacock revolution." By 1967, four agencies specialized in male models in New York, and the number was quickly growing.[8]

Advertisers of this period held lingering doubts about the appeal of men as models. The Marlboro man is one telling case. When Marlboro sought to change its image from a mild tobacco into a "cigarette with balls," advertisers ditched their use of professional models and found Darrell Winfield, a real cowboy, who in 1968 posed as the iconic Marlboro man. Advertising executives doubted that male models could convey the right image of tough, heterosexual masculinity, since, they reasoned, paid commercial models who pose as objects in front of the camera are implicitly feminized, and thus too "queer" to convey rugged and "authentic" manhood.[9] Marlboro men were deliberately not referred to as models but as "wranglers."

Since the 1980s, male modeling markets have expanded as the result of new men's markets in retail and grooming. Style magazines aimed at men took off in this period, despite marketing research that predicted the contrary; the UK's *Arena* became a hit in 1986, followed by *Loaded* and the transatlantic *GQ*, *FHM*, and *Maxim*, all of which appealed to newly fashion-conscious young men and "lads." Compared to their early twentieth-century illustrations and 1940s California Casuals, these new representations depicted men with ambivalently masculine looks—bodies subjected to plucking, grooming, and dressing to perfection.[10]

The Traditional Wage Gap

Male models' lesser earnings defy typical labor patterns. Women earn consistently lower wages than men, both between occupations and within them, and when men join the devalued ranks of women in feminized labor, such as in the care work and the "para profession," they tend to excel financially and advance to the top.[11]

To explain the traditional wage gap between women and men, mainstream economics emphasizes rational choice and individual factors, such as human capital differences between men and women and employee and employer preferences. In contrast to the orthodox economic paradigm of the market as a separate, static formation, sociologists argue that economic, cultural, and structural factors interact to shape market processes and outcomes. Markets, economic sociologists argue, are socially constructed sets of social relations, inseparable from culture. This means that markets are likewise inseparable from gender.[12]

Feminists' analyses of the workplace have theorized how wage inequalities reflect and sustain unequal social power of men and women. Since Rosabeth Moss Kanter's classic 1977 study, *Men and Women of the Corporation*, which found women in deferential, nurturing roles supporting men in positions of authority, sociologists have shown how gender structures organizations and shapes the people who work in them. Organizations reproduce gender inequality through such factors as occupational segregation and employer discrimination, the unequal division of household labor, and the cultural devaluation of femininity. Through a combination of these factors, men occupy the best-paying and the most prestigious jobs, while women are shuffled into lesser-paying fields where they likely hold positions with less authority than men.[13]

Women who do "women's work" typically earn lower wages than workers in other occupations. The cultural devaluation hypothesis contends that because women are devalued in our society relative to men, jobs associated with women, and especially those coupled with women's essential "nature" (such as being nurturing and expressive), are devalued by association. Men who do women's work therefore suffer a wage penalty relative to other men, though as Christine Williams (1995) has documented, when men join the ranks of teachers, librarians, nurses, and social workers, on average, they receive better rewards for their labor than women and are put on the fast track to promotion. Token males often "cash in" by virtue of being men in women's work, while token females at the masculine workplace don't fit in and don't feel welcome.

Of course, not all men are privileged over all women, but, rather, there are competing interests *among* men and women, not just between them. In any given context, argues R. W. Connell, "hegemonic masculinity" is culturally exalted over subordinated masculinities and all femininities. Gay men rank near the bottom of the gender order, on par with femininity.[14] Because the cultural valorization of hegemonic masculinity structures markets and work, gender is a liability for women, but a potential asset to men. Masculine advantage, if not endemic to the structure of workplaces, is something that workers produce and sustain through practice so that women hit the well-documented "glass ceiling," whereas men enjoy a promotional ride up the "glass escalator" in non-traditional occupations.

But the ride stops in a few rare fields. Fashion modeling is perhaps the most prestigious of them.

Display Work

Women outearn their male counterparts in another and related field, sex work, as feminist theorist Catharine MacKinnon bitterly observes:

> Aside from modeling (with which it has much in common), hooking is the only job for which women as a group are paid more than men. Check that out in terms of what we are valued for.[15]

Radical feminists like MacKinnon denounce sex workers' and models' wage premiums alike as evidence of women's sexual exploitation which, according to MacKinnon, represents the linchpin of patriarchy. While sociologists view such claims as reductionist and empirically flawed, there is a useful analysis here in the cultural premium on women's bodies on display.

Display occupations reward women over men, feminist scholars argue, because women's bodies have higher cultural value as objects of sexuality and beauty. Women's bodies have long been identified as passive objects of visual pleasure for the gaze, whether in newspaper advertisements, Renaissance paintings, narrative cinema, or modern fashion images. This positioning to the gaze plays out in women's work and life trajectories. Women have historically been more likely than men to trade in their physical beauty for economic security, and their appearances continue to bear greater significance in their life chances than men's.[16] Women can take up display jobs with seemingly natural ease, but when men get into pornography or stripping, they find a feeble heterosexual audience, prompting some male performers to go "gay for pay" in pursuit of a higher paycheck in gay venues.[17]

Men's bodies, conversely, are prized as active spectacles in professional sports, and while women have made significant inroads into playing sports, only recently have they begun to successfully challenge the gender gap in prize monies. In 2007, Wimbledon, the oldest major tennis tournament, awarded equal prize money to women players, despite club owners' persistent claims that remuneration is driven by "the market," not gender.[18]

Men's and women's bodies, of course, have different capacities, and their biological parts are, for the most part, not interchangeable. Most men and women do hit tennis balls differently, they have different reproductive abilities, and clothes fit differently onto their bodies. It is tempting to presume that these corporeal differences naturally lead to social ones, but social outcomes result from far more complex (and more interesting) processes. For instance, in the market for sperm and eggs, another market with reverse pay differentials, sociologist Rene Almeling found that while biological scarcity plays a role in pricing women's eggs higher than men's sperm, she also found that a cultural premium on motherhood plays a role in how eggs are valued. In other words, bodies take on cultural meanings (in Almeling's case, the valorization of motherhood over fatherhood) that influence how organizations commodify bodies in practice.[19]

In the modeling market, men's and women's bodies are commodified as "ornamental objects." Modeling work for women is like the professionalization of gender performance; they are "doing gender" par excellence.[20] Male models are also "doing gender," but they are in a contradictory spot. As John Berger argues in his classic *Ways of Seeing*, men act, and women appear. As professionally ornamental objects, male models exist in a cultural contradiction with masculinity on display. If display is gendered, then so too is the gaze. Film theorist Laura Mulvey has argued that even the way we watch film is gendered, with a split between the active/male and the passive/female, the masculine viewer and the feminine spectacle. It's a binary, she claims, that continues to effect the consciousness of how men and women see themselves—well after we leave the theater.[21]

The politics of looking, however, have undoubtedly shifted in recent decades. Mulvey and Berger presume a binary of male and female heterosexual consumers and producers, a stance that no longer holds among changes in gender representations since the 1980s. In 1982, when Calvin Klein launched its new underwear line for men, consumers gawked at a huge billboard in New York's Times Square featuring an Olympic athlete shot from below, with the camera scanning his muscular body, naked except for a pair of tight white briefs. He stopped traffic, and marked a shift toward the display of male bodies as sex objects in the mainstream media.[22] Today, images of men routinely promote style-conscious masculinities, so-called "metrosexuals," that blur the traditional binaries constructed between homosexuality and heterosexuality, masculinity and femininity. Iconic images of male bodies appear regularly in billboards and magazines and as publicly worshipped objects of desire. Within the changing terrain of visibility around masculinity, male models sit center stage—where they are, paradoxically, paid quite poorly compared to their female counterparts.

AT THE AGENCY: WHERE SUPPLY MEETS DEMAND

Each week at Metro a select set of models passes through the agency into the back of the office to see the accountants and pick up their paychecks. The accountant at Metro always has checks waiting to be picked up by a number of women, but he struggled to think of more than one man who regularly has a check waiting. His coworker, an assistant accountant, who sits across the office, gave up trying to think of the last time the men had more paychecks than the women: "I mean the guys are always, always, *always* making less than the women."

"Even if they do the same amount of work?" I asked.

"For the same exact work."

This was in February, during which time the men's board brought in less than one-tenth of the agency's revenue for the month, pretty typical, the accountants explained. At both agencies, men had far lower earnings than women. At Metro, men made up 30 percent of all represented models, but they brought in just 20 percent of the agency's revenue. At Scene in London, men made up 25 percent of the agency's represented models, and they made up 10 percent of the agency's revenue, an especially poor performance due in part to the "edgy" looks preferred by Scene bookers. Scene's male board was almost exclusively editorial, and it yielded few catalog bookings. The accountant explained that more than three-quarters of the board's total billings came from two annually renewable campaigns for Prada, which meant that with the exception of two male models, the board was unprofitable, prompting the agency to eventually discontinue its men's board.

Unpacking the wage gap puzzle begins with the bookers, since they are pivotal links in this market's chain of supply and demand, matching models with clients and negotiating prices. Bookers don't sell models at some predetermined market price, as of course none exists. Faced with high uncertainty in a volatile environment, bookers follow conventions and routines to determine a model's wage. Bookers always begin the transaction by naming the highest maximum fee they think they can justify on behalf of their model. Justifications are made based on the model's existing prestige, or *potential* for prestige, known as "buzz." Next, bookers actively negotiate with clients to keep the fee high. Finally, bookers activate their social ties with clients, calling in favors with old friends and pushing the boundaries of clients' payment histories to their advantage.

Hardly a quid pro quo exchange, value is negotiated between bookers and clients on the basis of reciprocity, trust, and shared understandings.

Bookers have enormous power in determining the worth of their models. They are aware of this, and they take pride in it. They are able to see value where objectively there is none. But whether they are looking at a man or a woman, it turns out, plays a large part in how they understand their models' worth.

It's "Just a Market"

More than half of the interview respondents were quick to inform me, as one men's booker did, "It's the one industry in the whole world where women earn more than men!" For the most part, bookers seem largely complicit with men's wage penalty and its seemingly neutral market underpinnings. "It's just accepted," as more than a few put it; "That's just the way it is." Another booker said that when his male models complain of lower rates, he tells them: "If you don't like it, then go get a pair of tits and come back!"

When asked to explain why male models earn less, seven out of thirty-three respondents simply had no answer; among these, six found it unjust, even "absolutely outrageous," and "disgusting," but always beyond their control:

> They get paid a lot less and I really don't know why. . . . You know, it's maddening! I mean as a booker, I can't do anything. I can't, you know, being a female booker, I can't tell my girls to get a lesser rate because I can't do that. (Carl, London booker)

> I remember saying to a few clients, "Sorry, we don't charge less for boys." But, you know, sometimes it worked, sometimes it didn't. And sometimes if the rate was so bad, then sometimes you'd run it past the boy and just say, "Look, we think you should turn this down, but, you know, we want to give you the choice." (Gretta, London booker)

And then, with a shrug, Gretta added, "The model always takes it." Some bookers criticized the gender inequality, but they claimed helplessness against the inevitable, rational forces of "the market."

But, again, what is "the market"? Models' earnings, of course, correspond to the gendered demand of fashion apparel. The size and the volume of men's fashion are on a much smaller scale than women's fashion. Women's ready-to-wear fashion is the dominant sector of the fashion industry—during Fall collections in 2010, for instance, Style.com reported that there were 288 designers for women's apparel, but just 91 designers for men's lines. In 2005, there were 89 US fashion magazine titles marketed to men only, compared to 184 fashion magazines for women. Among fashion direct-mailing lists, 355 titles were exclusively for men, versus 436 for women. Market research firm NPD Group estimates that men's apparel sales are just half of the $107 billion generated by women's apparel.[23] Male consumers also shop less than women: in 2004, according to analysts of the NPD Group, women purchased over one-third of men's apparel in addition to their own clothes.[24]

Given the smaller market value for men's fashion and men's weaker buying power, it seems that there is more to be gained from women modeling than men; after all, women's clothing sales generate double the revenue of the menswear market. It seems likely that a woman yields a higher return on investment from each hour modeling compared to a man. From an economic perspective, the wage gap for male models may seem like a rather obvious outcome.

Bookers see the wage gap as an obvious market-driven outcome. In fact, they could not understand why I kept asking about the wage gap throughout my research project. But the more they explained it to me, the less convinced I became.

Beyond Supply and Demand: When Men Consume More

I find three central flaws with the "just a market" explanation. Consider first that when women model for nonfashion products, such as alcohol and cigarettes, they still expect to earn more than their male counterparts, despite the fact that men are actually bigger consumers of both cigarettes and alcohol in the United States today.[25] As bigger consumers who spend more money on these products, men are important target consumers for alcohol and cigarette marketers. If wages were set according to consumer demographics, then we might expect men would be better paid for modeling products that sell to male-dominated audiences. Yet agents do not expect fees to work this way. For a national alcohol or cigarette campaign, one men's booker strives to get his models about $20,000–30,000, much less, he explained, than a woman's fee:

> It's usually a safe bet to say that the woman in a cigarette ad or liquor ad will get about $20,000 more than what the guy's finally decided on. (Ivan, New York, men's booker)

Bookers expect the inverted wage gap in alcohol advertising, even for models of equal status; in other words, unknown and unpopular women are paid more than unpopular men to advertise nonfashion goods. Reflecting on a different campaign for liquor, an accountant explained that a woman who was at the time a relatively unknown commercial model was paid about $15,000–$20,000 for a limited-run print advertisement. When asked how much the fee would have been had the model been male, he said:

> Oh, a fraction of it. Maybe four or five [thousand], certainly. I don't recall male models getting big, big money for anything that was not a significant worldwide campaign like a fragrance. (Leonard, New York staff)

A second irrationality in the market is evident when women and men appear side by side in advertising for *men's* fashion items. When a woman poses next to a man in a product such as men's cologne, bookers expect that she will *still* earn considerably more than the male model:

> Girls always get paid more than guys. Because, if you've noticed, every billboard has women. Women are the ones that sell the clothes, even in the men's advertising. Women sell men's cologne, and the guy is in the background! (Elle, New York booker)

When men appear in women's ads, they are typically featured as background props and are underpaid. When women appear in men's ads, they are featured as props front and center, and they are likely to be *overpaid* as such. If we expect male models are paid according to a straightforward relationship to the size of their consumer base and product sales, then we would expect male models in these kinds of jobs to earn more than women. A third irrationality to the rational market explanation appears in compensation for non-white fashion models.

A Counterfactual Pay Parity in Race

The issue of race, and its prickly pairing with inequality, provides a third counterargument that it's not "just a market" at work in models' compensation patterns. Non-white models—black, Asian, and non-Caucasian Latinos—make up only between 10 percent and 15 percent of all of Metro's boards, and just 5 percent of Scene's. This is so, bookers say, because there are fewer jobs and less demand for non-white models. Just a few "token" non-white models are enough, bookers reason, against their own politics, because that is typically the client's buying demographic. After all, white consumers spend more total dollars on fashion and apparel.[26] In other words, because non-whites comprise a smaller buying demographic, there is less demand for non-white models.

However, holding everything else constant, white and non-white models typically earn the same rate, job for job. That is, white, black,

Asian, and Latina models of the same sex with similar experience and editorial status will almost always earn an equivalent hourly or day rate. Race is not a bargaining chip for rate negotiations, explained Ivan, a men's booker:

> I've had lots of African Americans booked for Ralph Lauren, and I say, dude he's done RL, *they* love him, if *you* want him, it's $7,000 a day, end of story. "Well, you know, I don't know if we'll pay that for an ethnic model." Well, then go get yourself some cheap ass ethnic model who you don't really want representing your company, or pay him what he deserves to be paid!

This may seem counterintuitive, considering the fundamental ways race structures all labor markets, as we saw also in the last chapter. Fashion modeling has carried a legacy of racial discrimination in wages ever since black women made inroads into white advertising markets in the 1960s.[27]

Today, unequal pay for equal work on the part of whites and non-whites is almost unheard of, explained one men's booker: "I think everyone is too scared, because you have to be PC." On the few occasions that clients do not want to pay a non-white model an equitable rate, bookers refuse to accept what they see as prejudice:

> I had one client looking for a Latin girl and a Caucasian girl. Now the job was the same exact thing for both models, but they were going to pay the Caucasian girl more money than the Latin girl. Probably by a couple hundred . . . I'm like, are you *freaking* kidding me?! (Olivia, New York booker)

Ethnicity, as bookers made perfectly clear, is not an acceptable reason for a discount. Non-whites face entry barriers and fewer opportunities, but once they have secured their niche in the looks market, their earnings are, for the most part, not subject to discriminatory wage penalties.

Throughout the interviews, racial inequality was the one question most likely to bother respondents, making them awkward or outright incensed. When asked about sex inequality, however, respondents simply shrugged their shoulders, breezily offered an explanation, or cracked jokes. Modeling is a labor market in which race and gender intersect on different planes. Race provides a map of the overall structure of opportunities and access to the field, a form of inequality to which bookers are sensitive. When it comes to worth, gender is the most powerful determinant, though bookers seldom see this as problematic.

More Than "Just a Market"

These three cases—ads for nonfashion products such as alcohol, ads for male-targeted products such as cologne, and pay parity for non-white models—run counter to bookers' claims that the wages stem from consumer demographics and product sales.

We've already seen the elaborate social processes through which a model's worth becomes a fixed economic amount. Because models' productivity is unobservable, their wages are disconnected from consumer demographics and sales. A look's value emerges from bookers' and clients' negotiations and, crucially, their social relationships.

Few sociologists would suppose that wages simply bear a technical relation to the work being paid for. Rather, markets emerge through actors' normative understandings of the world. Prices and payments are tied to organizational constraints and to the moral worth and social positions of those getting paid.[28]

My aim isn't to reject market-based explanations but to foreground the social work—the shared understandings, beliefs, and conventions—that forms the basis of the market. The question then becomes, what (and whose) logic does a particular market follow? And with regard to the pay gap, what normative understanding of gender does the market absorb?

Bookers recognize the structural condition of demand uncertainty, yet their job is to cater to client demand. To navigate the tension, bookers must act *as if* they know what clients want, which, in fact, they have considerable power to shape. A model's worth can be trumped up not only based on how much the client wants him, but how much his bookers *think* that clients *should* want him. As it turns out, most bookers don't see much demand for male models, and so they are less likely to put up the fight to get them higher wages:

> There is not that supermodel male. I don't think they're worth less, but people feel that fashion is all about women. And they pay more to have that girl of the moment because there really is not that guy of the moment. (Lynne, New York booker)

There are exceptions. Men's bookers are sometimes able to outbid a woman's fee, on one condition—if the man is a more established name in fashion. A men's booker explained how he sometimes manages to get his star model the higher rate:

I've gotten away with it before, just by holding out and saying you can't have the guy. If they really, *really* want somebody, say, for example, Patrick. There's only one Patrick in the world. You can hold out and say, "No, you can only have him for this." But he's got to have the background. Patrick's done so many campaigns he's got campaigns coming out the wazoo. (Naz, New York men's booker)

The exception reveals the rule: the market rate is a product of social negotiation, of bookers "holding out" with their clients, something they can only pull off with belief in their model and in the strength of their relationships with clients. Hardly the straightforward result of static market forces, models' wages result from intricate social ties. Underlying these ties are cultural norms of gender.

MEN ARE WORTH LESS

"I hate to put it in this light," explained Kath, a booker in New York, "but it goes down to who's worth more." She was explaining to me her take on why male models earn less than women. "What I mean by that is," she continued, "who's got more editorial, who's got more experience, who we think has the most potential. I think that's really the bottom line."

Throughout our interviews, bookers explained the myriad ways in which they saw less potential in men than in women. They drew upon fundamentally gendered notions of men as "worthless" as models and, hence, literally *worth less* than their female counterparts. In their interactions with clients and with each other, they participate in constructing the value of models and modeling work both *among* and *between* women and men, and they uphold the norm that women, not men, make suitable display objects.

A Woman's Career

To most bookers, women and fashion modeling go hand in hand, while men and modeling don't make cultural common sense. I was surprised when Don, a senior booker and agency director, could not answer basic questions concerning the men's board: "I don't know," he said with a laugh when asked about the specifics of the men's hourly and day rates. "I run the agency, but you'd have to ask the guys' bookers." When asked why men earn less, he simply stated: "I do think it is because"—he hesitated—"women, it's a woman's career."

Some bookers just did not "get" male models, and one admitted to having been recently relieved of her responsibilities to scout men, claiming, "I honestly don't quite understand why a guy would want to be a model!" Another former men's booker joked:

> I don't get guys that want to be a model. . . . If you say you're a male model, it's like, dude, just say unemployed. It is the same thing! (Rio, New York booker)

Whereas girls are presumed to want to be models for reasons such as fame, riches, glamour, and self-validation, bookers imagine that men have questionable motives, such as vanity and suspect masculinity, most commonly in the form of queerness but sometimes, rather incongruously, hyper-heterosexuality. Several women bookers condoned the wage gap by claiming that male models do not need as much money, since male models are "just in it for the pretty girls." In a field that produces men as objects, male models may simply be incomprehensible.

Other bookers, when asked about the differences in men's and women's modeling, elaborated with broader social theories about the nature of sex, beauty, and fashion. They invoked the old advertiser's mantra "sex sells." Who better to sell it than women? As Ivan stated, "You know what? Girls are hot. They can sell anything. This is gonna sound really crass, but women buy things because they see women in ads and they wanna be like them. Men just wanna fuck the women. . . . They've got both markets."

Women, Ivan implies, in our gendered society are, in the end, just what Simone de Beauvoir long ago lamented—"the sex." Underscoring this is an assumption about the universal psychologies of men and women:

> But I think in the general psychology of men it helps to have a beautiful girl next to the guy in the advertisement than to just have the guy by himself . . . and I don't think that's necessary for women. (Leonard, New York staff)

As cultural intermediaries who maintain some social distance from final consumers, bookers filter commonplace ideas and assumptions about what consumers like and how they will respond to different looks. If bookers assume that men and women alike are psychologically predisposed to appreciate women as visual objects over men, then there is an instant and seemingly natural demand for female models over and above male models.

Or, rather, I should specify, there is a greater natural demand for *young* female models over male models. Bookers' colloquial use of "girl" in fact does describe many female editorial models who range from age thirteen to their mid-twenties. Male models are significantly older, ranging from age eighteen to forty-five. Almost all respondents explained the age gap with an appeal to sexist norms that women's bodies are better young than old, whereas age is an economic advantage for men:

> Men always tend to age better than a woman. They have the ability to go from being the young hip guy, to the young dad, to the middle-age dad . . . they can progress. But most girls shoot up and then plummet. Some of them can maintain it. But when you hit the heights at 15, your body is nothing like what it's gonna be like at 22, 24, 30, 40. Most men, at 22, are just gonna put on a little bit more weight, maybe lose some hair by 30. (Ivan, New York men's booker)

Their longer career arc, however, does not even out their economic disadvantages, for men who stay in the job past their early thirties find dubious benefits. Their work opportunities expand because their pool of competitors shrinks, but their competitors are understood to drop out because, as the director of a men's board put it, "After thirty, when they get a family, have a kid, they feel they need to get a proper job." The irony of the male modeling career is not lost on women models:

> You know, I'm like, this is the only place where I feel glad I'm not a guy. Because everywhere else in society, if you're a man, you have, like, so many more things for you, but in modeling, you're a girl, you make more money than guys. Rates are better for girls. Your career can take you to better places. Yes, as a man you can work longer, but who wants to be a model at forty years old, oh my God?! (Lydia, 32, New York model)

Unlike other types of women's work, there are no structural advancements or glass escalator effects for male models either within their agencies or in the larger fashion industry. Men can either stay in the industry, beneath women, where they are ridiculed and snubbed, or they can get out.

Gay for Pay

Fashion today is perceived to be gay by industry insiders and outsiders alike.[29] Everyone I interviewed—models, bookers, and clients alike—guessed that upward of 75 percent to 90 percent of men in the fashion industry are gay, *excluding* the male models. Working in an industry dominated by women and gay men, male models' sexuality is on the line. Bookers explain that men, just like women, have to "work it" to get jobs—that is, they have to flirt with clients.

This entails male models going "gay for pay," a phenomenon that sociologist Jeffrey Escoffier has found to be widespread in the porn industry, where straight men take on gay roles in higher-paying gay sex scenes. Gay for pay in fashion means strategically performing a homosexual identity at castings:

> I might be wrong, but this is pretty much a gay male industry. Not all of it, but there is a large portion of gay men that dominate this industry. And because of that factor, I feel that the male models know how to—not that the male models *sleep* with clients—but they know how to use it. Flirtation is a factor [they use] to their advantage. (Don, New York booker)

To some degree, bookers expect male models to enact the stereotype. One men's booker instructs his models to "work it" with clients. Most men's bookers claimed to never explicitly tell their models to flirt, though they all emphatically agreed that flirting helps men book jobs. This is similar to how women in modeling turn on the charm to win over clients. And it is the opposite strategy of gay men in other types of women's work (such as teaching and nursing), those who, in the face of homophobia and the pressure to hide their sexual orientation, have been found to play up their hegemonic masculinity.

Implicit in the term "gay for pay" is the suggestion that physical sex acts are part of the exchange:

> How many boys are *out* gay? Or gay for pay? It's actually kind of scary how many guys will experiment because they think they might get some work. (Naz, New York men's booker)

Few male models, however, are actually gay. At one agency, the director of a men's board did an unofficial count of his "out" male models, arriving at three out of one hundred men whose composites were on the wall. Heather, an agent, explained why she thinks the gay stereotype exists around male models:

> The funny thing is, a lot of people think they are, and I understand why, because guys are all up on themselves like girls are. They really aren't up on themselves. There are not as many gay ones, really, as I thought there would be. There are not many at all.

Given the stereotypical conflation of homosexuality and femininity among men, the popular image of a man engaging in such feminine work suggests a queer identity.

Ivan, a gay man who directs a board of one hundred and forty male models at an agency in New York, took delight in unraveling the myth of the gay male model:

> That is a blatantly false stereotype! Most of them are not, and not only *not* gay, but so not gay even after, like, seven cocktails, still not gay! Passed out asleep on the bed and still not interested! Not that I've tried [laughs]. A lot of them are very comfortable with their sexuality, and you have to be, because the business is run by gays. (Ivan, New York men's booker)

Indeed, male models must be extremely comfortable with all types of sexuality. As objects of visual pleasure, models are paid to be desirable goods for consumers, clients, and even for their bookers. They must project sexiness. This became all too clear the day I sat beside Naz, another director of a men's board, at the booking table. Between phone calls and e-mails, I asked him to explain the phenomenon of gay for pay.

"Women do the same," he abruptly said. "Why do you think women wear midriff tops? Guys do exactly the same. I mean, *hello*, look at this picture there of that guy with that tank top on." He swiveled around in his chair to point to a composite card on the wall, this one featuring a sultry young man in a loose white tank top. "What does that say to you?"

The model's muscular arms were clasped over his head as he gently leaned on a cast-iron fence. His head was tilted up in defiance, and he glared right back at me with full lips slightly parted—it was sexy all right, but his eyes had a hint of sadness. I was reminded of the famous Buffalo stance of *The Face*, circa 1989, when stylist Ray Petri created the new look of moody masculinity—a strong and sensitive guy. This young man was not dripping with overt sexuality, like the oiled-up hunks in Bruce Weber's Abercrombie & Fitch ads; rather, there was a softness about him.

"It says gay?" I offered to Naz.

"Yeah! And most of the clients are. You look at the woman's side," he said, pointing to a nearby composite card featuring a young woman, also in a white tank top— her hair wet, her arms and chest glistening in baby oil, her head tilted down, eyes glancing mischievously up at the camera. Her index finger was even resting on her bottom lip.

"I mean she's got her finger in her mouth! Is that really necessary? What is that selling? At the end of the day, they are a commodity," Naz finished triumphantly.

So while male models are not gay or necessarily perceived as such by their bookers, they are "queer" in the sense that they violate hegemonic masculinity. Male modeling is, as Joanne Entwistle (2004) points out, a kind of "queer" work, because it involves largely straight men and boys becoming objects of a gay male's gaze. As display objects, male models lack claims to hegemonic masculinity, putting them closer to being on a social par with women. Financially, however, they are fall below women.

Resisting Display for Pay

Based on these discourses around men, sex, and bodies, it seems that bookers see women as being better suited for modeling because of the close alignment with bodily display. Acting, dancing, athletics—in these other physical trades, the body is also offered up for sale, but as active bodies, not passively visual ones. Even art models, who are poorly paid, about $10/hour, define their work as being more than display objects. Art models see themselves as collaborators in the craft of artistic production; they see their labor as both physically demanding and active. Importantly, the artists who hire them agree, and they compensate men and women equally for equally valued labor. Ironically, art models rebuff posing for photography, which they experience as a passive role too far from the creative production process. The difference can be seen in art models' language: a photographer "takes" their picture versus a painter who "creates" or "makes" an image of them.[30] Actors, athletes, and art models make a living with bodies perceived to be doing something. The model's body, conversely, is just for show. Of course, as we saw in Chapter 3, models disagree, noting the hard mental and emotional work it takes to secure bookings. And yet in commonly bookers' words, models are passive spectacles, just "commodities" and "the sex."

While women have a long history as bodies for consumption and for display, men are only just getting started. Since the 1980s, with CK men in their bulging briefs and athletes like David Beckham relishing their roles as sex idols, male bodies have increasingly been offered up as sights for women and gay men's eyes to feast upon. And yet bookers remain firm in their resistance to acknowledge these new possibilities. They continuously drew on traditional stereotypes of women as the narcissistic shoppers and on men as manly "dudes":

> Yes, it's one of the only industries in the world, and porn, I would imagine, where they get paid less. Because more girls buy fashion magazines, more girls like makeup, more girls like clothes. It's a women's industry. I don't know too many dudes running around buying skin care lines, but I know every single woman does. (Rachel, New York booker)

Boys Are Just Cool Like That

Because bookers consider modeling less valued work for men than for women, they tend to view male models as unprofessional. In London, an accountant repeatedly called for owners to drop the men's board with appeals to gendered notions of professionalism:

> Well, they just don't make any money. They've got a different mentality. The girls seem to take it more professionally than them, you know, especially the English boys. It was just a joke to them. (James, London staff)

Several expressed that they felt men couldn't develop the craft of modeling in the same way women could:

> You can't push the figures for the boys like you can for the girls. Because I don't think with the boys it's a craft. With the boys they *are* just cool like that. They just come in; they don't have to learn anything. . . . The more they learn, almost the worse they get, you know. So it's a really different skill. The girls have to learn how to walk in high heels, present themselves in front of the camera; the more a boy poses, the less—*easy* he looks. (Helen, London booker)

Thus bookers will accept lesser payment for men because they think that men have less to offer as models. Their looks cannot be crafted to perfection like women's, and so they are, as the London accountant put it, "not taken so seriously."

To bookers, male models' lack of professionalism makes cultural common sense. After all, modeling is a widely shared ambition among young women, and popular media regularly portray modeling as the pinnacle of women's employment. Furthermore, women are schooled in becoming ornamental objects through early childhood socialization. This is an integral part of how girls learn to "do gender" but the opposite of how boys learn to perform masculinity. Modeling may therefore seem to attract more serious women than men, leading bookers to assume that male models just don't have valuable assets.

Devaluation in Practice

These assumptions set the terms for how bookers think, talk, and manage their models in practices that are generally geared toward supporting women's careers over and above men's. Agencies invest money to pay for women's start-up costs, such as visas, airplane tickets, pocket money, and portfolio pictures. These costs can add up considerably, up to $6,000 for women at Scene and $15,000 at Metro. For men, however, the debt allowance is minimal, and male models simply go without many provisions:

> We make them get part-time jobs, we're not an ATM machine. . . . We watch it. Not because we're being cheap, but because we want them to make money, not owe money. We try to keep them below $2,500. (Missy, New York men's booker)

Given their fewer work opportunities, male models must be extra personable and charming to find steady work. Men with bad attitudes are not tolerated, especially given bookers' mantra, "It's not enough to be booked but *rebooked.*" Because each man is literally worth less to the agency than many, and probably most, of his female peers, bookers drop men more swiftly and with less sensitivity than they drop women.

On one level, this is simply a prudent business strategy on the agency's part, given the dismal prospects for male models to earn enough money to pay back their debt or, indeed, to reward their bookers' patience. These differences also reveal lower expectations based on gender. Bookers see men as less competent, as a drain on agency resources, and as not being worth their investment. Expectations are self-fulfilling, a sociological maxim that is especially true in a cultural production market like modeling, where gatekeepers' expectations and perceptions are directly tied to models' career outcomes.

THE CLIENTS: GENDERING BUZZ

Clients whom I interviewed were equally skeptical of male models. Like bookers, clients viewed male models with some confusion, especially since the rewards for men are so few. David, who casts top Fashion Week shows in New York, usually books a few men each season, and he usually has his pick of men to choose from, even though he does not typically pay male models to be in his shows. So why, then, would they want to walk in his show? This question stumped him: "Exposure, I guess. Or, I don't actually know. Why would they do it?"

The feeling is that something must be wrong with these men for them to debase their masculinity and career options for a shot at modeling, which is, clients noted, a very long shot for a viable career for men:

> I think it's demeaning to a man, isn't it, to be a model? I think, to sort of live off your looks like that is something that maybe doesn't sit comfortably with a lot of men. . . . It's sort of a young man's job. It's okay until you're sort of,

you know, maybe if you're at college or you're doing something else. (Umberto, London photographer)

Tellingly, this photographer slips from personal to plural pronouns, taking a little distance between his own views, "I think," to those of an implicitly homophobic public, "a lot of men."

Again, like bookers, clients agreed that there's less craft in men's modeling, because men's looks are not something to be perfected and played with like women's, as a London photographer explained:

> Yeah. I think it's a bit easier for a man . . . I don't know. For me it seems—I think men just have to look a bit more broody. I think it's much easier for men to model than a woman. (Chloe, London photographer)

Clients generally view male models as "easier" or, at least, "simpler" looks. They tend to have fewer expectations of male models—there is less desire to create striking fashion images or to break beauty canons with male looks. Male models should be in and out, with no fuss, explained Hall:

> I mean I hate to say it, but I don't think people expect quite the same thing out of male models. . . . I expect professionalism. I won't put up with his tantrums like I would a female model. (Hall, New York photographer)

When it comes to pricing, clients also explained wages as a function of the market, but they conceived of the market as being, in large part, constructed by bookers. Bookers name a fee that is either compatible with their budgets or not, and negotiations ensue. Because bookers are likely to demand more money for women than for men, the client will give a larger chunk of the advertising budget to hiring women over men. Rarely do clients insist on paying equal rates to men and women; rather, they follow the bookers' leads.

But why do clients tolerate paying so much for women models when there are dozens of other models and agencies that surely offer cheaper models? In response to this question, clients appealed to the same kinds of buzz that bookers work to construct. In the editorial and high-end advertising and catalog circuits, clients are hoping to score the hottest new look, the best new model with the most buzz, and the greatest editorial prestige and symbolic capital. At this high end of the market, clients are looking to bookers and to each other to keep on top of the trends, to be in the "know," to pick the right look. Clients show passion and excitement for finding the next big look, but their excitement is considerably stronger for women than it is for men.

Clients express drastically less passion to find the next big men's look in fashion. Consider Oden, a straight man who has devoted twenty-three years of his life to the fashion modeling industry, first as a model, next as an international scout, and now as a casting director for luxury-brand labels in New York. I say he "devoted" these years because like many of the men and women, gays and straights alike, whom I interviewed, Oden brings a sense of love and passion to his work. He relishes the chance to discover a new look and thereby "break" a catwalk or magazine star. He explains: "What this fashion business is—because I come from scouting—is really to find models. I've been doing this for twenty years, something like that, and it's always been my major thing, try to find the next big girl."

Oden uses his authority wisely and forcefully. He was very animated talking about his passion for finding new looks, explaining that the first thing he does when he's found a "great new girl" is pick up the phone and call the booker, to pay the booker "respect" for a good eye. Next he calls his friends within the editorial circuit in Milan, Paris, and London to tell them that "a gorgeous girl is coming" after the shows in New York. "One of the big, big things is spreading the word about the girl," he says.

But does he do this for a great new male model? Oden paused when I asked him this, and he thought for a moment, and then said:

> Uh, no absolutely, I *would* do it, but my background is a scout for woman. And for me, a piece of clothes can make the woman look gorgeous, make the woman look sexy, make the woman look a *woman*. A nice suit is great, but I can look the same in that suit.

Clients and bookers—those crucial players in naming a model's price—are much more excited about women than men, and they are more willing to participate in the buzz for women. This greater passion for women models gives their bookers more leverage to ask for a higher rate. The buzz that is so integral to ratcheting up women's fees is missing for men. With little symbolic currency, bookers have a harder time boosting men's rates. Ivan explained:

> The women at least have a little bit more leverage, because usually when they're getting ready to book a girl, the client really wants her. Like wants her to a point where she has done an extensive amount of runway or an extensive amount of editorial, is working with the right photographers. There's much more of a dance, so to speak, that gets a girl to that level than a guy. (Ivan, New York men's booker)

If, as Ivan explains, it takes a dance—an orchestrated collective action of invested players—between models, bookers, and clients to build the excitement and buzz that yield women's high rates, then for men it takes a snap of the fingers:

> Like the guy they're probably like, "Okay, these are the four guys we wanna have, let's pick one that goes right with the girl." The girl, however, is just like, "We *need* to have Gemma, because look at what Gemma's done in Paris, look at what she did in Milan, she's in these editorials." She's got the background they want, so they're gonna want her. With the guy, it's like, "Okay, whatever, he's hot, stick him in the ad [snaps his fingers]. He's not available? He wants too much money? Well, screw him, let's get some other guy in there." That's quite seriously how it goes down. (Ivan, New York men's booker)

When selecting their male models, clients are generally less choosy and less attuned to the circuit and to fashionable taste. Compared to most castings for women, men's castings are easier and rather blasé. Any guy will do.

On the whole, many clients didn't give much thought to why they pay male models less. They claimed to just be following the way things were done—if it penalizes men, then, well, it's good for women:

> It's the one industry where women are actually coming out on top after years and years of sort of suppression and of women's lib, and fighting for rights. . . . I don't know who made those rules. It was a woman, probably. (Jordan Bane, London casting director)

Contrary to Jordan's suggestion that women are behind men's lesser earnings, the wage gap is not a "rule" that any single person makes. Rather, it's a convention that bookers and clients alike describe as a tradition:

> I think probably because women have been modeling for so much longer. It was always a women's thing, and then all of a sudden men's fashion comes over. I think it's wrong, but that's the way the clients look at it. (Olivia, New York men's booker)

While appealing to tradition and the market, bookers also *make* those traditions and reify market relations by accepting lower rates for men. I found it to be a widespread practice for women's bookers to use men's rates as the basis to boost women's fees. In other words, women's bookers resist equal wages, and in fact they perpetuate men's lower wages. One women's booker explained what he does on the rare occasion when his client pays an equal rate to men:

But my thing is, like, if I ever hear about it I would be like, "Why did she get the same rate as the guy?" I even do that too, because it's known . . . that's already out there, so I play that. I play that out, and I'm working for the girl. She is a woman, so of course I'm going to try to get her more money. (Christoph, New York booker)

It's very rare that the guy gets paid what the girl gets. The agency will always use that to get more money. Like a booker will say, "Oh, you are paying the girl more, right?" Normally, that's just how it's done. (Elle, New York booker)

Bookers rationalize the gender wage gap with orthodox notions of "the market," which they understand as a set of neutral laws—supply meets demand. But orthodox economics is not well suited to explaining value in anything less than an idealized market setting. Modeling is an absolutely *imperfect* market; it is comprised of sets of social relationships organized around the management of uncertainty, and social relationships are always rooted in shared cultural norms, and so this must be in order to function. Since this market is so uncertain, bookers imitate and look to each other and to clients for signals of what is going to sell and at what price: What is a fair rate? What did we charge last year? As a result of imitation among high stakes, wages can become "locked in" to conventions, and a deviation from conventions risks being perceived as unfair, thereby breaking clients' trust and losing the job.

Here we have a structural force in the market: because everyone's networking, and imitating each other, these conventions become institutionalized as tradition.

It becomes risky for bookers and clients to go against these conventions. "Tradition" and "the way things are" figure prominently in the accountants' explanations for men's wages:

You're always gonna charge the going rate. I mean, they pay what they can get away with paying, and we bill what we can get away with billing. It all goes to what the market rate is, like anything else. It's also now just the way things are. When the client calls up, they're booking a guy and a girl, they know after doing a thousand dealings with bookers that they're gonna pay more for the girl than the guy. (Joe, New York staff)

Clients largely confirmed that this is, in fact, now what they expect. Frank, an advertising casting director, was a model in 1995, and he recalled one job in which the woman in the photo next to him earned five times his rate. Now on the other end of the market as a client, he explained how rates are automatically gendered:

I mean, you will never have an agent calling and saying, "How much is the girl making? You need to match that." It's taken for granted that he's gonna make a little bit less. (Frank, New York casting director)

The imitation mechanism and the preponderance of these "rules of thumb" lend a structural durability to the wage gap. From a conventions perspective, wage differences are not the outcome of market forces. Rather, market forces work around already socially entrenched norms. The social meanings of male and female bodies on display set the terms for how bookers and clients collectively find communal agreement on the value of looks.

THE BOYS: MONEY FOR NOTHING

Agents devalue them. Clients mock them. And the market—as a conjunction of culture, social ties, and institutionalized conventions—generally punishes them. Male models know all of this, and for the most part they accept their lower pay and undermined potential, adhering to discourses that draw on traditional tropes of masculinity. The "boys" redefine their "worthlessness" as a privilege and a perk, and in the end they too devalue their own labor to resist a feminized role.

Chic (and Chick) Dreams

Many girls dream of becoming models. Boys, on the other hand, dream of becoming world-champ athletes, not catwalk superstars, even though there has been a noticeable shift in advertising in recent decades celebrating (and selling) male beauty. It would seem that male modeling, based on the changing representations of modern masculinity, might look like a pretty good job to younger generations of men, those born in the 1980s and later.

Out of the twenty men with whom I spoke, nineteen never thought to pursue fashion modeling. Rather, they talked about falling into the business, mostly after encounters with scouting agents (in twelve cases) or through the encouragement of friends (seven cases). Several also stated that modeling "just fell into" their laps. Such "falls" into the field usually happen at a young age, between eighteen and twenty-one, at a time when modeling seemed to beat the available work alternatives, which ranged from working in nightclubs, shops, and restaurants to not working at all as students:

I wasn't making a lot of money, but I was traveling around for free all over the place, so you know, it was better than working at the club that I was working at, and I was making a little bit more money than I was at the club, but not that much more. (Cooper, 28, New York model)

Most men spoke of their ambivalence toward the job. Though they said they liked the perks, they denied that modeling was something they really wanted to do. John books steady catalog work and was among the top-earning men I met, making approximately $50,000 a year. When an agency provided him with a plane ticket to Chicago and a place to live at the age of eighteen, he pounced on the chance to leave his small hometown in Oklahoma, abandoning a full sports scholarship to a local college. Modeling has permitted him to travel all around the country, to work with top photographers, and, by his own account, to party like a maniac. And yet he scoffed at the thought of giving advice to boys who want to model. "I think it's the dumbest business ever," he said. "It's like, you don't strive to want to be a model; that would be weird. It's kind of something I fell into, and I'm making money, and that's it."

Just one male model I interviewed, forty-four-year-old Michel, pursued what John considers the "weird" dream to model. Michel left his working-class factory job in an industrial village of France in search of an easier, more glamorous life. He turned his bodybuilding hobby into a lucrative career in middle-market advertisements and internationally syndicated television commercials, and last year he made approximately $70,000. Michel's next dream is to become the national spokesman for a commercial brand; he is the only man I interviewed whose future goal is yet more success with a modeling career.

In contrast to Michel, most male models approach their time in the industry as a stepping-stone to careers in the creative industries. Male models envision futures in music (six in my sample), film or theater (four), or fashion and advertising (four). One male model in New York explained that he stays in the business, despite knowing that he earns far less than women, because it is great preparation for his next venture as a musician:

I never really looked at male modeling as a career, you know. I looked at it always as more a stepping-stone into more creative outlets. Which is a, you know, really my primary interest. I looked at it as more of a way to open a lot of doors to meet some people. And of course, you know, have a great time. (Andre, 22, New York model)

In addition to opening doors and social networking, modeling offers men a fun "adventure" and a "cool ride" for minimal effort. As Noah explained, "You get paid to sit in front of a camera, and there's hot chicks hanging around! That's a perk too."

Such comments underscore men's weak commitment to the market, and the temporality of what will probably amount to a short stint. Women, however, are more likely to pursue modeling for the economic rewards. Women's modeling is an end in itself. And no woman, it is worth mentioning, noted "hot men" as a motivation to model.

Men do not see modeling as an end in itself but, rather, as a means to an end: to travel, to make money "on the side," to figure out what they *really* want to do for a living, and to get established in the creative industries. Oliver, an aspiring London musician and model, summed up that modeling is "just like candy every now and again."

Doing Nothing

Once in the job, men have to manage several problems arising from their devaluation. First, devaluation means financial difficulty. It is hard to make a living as a male model, especially as the work is only available in global cities such as London and New York, where the cost of living is high. To manage the poor pay and irregularity of modeling work, men tend to work flexible second jobs. Eight men in my sample of twenty made a living from modeling alone, compared to twelve of the women. To get by, Oliver teaches private guitar lessons, Brody is a DJ, Ryan is a fitness consultant and a waiter, JD works for a magazine, and Edward works for a production company. So while several male models demarcated modeling as "side money" or "something extra" and "candy," many actually worked side jobs to keep themselves in the market.

A second challenge for the male model is the stigma of his occupation. In addition to being literally devalued in the market, male models are socially devalued. Several men confessed to me that they thought male models were predominantly gay before they were ever familiar with the industry. Another popular image of the male model is that of the self-absorbed idiot in the 2001 hit movie *Zoolander*, which starred Ben Stiller as "professionally really good looking." Gay and vain are two labels that men try to avoid by downplaying their involvement in the industry, especially when faced with the frequent conversation starter, "So what do you do for a living?" Owen, an edgier London model, learned how to answer this question the hard way. He initially revealed his line of work when meeting new people, until it became apparent that no one believed him: "People said, "What, *you're* a model?!""

Women reported a similar reluctance to reveal their work as models (mostly because they didn't want to appear to be boasting), and all models are likely to say that they are students or that they work "in advertising."

But while women and their families back home tended to feel a bit of pride for their role in fashion, most male models wanted to keep quiet the news of their accomplishments in the industry. As Owen put it, if he were to tell the lads back home in East London about his modeling career, "I'd be shot on site!"

Other men try to downplay their fashion careers and play up the perks and "easy money" earnings. For instance, twenty-two-year-old Ethan tells most people back home that he's a caterer in New York, which is pretty close to the truth. Upon arrival at his new agency, bookers handed him several business cards for catering companies seeking attractive part-time staff. After five months of modeling and catering, Ethan headed back home to Tennessee with $6,000 cash saved from catering and $1,000 in debt to his agency, despite booking quite a few magazine and advertising jobs. His friends back home, he explained, lovingly disrespected his modeling career with lots of *Zoolander* quotes:

> They give me some hell for it, but I don't hide it. . . . Even when I did it in college, they'd make fun of me for going on castings and stuff, but then when I'd book something, I'd be like, hey, I'm getting paid $500 today to do nothing!

Ethan hints at the third and fairly general problem of devaluation: men feel personally dissatisfied with the work. It feels like "doing nothing," they said. Modeling can be at times boring and intellectually light for men and women alike. Men bear an additional burden because modeling puts them in the awkward position of relying on their looks, which to men is "nothing" at all:

> Here you're in a business that is based around nothing, except for looks, essentially. . . . I mean I was always an athlete, so you know, there was always kind of, okay, you can work harder and you can be a better player. You know, you can practice more, whatever. But with modeling, I mean you really, your entire destiny lies with clients. . . . So, I mean you get good at selling yourself just on your looks, which is kind of ridiculous. (Andre, 22, New York model)

Thus I largely found that men don't think too highly of their own work as models. To Milo, a twenty-six-year-old actor with five years of modeling experience, modeling is "not like some huge skill that I feel that I've developed, even though there is a skill to taking a good picture and knowing how to make yourself look good, but it's not, like, you know, a *surgeon* or something."

Crafting the Male Look

"Girls," explained Frank, a casting director in New York and himself a former model, "are judged for their looks from the day of birth." It is, he insists, "a plague in a woman's life from the beginning." Men, he said, are a different story, meaning that men and women enter the project of crafting the self into a look from different starting points. Because the overwhelming majority of men enter modeling through the scout's push, not by following a childhood dream, they come to the field with a masculine orientation to their looks. That is, they probably have not looked at their bodies as moneymakers, as tickets to upward mobility, as display objects, or as projects to perfect, as women are socialized to do more generally. Despite having less social preparation to be aesthetic laborers, men generally get less training in these new ways of "doing" masculinity. They "sink or swim" on the catwalk and in front of the camera:

> And I went to some show castings, I didn't know how to walk or anything but I've had to gradually pick it up. . . . I just sort of like watched what the other guys did, and I asked them in the agency, and they were like just develop your own walk. (Edward, 22, London model)

Although men spoke about modeling as not really being "work," in fact, they recognized the importance of cultivating a bodily craft, one that requires practice and skill. They framed these skills, however, as somehow different from and *inferior to* women's modeling. In the end, male models seemed to agree that "boys are just cool like that," as the London booker earlier proclaimed. For instance, a male model who dates another woman in the industry explained:

> I think certainly from a boy point of view, there's not, there isn't much you have to do, you know. It's different for girls. Like, my girlfriend explained, in Paris you have to go to the castings looking a certain way, whereas in London and New York I can just kind of rock on to an extent, looking casual. (Lucas, 26, London model)

Lucas picked up on the expectation that women should be more decorated and done up. Of course, an interview is partly a performance too, so these men may be following gendered scripts to seem disinterested in things largely defined as feminine.[31] In this case, they aligned themselves with the expectation that they do not preen over their appearance. They had few reservations, however, discussing the expectation that they flirt with clients to get jobs.

"Everyone Has to Play His Cards"

Women have long been expected to perform emotional labor in service industries and to use their gender and (hetero)sexuality to increase profits by flattering and enticing (male) customers—most noticeably in the mostly female cabin crews studied by Arlie Hochschild (1983). In fashion modeling, both men and women must turn on the charm to woo clients. This takes a distinctive form for the male model, who deploys special tricks of the trade by flirting to advance his career. Men learn largely on their own that they can increase their chances by using gender to their advantage through the strategic application of their sexuality.

Like bookers and clients, male models recognize that they work in an industry with a high number of gay men and women, and they disavow the stereotype that male models are gay. Therefore, a largely straight male population has to learn to be comfortable on display for gay men. Several models talked of overcoming their initial homophobic hesitations; this was especially the case for young men coming from rural or suburban backgrounds. In addition to learning to become comfortable around gay men, male models have to learn how to work it, and they use the high proportions of gay men to their advantage. It is a widespread practice for straight male models to flirt with gay clients, and to flirt shamelessly. As Ian said, "Everyone has to play his cards":

> How to explain. I just give some gay persons, you know, like a smile or something to let them think something. . . . It's just to give them a little bit of hope you know. I don't ignore them. I play with them, because in life you have to seduce people, especially in castings. Sometimes you have five minutes and you have three people looking at your book and you, and you have to *seduce* them. They can be guys, gays, girls, lesbians. (Ian, 25, London model)

No one teaches the male model this art of seduction. He learns it on his own. As Ryan put it, "It's common sense," and everybody does it. It often takes the form of "playing along." For instance, Ethan passively let a gay client flirt with him at a party. Just as likely, models also take the initiative, as when Michel winked at me and smiled a mischievous smile as he explained, "I'll give him a look with my eyes. Aha, *hi!*"

Male models play a game of coquetry by seeking the favors of men, but with insincere affection. It is a form of play, notes Georg Simmel, because the coquette artfully balances making both an offer for sex and refusing it to her suitors.[32] But coquetry is also dangerous, for the flirt runs the risk of having to make good on the offer. Many men recounted uncomfortable moments of having to iron out their ambiguous sexuality. Oliver had to tell a client bluntly "I'm not into that" when flirting led to an outright sexual proposition on a photo shoot. In a more intense confrontation, Owen physically pushed a photographer away and stormed out of the studio. Even without flirtatious efforts, male models experience an onslaught of sexual advances from clients. They shared several stories of implicit invitations of sex in exchange for work, as Michel, the forty-four-year-old model in New York, demonstrated:

> Many times, many photographers like me a lot. And you have to fuck, fuck, fuck *first*, and *after*, you do the job. So yeah, one time, I met a big photographer, in his big, big loft, and I come over, and I say, "hi," and he says "hi"—

—and here Michel leaned into me and reached for my hand, which I offered, because it looked like he wanted to shake my hand. But instead he pulled my whole arm into his chest, down his body, and toward his crotch. I jerked my arm back, and he looked at me with raised eyebrows:

> "Aha, *hi!*" And he was a big photographer, big and famous. And I said no. What can I do? It was a big photographer, and um, I could play the game, but I did not, I cannot, I'm sorry! So I lost a big, big job, yeah.

Almost every single male model had similar stories to tell of unwanted sexual advances from men, though most of these stories recounted the experiences of friends. If, in fact, pressure to be gay for pay is as widespread as models indicate, then the shortage of first-person accounts suggests a reluctance or an embarrassment to talk about one's own sexual ordeals.

Accepting the Wage Gap

Male models know that culture and conventions work against them, and they expect no less than to earn less, regardless of the job, the product, or their own editorial experience. Preston recounted the tale of his friend, a "top guy" in London, who booked a campaign with a "big model," by which he meant a big female model. Each earned $10,000 and $60,000, respectively. This must be a clothing line for women? It was not, he told me, and furthermore, my question was irrelevant:

You just assume they're getting paid more most of the time. If they're not, your booker will tell you because they'll be pleased and proud of the fact you're getting more money than the girl. (Preston, 21, London model)

But clearly, it takes a lot of work to be a male model—emotional work, identity work, physical craft, and even sexual work, walking dangerous lines of desire. So why do these "boys" take anything less than an equitable rate? When I remarked that he seemed surprisingly at ease with his relatively low wages, Milo shrugged and said, "I devalue what I do in some way so, I don't—you know, if someone doesn't pay me as much as I think maybe I want to be paid, I can understand, because in my mind, I'm not doing that much."

Another common explanation among the men I interviewed contextualized their modeling wages in the rest of the labor market framed by masculine advantage. Fashion modeling, these men concluded, is in some way a bit of "justice" for women: "Plus you can't really complain because guys make more in almost every facet of the world, so," uttered Parker, a business college graduate and model of seven years.

Men also tended to make sense of their pay penalty with appeals to market-based explanations, including women's greater buying power as fashion consumers, and, most tellingly, as inherently superior models than men. Toward this second line of reasoning, male models pulled on gendered norms that women, not men, are the rightful recipients of the gaze and the more valuable visual commodities.

"I think it's a woman's occupation type thing," explained nineteen-year-old Joey. "They're the ones who should be doing it. Women are beautiful." The implication, of course, is that men are not beautiful, nor should they try to be. Men will take any pay they can get, because they don't think they should get anything:

For most guys it's like a given, the money is, like, however little it is, they still can't believe it, you know? It's like, "*What*, you want me to pose and I'm gonna make, like, $200 for it?" I did this, like, DKNY ad, and people were coming up to me telling me how much I had been ripped off. I was a waiter at the time [and] I was like, "Are you kidding me?" Like that day, instead of standing in front of a camera, I would have been waiting on tables and [made] ten times less than what I made. (Frank, New York casting director)

Ultimately, by effacing their own labor, male models sell themselves short and expect lower compensation:

Yeah, it's happened a few times. I don't know what job it was for, but I mean, more power to [the women]. If they can make more money than us, it's great. . . . Why do guys at some places make a hell of a lot more than a girl does, right? Because they're better. (Ryan, 25, New York model)

Ryan's remarks stand out because of his blunt assertion that any wage differential is merited. In this he draws from a conservative economic idea that one's human capital (i.e., skills, education, job tenure, and overall abilities) neatly matches one's earnings. The best worker (male or female) will be rewarded with the highest wage, according to the market's hard, precise calculations. Given the myriad ways that male models distance themselves from display and devalue their own modeling work, it follows that Ryan would of course expect a woman to outearn him—just as he probably expects to outearn women in labor markets beyond the fashion world.

For the most part, the "boys" spoke with congratulatory tones, a kind of "*You go girl*" spirit and encouragement for women to finally bask in their well-deserved dominance. A few men even conflated this advantage with what they perceive as women's greater power in society:

It's very easy to understand. What rules the world? Sex, power, money—stuff like that. And sex is girls. It's not guys. (Ian, 25, London model)

Women get more respect in this industry, and women rule the world at the end of the day. . . . Like, why are rich men wantin' money? One of the biggest reasons is to get women. And why do clubs always want girls in the clubs? Because rich men will come and buy them drinks! It's all linked to women. At the end of the day, even the most powerful men in the world, they all go home and get run by women! It's just fact, they are more powerful, so of course fashion's the same way. (JD, 22, London model)

Such sentiments exemplify what sociologist Judith Stacey has called a postfeminist turn in culture, in which feminist ideas of equality have been incorporated into popular discourse only to be revised, depoliticized, and, ultimately, undermined.[33] How innocently "the boys" ignore the systemic nature of masculine privilege and its historical legacy in structuring institutions ranging from law, family, work, and education; how happily they celebrate women as "rulers of the world," as "the sex," the eye candy, and the possessions! Modeling is a safe place for women to excel because they are not a real threat to men's structural dominance. In fact, they confirm it, and they bolster it, by *proving* that women are better suited as bodies to look at:

I think it's great that in one industry, the industry in which they deserve it the most, namely, female beauty, they should be paid more. Because Christ, I mean the most beautiful man in the world can never come near what these beautiful women are, the gift they are giving to men across the world, and to women for that matter, you know. (Ben, 29, London model)

This was said by a man who only moments earlier in our interview told me about a campaign he booked for sunglasses that paid him $5,000 for a day of shooting. The woman standing next to him in the photo earned $100,000 for the day. But Ben does not mind—quite the contrary. He's happy for women to challenge the gendered order and to claim their rightful place as superior visual objects. This is, of course, no real challenge to gender at all but a thinly veiled reproduction of traditional sexist norms.

REAL MEN AND FALSE EQUALITY

Economic values tell us much about social ones. In the modeling industry, the lower rate for a man's look tells us that masculinity and modeling are culturally at odds. As Susan Bordo (1999) has argued, there is something feminine about being on display, even as male bodies increasingly share the spotlight with women in pop culture. Yet in the way they talk about male modeling, bookers, clients, and even the models reveal some discomfort with masculinity on display.

Historically, bodily capital has been a woman's trade and a man's purchase. Like sex work, fashion modeling promotes femininity for the gaze. What appears to be a form of wage discrimination against men in this market may in fact perform a wider social service to masculine domination at large by resisting and *protecting* hegemonic masculinity from commodification and display. "Real men" don't model, because models are inherently feminized for the gaze. Advertisers are more likely to hire athletes and actors for men's fashion campaigns, since recognizably talented men make for more suitable icons than just plain beautiful ones. Even the term of the modeling product—the "look"—is steeped in gender, for looks are not something that men *are* but something that men *do*, and they do it *to women* in ubiquitous and public ways.

Bookers and clients live with and understand these cultural tropes, and it is through this lens that they interpret consumer values and do the work of brokering male models. How these producers interpret men's status as bodies will set the terms for male models' status in the market. "The market," which bookers say is the rational operation of supply and demand, is not a complete explanation for men's wages. But they mobilize "the market" as a concept to justify the gender gap, even as they actively construct that gap based on their *interpretations* of men's and women's differences. Men's wages are then misrecognized as a natural market outcome that just so happens to reward women.

Sociologists have argued that employers implicitly take the sex composition of a job into consideration when paying their workers; the greater share of women employees, the less likely the boss values the work.[34] Male models add to this theory by showing us how important the cultural contours of the job are when employers determine the worth of their labor. Employers are sensitively attuned to the sex appropriateness of a job. It is precisely for this reason, other scholars have found, that men in so-called women's work, such as nursing and teaching, ride to the top of their fields on the "glass escalator," promoted into more appropriate positions of authority and management. Although men may be able to advance after embracing some aspects of women's work, like nurturing and caring work in fields like nursing and social work, they are heavily penalized for putting their bodies on display in the modeling market.

From fashion, we can move toward a more general theory of men's display value: the more a body is objectified for display, the greater women's relative market value. Similarly, the less recognized talent or skill is involved in the body work, the greater men's wage penalty relative to women.

Consider jobs that require a good deal of body display but not much recognized talent: stripping (as opposed to ballet dancing), porn acting (as opposed to stage and film acting), and prostitution—all fields in which women can expect to be paid more than men. Women engaged in sexually explicit work such as stripping and prostitution are rewarded for reproducing the display value of women's bodies, but men in such positions are penalized. Similar to the male stripper and porn actor, male models violate the heteronormative gender order. Beyond sexy and seemingly marginal markets such as fashion, a theory of the relative value of men and women in display work is important for the study of gender and aesthetic labor, especially given the growth of the "style labor markets," from tourism to retail. If "looking good" is rising in importance in the service sector as much as sociologists think it is, men's display value would seem to take on greater significance.

Building upon a broader sociological theory of the market, I have argued that economic forces such as consumer expenditures can explain only part of the wage gap puzzle. Markets also require social interaction, shared meanings and culture, and institutionalized routines to make uncertain actions a bit more predictable. Together, economic, cultural, and social structural forces enable market exchange. Working from the shared understanding that men's bodies are—and *should be*—worth less than women's bodies, bookers, clients, and even models themselves collectively construct the inverted wage gap.

Unlike the race gap, men's wage gap is not recognized as problematic. Instead, it is celebrated as a gender victory for women. This positive spin is part of a postfeminist discourse on the rise since the 1980s. In the aesthetic economy, I've found, gender inequalities disguise themselves as playful and progressive. Indeed, they even fit with bookers' and clients' cosmopolitan dispositions for progressiveness, but only because they fit within entrenched constructs of men's and women's worth.

The irony, then, is that although modeling is the deviant case, a place of putative feminine privilege, it actually shows an entrenched pattern of gender inequality more generally: women are more valuable as bodies than are men.

CHAPTER 7

Exit

As I finish writing, Sasha and Liz are now twenty-seven years old. It's been five years since I met them, since I began modeling in New York for what was, in the beginning, a graduate research project. While both women have traversed through the New York modeling market and beyond, they have landed in very different places.

Three years after our interview, I saw Sasha on TV in a national commercial for a well-known retail chain. The "Virus" from Vladivostok was easily recognizable with her strangely large brown eyes and bobbed hair. I caught up with her over dinner and learned that she expected to gross $250,000 in 2009 from modeling jobs. Since leaving London, as she had put it, "poor as a little mouse," she arrived in New York to a warm reception by commercial clients. She has since crossed over from the editorial to the commercial circuit, now booking high-end catalog work at $5,000 a day. She recently purchased a flat back home for her family in Russia, paid for in cash. Today she rents a large apartment in downtown Manhattan and has recently enrolled at an elite private university to study acting and filmmaking.

Liz, in the same span of time, has gone flat broke. She is in the same stagnant position in the modeling market today as she was four years ago. After her second year at Baruch College in New York, Liz quit school and moved to LA in pursuit of just the kind of television commercials Sasha has secured. After an early "lucky break," Liz booked a national campaign for shampoo and was finally able to make a living from her modeling income.

But it wouldn't last. Just as things were going well, she got sick. She was diagnosed with a stomach tumor and underwent two procedurally straightforward but financially disastrous surgeries. Without health insurance, Liz paid out of pocket, draining all of her past years' earnings. She has since filed for bankruptcy, moved back home to Pleasantville, New Jersey, with her parents, and has taken up training as a yoga instructor. She commutes to the city to attend the occasional showroom casting, but she hasn't booked a job in months. She is waiting for her agency to drop her any day now.

The same freelance work arrangement both women once enjoyed for its freedom and flexibility provided economic advancement to Sasha, but it derailed Liz. Neither of them, nor the other thirty-eight men and women in this study, have yet to reach the heights of supermodel celebrity associated with their trade, though several have come close, and a few lingered on its edge for a fleeting moment. Why have these forty models not reached the top of fashion's hierarchy, such that you, my reader, would not recognize their real names among the sea of their competitors? Why does any cultural object succeed among the thousands of competitors who fail?

"I mean, obviously, if you're a model with a reputable agency in New York, you have the looks," Liz once said to me in the early days of our acquaintance. "I don't know what makes one person better than the other. I think people know it, and people always ask themselves that, but they could never verbalize it."

Yet the very fact that bookers, clients, and even models cannot articulate just what this special quality is means that it does not exist as a physical property. This special quality exists in the social positions and relationships among the producers themselves. It resides in the social world of cultural production, composed of vibrant exchanges and ongoing negotiations in the editorial and commercial circuits of the market.

By decentering the models and moving outward and away from their enchanted images, we can study the look in its social components. The look happens through the convergence of strategic work by models, agents, and clients as they collectively grope for the look amid uncertainty. Models learn to pick up and embody what bookers and clients want from them; bookers tune into clients' tastes, and clients tune into bookers and each other. Like models, the careers of bookers and clients depend upon the cultural and social capital they secure by working in fashion, developing social ties, and sharing common values. All of the players in this world are seeped in norms of white bourgeois culture. They come into the market immersed in invisible prejudices that devalue non-whites and men relative to their white female counterparts.

By pulling back the curtain, we find that organized collective action, not mere individual talent, makes or breaks careers in fashion. Each player in the fashion world moves in anticipation of others' moves. The success of any model is not based on an internal trait known as beauty, because beauty has a social life.

SUPERNATURALIZATION

This book has shown the complex social production of that which appears natural. The social processes of naturalizing value that I have traced here can be found in a range of other social valuation systems beyond fashion. What, after all, are classifications by race, gender, or sexuality but the production of value in the realms of desire, acceptability, and legitimacy?

Race and gender, in our contemporary postracial and postfeminist era, are the things we cannot say and cannot see. Yet they are operating. Even within fashion, a world where producers proclaim cosmopolitan liberal identities and assert desires to *not* be racist and to *no longer* need feminism, we see the everyday practice of racism and sexism in hidden, taken-for-granted assumptions of beauty, bodies, and worth. Such assumptions lead producers to think that a man who would show his body must be gay and is indeed "worth less" than a woman. Such assumptions also conclude that "really good" black models simply don't exist; meanwhile, they leave unquestioned an implicitly white standard of beauty. The troubling illusion, for the fashion world and beyond, is that racism and sexism are things of the past. Here is the spell cast upon all of us—producers of culture and consumers alike—who celebrate diversity and femininity but simultaneously place a higher value on whiteness, on the commodification of female bodies, and on upper-class ideals of desirability.

These tacitly held values are enacted all the time, and usually without notice. But while they are naturalized, they are also glamorized. Glamour is that seemingly magical aura that surrounds a winning cultural product. Glamour makes the look appear as if it is a miracle or a spontaneous accident, thereby effacing the entire social life of the market

FIGURE 7.1. Fashion Week at Bryant Park, New York City, 2008

that has produced it. Fashion is not merely the naturalization of social processes, but, in actuality, it is the *supernaturalization* of miraculous successes.

This social alchemy brews in the editorial game, where the "winner takes all" of the spectacular jackpot, having climbed the steep stakes of unpredictability. The editorial winner seems to have achieved the impossible; she will be seen as an apparently supernatural exception. This fantastic success is understood to be distinctive, not simply better than the rest, but qualitatively different from them: you will know it only "when you see it."

In the commercial circuit, in contrast, there is no such potential for hitting the jackpot. There is no magic. There is no illusion, no *illusio*, or belief in the game, and the passion for playing is diminished because the path to success is obvious and relatively predictable.

Uncertainty and glamour, therefore, go hand in hand in the field of fashion modeling, for the winning editorial look does not happen magically but from a kind of collective misrecognition that mistakes uncertainty for magic. What looks like uncertainty, in the discourses of the models and bookers and clients, is in fact the misrecognition of a process of invisible work that creates, *as though by magic*, glamour.

In the fashion modeling arena, both forces of naturalization are at work: we see the invisible work of normalizing race, class, sex, and gender in the everyday application of taken-for-granted valuations of beauty, and there is the invisible work of exalting the miraculous, which legitimates the winners and the entire game that they have so skillfully manipulated.

MARKETS AS FASHION

Cultural intermediaries work at the intersections of culture and economy. They are at once making cultural decisions, interpreting and constructing taste, and simultaneously making economic decisions around appropriate market transactions. A key part of their work is the paradox of "pricing beauty": they construct economic value where, objectively, none exists.

To study the cultural economy is to break down analytic distinctions between culture and economy, and to think about economic calculations as always fundamentally rooted in cultural values and social processes. Much of the sociological thinking about culture industries treats them as anomalies, as though art and fashion markets have special and unique properties.[1] But consider the opposite frame: all markets contain an element of fashion. As a labor market, modeling is prototypical of precarious work in the new economy, with its rising importance of soft skills. Classifying people into looks happens to all of us all of the time. We all do aesthetic work and are judged for our performances, but with less transparency than in modeling work.

Modeling is a great case, because it gives us access to a market where there are fewer pretenses and more acknowledged ambiguities. All markets have varying degrees of demand uncertainty and unpredictability in outcomes. "Nobody knows" in fashion any better than in other speculative markets such as finance or real estate. The editorial client who "just knows it when she sees it" is strikingly similar to the journalist who has a "nose for news" and the basketball player who has "court sense" and the day trader who has a "killer instinct" on the trading floor.

All markets are predicated on some uncertainty. Fashion producers acknowledge this ambiguity in their day-to-day activities, and their careers are defined by their ability to manage it. But the ambiguity they face is generic; it is shared across all market settings. They must coordinate with other producers, and, together, they give legitimacy to conventions—conventions that, as the world witnessed with the

2008 economic meltdown, can be deeply flawed and dysfunctional. This book is a challenge to everyday assumptions about seemingly natural market outcomes, because it pushes us to think about *all markets as fashion markets* and all economic actions as rooted in social conventions.

TIMING

"It's timing," a booker, Rachel, immediately responded when I asked her why one model makes it while thousands of similarly positioned contenders don't. "And the drive enough to do it," she paused. "The team you have behind you. But mostly, it's timing."

The most frequent answers models, bookers, and clients offered to the "million-dollar question" were two small and simple words: luck and timing. Luck, as I have shown, does not operate blindly, and it is certainly not dumb. Luck is rooted in an organized production process within which actors strategically fight to change the game in their favor. Timing is the precise coalescence of these strategies to produce a winner. It is the alignment of the model's aesthetic labor, the booker's promotion, and the client's preference, all within the right set of cultural conditions.

To summarize the steps that make the look happen, let's move backward against the grain of this book's analysis, from culture to practice. Models' looks must first resonate with contemporary cultural values set by race and gender relations. Liz and Sasha are slim, tall, white women; their bodies fit within entrenched Western norms of female beauty, historically the exclusive domain of white bourgeois society. Today, because a black First Family lives in the White House, we can expect both change and resistance to these norms. Ethnic diversity will likely expand most quickly in the commercial circuit of fashion, where producers are sensitive to middle-market consumer desires and expectations. Such progress is likely to be slow and limited in the avant-garde circuit of editorial fashion, where producers produce for each other and appease their own insular, high-end taste within a closed elite network.[2]

Cultural production has a complicated relationship to culture and to current events such as Obama's election. The Obamas are, of course, themselves elites and exceptions to the shared narrative of class disadvantage among non-whites in America. While their triumph does not change systemic institutionalized racism, it does open up a space within the public imagination to see black as beautiful and high class. Yet this does not automatically filter into fashion, because as a cultural production system, the fashion world absorbs shifts in the social terrain through organizational constraints, production routines, and conventions. Racism, and anti-racism for that matter, does not straightforwardly dictate how producers create fashion. Producers certainly reflect on the cultural changes of their time, and, indeed, many bookers and clients expressed candidly their discomfort with what they perceived as a white bias in fashion. But such reflexivity is mediated; how producers apply it in everyday practice differs according to the different bundles of conventions and social relations that structure the editorial and commercial worlds of production. Editorial producers end up reproducing racist or sexist ideals as part of a collective dynamic that once in place becomes a hegemonic world of relationships and conventions.[3] Worlds of cultural production lend durability and traction to patterns of doing things, such that over time it becomes hard to change course.[4] The look, therefore, does not simply reflect culture; it cannot be reduced to a simplistic representation of contemporary values. Culture is mediated in the routines that people follow.

For any look to make it big, it must fit within the spectrum of possibilities of beauty that each culture subscribes to. Next, it must impress bookers and clients at the right moment. Sasha believes that a model rises to the top of fashion's hierarchy almost through a flippant series of coincidences: "You were pushed in the right time by the right person or right day," she said. While clients collectively group for what casting director Jordan Bane calls a "needle in a haystack," bookers are working on building their models' buzz to raise their cultural, and therefore market, value. Sponsorship by high-status producers can trigger the Matthew effect, in which the "rich get richer": as popular models tend to accrue more popularity, they become the winners who "take all."

"If you catch that wave, you gotta ride it!" exclaimed Daniella, a struggling Australian model once so full of editorial promise. Following through on lucky breaks is the third key to timing. Models must be ready—in the way teenagers usually are not—to deploy the skill and wit necessary to sell themselves as corporeal and personable goods. Additionally, they must adapt quickly to the anti-economic logic of the editorial circuit that subverts their short-term financial interests with an eye toward the long-term editorial jackpot.

It takes practice to master aesthetic labor and time to game the logic of the editorial circuit. Yet time is forever working against the model, whose expiration date looms large. Paradoxically, the models who have accumulated the necessary embodied knowledge, confidence, and know-how of the field are unlikely to be the fresh faces editorial clients want. By the time the model is socialized to ride out a lucky break-through, her or his tide of luck has probably washed away.

While models hope to catch the waves of social excitement to propel their careers, the entire fashion industry hinges on the ebb and flow of consumer capitalism. My time in the field was characterized by a particularly golden economic age for global cities, a time when financial miracles were commonplace and easy to believe in. During the 2003–2007 economic growth of real estate and finance capital, winner-take-all markets grew and generated enormous sums of money, sums that would evaporate in the wake of the 2008 economic crisis. In 2010, a new sense of precariousness and vulnerability pervaded the market, especially in those markets linked to luxury consumption. This sense is especially acute among the bookers at Scene, who lost their jobs in the wake of the global recession when Scene closed its doors after nearly thirty years in business.

I returned to the office not long ago, passing through London for a sociology conference. The sky was a typical London grey, but the street leading to Scene's office was unusually deserted. The office itself was solemn from the outside, the front window shade pulled shut. Helen, who had founded Scene, led me in, and amid our excited chatter— *"Hello Darling*! So good to *see* you!"—the agency was still and quiet. Shelves once lined with portfolios and magazines were bare, the black-and-white portraits of fashion icons once decorating the walls had been packed away, and only a few office chairs and the booking table upstairs remained in place. The rows of models' cards had been emptied, leaving the great wall blank. A single computer remained at the booking table, where the agent Fria was sending e-mails, still managing two or three "big girls" through their transition to new management.

Helen served me a cup of tea, and she and Fria began to explain the agency's downfall. Scene had been silently suffering for the last few years due to a drop in revenue from television commercials. Because of TiVo and satellite TV, television advertisers drastically cut their budgets for models. In the past year, Scene was lucky to negotiate $15,000 for the unlimited worldwide broadcast of a commercial featuring its models; ten years ago they would have gotten at least that amount for limited usage in London alone, and several times that amount for worldwide broadcasting rights. While bookers positioned Scene as a boutique house of "cutting-edge" editorial looks, they had always steadily accrued assets from a handful of commercially successful (though of course nameless) models, assets the company used to attract a wealthy financial backer and expand into a chic East London loft. The steady accruement of symbolic capital masked the slow drain of Scene's economic capital, until the plug was finally pulled during the 2008 economic crisis, when all advertisers cut their budgets, eventually catalyzing its closure.

When I asked Fria how she felt about closing shop, her reply surprised me. She was initially depressed at the thought of no one taking notice of Scene closing. She worried that nobody would care.

"Everyone has those moments, you know," she explained. "Fashion can seem so inconsequential." What if, in the end, her life's work would prove forgettable?

Fria recalled a recent conversation she had had with a Russian model named Katia, who had come to work in London under Scene's care when she was a teenager and was now grown up and fairly wealthy. As Fria bemoaned the end of her booking career—"I could have done something worthwhile in the world"—Katia replied to her, "Like looking after children in Africa or something?" Yes, Fria agreed, that's the kind of meaningful work she could have been doing all this time.

"What do you think you've been doing all this time?!" replied Katia, the story goes. "How many houses for girls, and houses for girls' mums, have you helped to get all these years?"

As Fria told me this story, she looked genuinely touched, and acknowledged that, indeed, she had created a lot of wealth for a lot of women from around the world. I was touched too, even as I recalled the stories models shared of Fria's critiques about their appearances and bodies. In no time, the bookers at Scene were overwhelmed with phone calls and e-mails expressing grief and gratitude from models and clients. The managers were also pleased that all of the bookers were able to quickly find new jobs at other agencies around town.

Our teacups almost empty, we talked about what our lives will be like after fashion modeling. Fria plans to move to the south of France, where she will "enjoy life" and learn French on the beach. Helen tells me, in her big husky voice and tired eyes, that she is developing screen tests for TV programs and will now finally have the time to write her memoir. And so the creative industries get yet another recruit. For my part, I will be a professor of sociology, which they proudly announce is a "first" for a Scene model.

I thanked them both, and with a mix of pride and nostalgia, I stepped outside into the gritty sidewalks of East London, looking up at the loft office that was Scene Management, nestled among gleaming office suites of brick and steel, almost every other building on its street with a "For Rent" sign behind darkened windows.

WISHING

Work in a glamour industry dispels any earlier enchantment with its cruel volatility and waves of rejection. Working in this glamorous world ensures models an entrepreneurial relationship to their personhood; they will be their own bosses in selling their personalities and bodies—strict bosses, especially for women, who must oversee their bodies to impossible measures of perfection. The model will have a flexible schedule and yet no time off; she must work on herself all the time, at every meal, every night out, and every casual backstage interaction. In securing a position among the most celebrated trades for women, models relinquish their self-control to unmanageable factors such as social status, network structure, taste, and timing. Upon entering the market, models quickly realize the dream is not all it's cracked up to be. Realizing that fame and celebrity probably lie beyond their reach, models take up a career that becomes a series of readjustments of their dreams, now broken down into baby steps of wishes for success in the short term.

Models refocus their goals and desires onto the pursuit of immediate thrills. They adjust their goals from the pursuit of the long-term editorial jackpot to the daily chase of small-scale delights won by booking a particular job or producing a particular picture. Modeling becomes not so much the pursuit of a career but a series of jobs and job interviews, each with its own promise to spur the next. In this way, the freelance aesthetic laborer continually re-enrolls in the pursuit of an unlikely breakthrough.

Any model's career ends up being the chase not of those glamorous heights about which she or he initially dreamed but of the mundane subsistence that she or he can reasonably expect. For women, there are more pleasures, thrills, and compliments in becoming an ornamental object. For men, the enticement is more firmly rooted in an imagined easy life and the illusion of easy money, filled with a favorable hours-to-pay ratio and global travel. Models drift from one job to the next, making just enough money to keep working toward the next break, the next campaign, or the next option by Jordan Bane, the next editorial, the next show. They know that their chances are slim but are, at least, equally thinly distributed.

"I wasn't complaining," said John, the twenty-one-year-old Oklahoma native, as we sat in his cramped New York two-bedroom apartment, littered with cheap furniture, overflowing ashtrays, and clothes piled onto the mattresses of his three roommates: "It was enough to stay alive and eat and everything."

Such wishing can have both wonderful and disastrous effects on one's life. For Sasha, modeling was an obvious way out of the limited opportunities in her hometown. "But like in my country," she told me, "it's very difficult to make it big in a career, unless you have good connections from a rich family or some other exceptions like you're a big-time genius, you know?" Not having either, an invitation to model in Tokyo was a clear route to upward mobility. Sasha artfully navigated the editorial and commercial circuits, building enough editorial prestige to increase her catalog day rate and eventually to land television commercials. She no longer does the Fashion Week shows, of which she says, "Waste of time. To be on the runway and feel like a rock star is nice, but it's better to be able to look at your bank account and not feel depressed!"

The opposite of downward mobility happened to college-bound Liz. For her, modeling was a distraction. Had she finished college and landed a professional job like her three siblings, she probably would have been in a better position to handle her impending health care emergency. Now the only one in her family without a college degree, Liz is training to be a yoga instructor, another freelance job with the kind of flexibility that still appeals to her entrepreneurial ethos.

Just as modeling can close some doors, it can open others. Most commonly, modeling teaches young women and men about work in the cultural economy, where freelance arrangements are the norm, no day is like the last, and labor itself becomes a lifestyle to consume, a type of "work consumption." The models in this study considered future career opportunities largely within the cultural economy as actors, musicians, advertising designers, magazine producers, and photographers, and, less conventionally, as event organizers, DJs, and club promoters. In addition to the creative industries, the male models planned to go back to school, teach physical fitness, and go into business for themselves in fields as diverse as nutrition and information technology. For women, a stint spent modeling would be more of a disruption of their lives because they are recruited at the high school ages of thirteen to eighteen, whereas men can enter the market after their college years with plenty of time remaining on their career clock.

Most models, it probably goes without saying, do not wind up in academia with PhDs. And few PhD students wind up in fashion modeling—they're deemed too old. By showing the construction and reproduction of these beauty ideals, sociologists can suggest their arbitrariness and critique their unfairness. But this research has also been an exercise in wanting to embody those beauty ideals. Sociologists are no less enmeshed in the ideologies and practices of body management; indeed, I spent two and half years pursuing them, and then, finally, letting go.

EXIT

"If I was a feminist," Clive, the New York stylist, once told me over coffee, "I would be sitting here saying that fashion is really sad, and really disgusting, and to a certain degree I can understand that." Clive talked with me in a Starbucks downtown, and he had already spent a good portion of our interview sympathizing with the hardships of selling one's body and self as goods for consumption in what amounts in, in his words, a "meat market." I nodded, agreeing with his acknowledgment of suffering and duress, but there was more to his point of view than sympathy.

"But also," he continued, "fashion is so fun! It's *so much fun*. And if everybody can go out there and model, *great*! Do it. You have a ball!" Clive, in his recognition of the complexities of social meaning within the realm of personal experience, is being very feminist. In a simple form, feminism recognizes the depth and worth of women's and men's experiences, and all of the contradictory pleasures and oppressions that exist simultaneously within a single practice. I agreed with Clive because I too had had a ball at moments throughout my time in the fashion modeling market. Like my interviewees, I felt daily titillating thrills and incredible highs by embodying a dream that I had dreamt since devouring my first *Vogue* magazine at age thirteen. And there I was, age twenty-three—but, in model years, frozen in time at age eighteen—living out the fantasy but having to readjust it day by day to seek pleasures in the moment amid so many harsh disappointments.

My own exit from modeling came in an e-mail message from my booker at Metro, with the subject heading "Hey Doll!!!" It read:

> I need to chat with you about your future here at Metro. We are cleaning our boards and deciding what to do about some of the girls, of which you are one. I know modeling is and has not been a priority and we totally understand and get it. At this point, we are taking you off the board because there is not really a point to ordering more cards and incurring expenses when you are not available. I am sure you understand. . . . I have your file here and your last check. I can send it to whatever address you want or I can keep it for you to come in and get. Let me know babes and big kiss!!!!!!
> xoxoxoxoxoxoxxo

It was a soft letdown, a single paragraph that began as a "conversation," a deliberation in the works, only to conclude abruptly with my closed file of pictures and a final check for $150 that I would personally pick up at Metro's office between a series of hugs, well wishes, and promises to keep in touch. Then I was shown the door, and I stood outside on the buzzing Manhattan street. This was my exit from the field, and I once again felt that familiar jolt of pride and excitement, as always, edged with a slight sting of rejection.

Fashion promises a life of being extraordinary. It is a promise sustained by a handful of success stories but predicated on a thousand invisible failures. Those who work in a glamour industry will find that the magic inevitably vanishes. The backstage secrets are revealed.

The Precarious Labor
of Ethnography

This is a book about the production of glamour. It's about all of the invisible work it takes to construct a seemingly effortless and natural look, and while not intended as an exposé of the modeling market, this research has exposed processes and practices of evaluation that would otherwise go unseen. Fashion is not unique among industries for keeping secrets in its closet; as the sociologist Everett Hughes has noted, all trades have an underside that insiders wish to keep hidden from outsiders.[1] This is no less the case for the trade of ethnographers, and the production of this book has its own backstage secrets.

The moment I stepped foot into Metro's office, I walked into ethical, feminist, and practical research dilemmas, not all of them successfully resolved. As an outsider coming from a historically critical discipline, I feared any modeling agency would shut the door in my face if I immediately stated my intentions to observe their work. After all, the modeling industry weathers a good deal of negative attention in the media and in feminist and cultural commentary. So to get my foot in the door, I did not disclose my intentions as a researcher until I was able to establish my position as a model at both agencies.

This led to an enormous amount of anxiety in my first few weeks in the field. Deception is obviously bad ethics, but it can also compromise the quality of data that one is able to collect.[2] For weeks I wrestled over a strategy to "come out" to agents. Finally I asked my booker out for a coffee, where I explained my real interests in signing up with the agency. To my surprise, he thought the idea was cool, and he offered me several thoughts on the psychology of beauty and aesthetics—topics he found really interesting. Afterward I also spoke with managerial staff and secured permission to record observations of my working experiences. Almost nothing changed in my work at Metro aside from my explicit purpose in writing about my experiences while modeling. Even after speaking individually to each staff member about my project, nobody acted noticeably different around me, aside from the occasional line, "Don't write that down," issued when someone made a crude joke around the office. I usually did not take notes openly at the agencies or at castings, so as not to disturb the normal work setting of participants.

Disclosure to clients was a different kind of problem. It would have been pretty awkward to first introduce myself to clients at castings as an eighteen-year-old model, as bookers had instructed me to do, and then ask for permission to observe the casting for my PhD research. This wouldn't have gone over too well with the agents either. And it wouldn't have been good research practice, if the point of ethnography is to learn about the social world as it unfolds *in situ*. When appropriate, I handed out a sheet of paper explaining the project to people, careful not to disrupt normal business routines. I have also taken pains to hide the identities of all those I wrote about, changing key details and dates throughout this book. By gaining access to the industry from the position of a model working within it, I was limited in how much I could openly engage with clients, which is why I decided to interview a sample of them.

Because casting sheets often contain contact information for clients, including phone numbers and addresses, I could easily follow up with interview requests after castings so as not to interrupt the natural work setting. Asking for interviews as a model was at once an asset, granting me access to an exclusive world of producers, and yet it was a potential distraction from my being perceived in the interview as a serious researcher. To manage the tension, I conducted interviews toward the end of my time in the field, when I was no longer working in New York and was in my final weeks in London. In London I had the good fortune of securing an interview with one well-connected hairstylist who shared an enthusiasm for my research, and he helped introduce me to some of the biggest names in the business in London.

Even after disclosing our researcher status, ethnographers maintain various degrees of honesty with their subjects. In methodological terms, I took what Gary Alan Fine has called "Shallow Cover," a term he borrows from espionage practices.[3] Under Shallow Cover, my presence as a researcher was in the open, but I didn't announce the foci of my research; partly this would have compromised the project, but also, as is typical in the grounded ethnography approach, I didn't know my theoretical questions or analytic foci until spending considerable time in the field.[4] Thus my participants were in a grey area between being informed and uninformed. This is in some ways an ideal position, mostly since it doesn't limit the kind of access one can get. In other ways, however, this is the worst position, because at times I felt like I was spying on people who had generously welcomed me into their world.[5]

Adding to the problem was my strong rapport with bookers. At both agencies, public displays of affection between models and bookers are routine; walking into Scene on any given day, I could expect to be kissed on each cheek by several bookers and hear "Hello, Darling!" followed by a barrage of kind words from everyone else. I found myself also hugging, kissing, and endlessly chatting with the very people whose work I was, at least in the back of my mind, expecting to critically analyze in my future writings. In Goffman's words, this would make me a "fink," a dubious character.[6] Callous as it may seem to have used my personal relationships with bookers as an instrumental resource, it should be remembered that the *use-value* of social ties figures prominently in the modeling market. I looked at my bookers with the same exploitative interests with which they looked at me.

Bookers and clients commonly met my requests with curiosity, if not excitement, to be a part of a study. Bookers in particular understood their interviews as "helping" me with my schoolwork, not an entirely thorough interpretation but also not one that I tried to discourage. I attributed their breezy treatment of my dissertation to two things, both concerning the research site itself. First, as a model, I was automatically infantilized and trivialized. Even in my first month, bookers were introducing me to clients as an NYU freshman, although I had repeatedly told them that I was in my first year of a PhD program at NYU. It's probable that any model persona is simply incompatible with a doctoral researcher writing a critical thesis. But there is more to the story than this: I was also genuinely *welcomed* into their world because I worked hard to be a valuable look for both agencies.

YOU'RE EITHER IN, OR YOU'RE OUT

Gaining access to the backstage work of fashion as a model had a number of advantages. If, as Goffman has noted, a goal of the ethnographer is to "tune" her body into the field and field participants, to be capable of feeling as they feel, then there was no better way to understand this world than to accept the unique opportunity to join in the work itself. As an insider, I didn't just conduct participant observation; I was an observing participant.[7] However unique this might have been, this insider position raised a serious set of problems. Feeling what participants felt meant that I too was subjected to heightened insecurities. My very presence in the field was legitimated by someone else's assessment of my "look." Working for my informants as a freelancer in a highly competitive market placed me in an especially precarious position. I desperately wanted my bookers to continue our working relationship, as my dissertation hinged on it. Thus even after disclosing my status as a researcher, I was still continually anxious around my participants, because as a model I could be "dropped" at any moment. Furthermore, my participants belonged to an exclusive world of powerful tastemakers. American sociology originates in the study of marginalized people, and the early Chicago School ethnographies centered around gang members, hoboes, and the ghetto— people, in other words, who had less social status than academics. Marginalized people continue to attract a large share of ethnographic interest, which is partly a matter of access; it's hard to get privileged people to talk to us. Hence I felt beneath my research subjects, as a sociologist, as a graduate student, and as one of thousands of young women trying to secure a place in the modeling industry.

Given my tenuous position, I took extra pains to be polite, courteous, and professional. I showed up usually on time and I was an aesthetic worker par excellence with a cheerful demeanor whenever dealing with bookers and clients. I spent a lot of emotional labor in a focused effort to be likable and, so I hoped, less replaceable. This meant I also spent a lot of time agonizing over my appearance, something I had not anticipated when I headed into grad school. I deferentially went to the gym to "get stuff off," as one booker advised in my first days in the field, and one year into the fieldwork, I was genuinely worried about my 36" hip measurement, which nearly excluded me from Fashion Week castings. Picking out clothes in the morning was terribly stressful—trying to dress in a way that (1) showed my body, (2) made me appear thin and young, and (3) would not draw too much attention from classmates or professors in my graduate seminars.

With all these anxieties, my insider subject position gave me a firsthand account of what it felt like to work, day after day, in a job that might disappear at any moment. From here I was able to experience not just the uncertainty of the job's *form* (the structural precariousness as freelance labor) but also the ambiguity of its *content*, specifically in trying to figure out how to do the work well. My insights into these multiple uncertainties may not have been possible without myself transforming into the aesthetic laborer. But by following Goffman's advice, I came out of the field with a perspective shaped, in part, by a model's position, which likely influenced how I saw the work of my other interview respondents: the bookers and clients.

Feminist sociologists value equality and sharing in the knowledge-production process, and many have argued that ethnography represents a methodological ideal because the researcher and the subject can work together and share in the craft of sociological knowledge.[8] While I support this goal in the abstract, once in the field I never felt particularly powerful relative to those I studied. In fact, with the bookers and clients, I felt the opposite: vulnerable. For this reason, I did not feel obliged to share my interpretive authority with my participants. As Stuart Hall has noted, representation is about power. Fashion's gatekeepers have tremendous power in the modeling market relative to the models they manage. They also have considerable power to shape the values and aspirations of the millions of people who admire (and/or despise) the looks that they produce. In representing the backstage world of the fashion modeling industry, I too have a stake of power, which can be used most responsibly when ethnographers attend to their own backstage practices.

Notes

1. All names of persons and organizations are pseudonyms with the exception of a few interview respondents who requested I use their real names.

2. Quotes presented in this book come from tape-recorded statements during interviews and also handwritten notes I took during informal conversations. In cases where direct recording was impossible, for instance, fieldwork encounters, I took notes immediately after all interactions and typed them into my field journal within twenty-four hours.

3. Frank and Cook 1995.

4. On the history of glamour, see Wilson 2007.

5. For a history of modeling, see Evans 2005.

6. Wacquant 2004.

7. Mears and Finlay 2005.

8. On "creative" economy, see Currid 2007; on "aesthetic" economy, see Entwistle 2009; on "cultural" economy, see Lash and Urry 1994; Scott 2000. Sociologists studying the cultural economy have examined art (Plattner 1996; Velthuis 2005), music (Hirsch 1972; Negus 1999), television and film (Bielby and Bielby 1994), and fashion (Aspers 2005; Crane 2000). In addition to analyzing the economic dimensions of cultural products, studies of the cultural economy have also examined economic institutions as cultural practices, notably in cultural analyses of the financial sector (see Abolafia 1998; Du Gay and Pryke 2002; Zaloom 2006).

9. See Bourdieu 1993a; Faulkner and Anderson 1987; Menger 1999; Peterson and Berger 1975.

10. See, for example, Etcoff 1999.

11. I say "producer" to describe models, bookers, and clients in order to foreground the idea that this is a production market composed of producers of a good.

12. This tension between creativity and commerce comes up in all kinds of culture industries, from Renaissance painting (Berger 1973) and contemporary art markets (Velthuis 2005) to the literary field (Bourdieu 1993a, 1996), book publishing markets (Thompson 2005; Van Rees 1983), and, of course, fashion (Aspers 2005; Bourdieu 1996; Crane 2000; Kawamura 2005).

13. I take inspiration here in Viviana Zelizer's theoretical agenda and her concept "circuits of commerce," see especially Zelizer 2004.

14. On uncertainty in creative industries, see Bielby and Bielby 1994; Caves 2000; Hirsch 1972; Peterson and Berger 1975. For an economic account of pricing in cultural markets, see Karpik 2010.

15. White (2002), for instance, has argued that uncertainty characterizes *all* production markets. See Lears 1994 and Zukin and Maguire 2004 for social histories of marketers coping with uncertainty.

16. See Simmel 1957.

17. Gisele's income reported in Bertoni and Blankfeld 2010. The U.S. Department of Labor surveys combined characteristics of fashion and artists' models. These figures should therefore be taken as rough estimates. See "Occupational Employment Statistics" (41-9012 Models) at www.bls.gov/oes/current/oes419012.htm (accessed April 1, 2011).

18. Kalleberg 2009; Kalleberg, Reskin, and Hudson 2000.

19. Massoni 2004.

20. Hirsch 1972.

21. My approach is similar to that taken by Joanne Entwistle (2009, pp. 51–74), who also analyzes the social production of value in her study of fashion modeling, which she importantly terms the "aesthetic economy." Entwistle uses the term "circuits of value" to describe the interplays of editorial and commercial fashion production that valorize models into high-demand looks. But whereas Entwistle draws mainly on Bourdieu and more recently Michel Callon and actor-network theory to outline the structure and linkages in the aesthetic economy, she overlooks the interpersonal connections and conventions crucial to the valorization process. This study picks up where Entwistle leaves off, and examines the role of social interaction, relationships and shared conventions among and between actors in editorial and commercial fashion circuits.

22. For journalist accounts of models, see Gross 1995; Halperin 2001; for historical accounts, see Brown 2008; Evans 2001; for cultural studies, see Bordo 1993, 1999; Craig 2002; Dyer 1993; Goffman 1959; hooks 1992. A few notable sociological studies of modeling include Soley-Beltran (2004) and Wissinger (2007) on modeling work as commodification of the body and affect; Entwistle's (2004) interview study with male models as sexual objects and her (2009) study of modeling as part of an aesthetic economy; Mears and Finlay's (2005) article on modeling work in the Atlanta fashion market; Mears's (2008) ethnography of modeling work as gender performance; and Godart and Mears's (2009) network study on status hierarchies among catwalk producers.

23. On London, see Freeman 2010; on New York, see Center for an Urban Future 2005.

24. Data on New York fashion from NYC Economic Development Corporation, "Fashion Industry Snapshot 2011." See www.nycedc.com/Fashion (accessed April 1, 2011).

25. For an overview of cultural intermediaries, see Bourdieu 1984, pp. 318–71, and Featherstone 1991. See Hirsch 1972 on gatekeepers in culture industries. For empirical cases, see Crewe 2003; Negus 1999; Nixon 2003; Skov 2002; Velthuis 2005.

26. West and Fenstermaker 1995; West and Zimmerman 1987.

27. For feminist critiques, see Bordo 1993; Hesse-Biber 2007; Wolf 1991. For intersectional analyses, see especially Craig 2002; Hill Collins 2004; hooks 1992.

28. On Naomi Wolf, see Wolf 1991, p. 50. An alternate reading to beauty and body trades follows the poststructural consideration of subjectivity and resistance in women's lived experiences. Third-wave feminist theorists have since redefined many sites previously thought of as exploitation and objectification as playful expressions of women's empowerment, from sex work (Chapkis 1997) to cosmetics (Bordo 1993, especially pp. 245–75). In this reading, fashion models are one of many celebratory sites for women to reclaim the right and enjoyment to display and sell the body. Various interpretations of what models might (or might not) mean are limited to address actual worker subjectivities (see Mears 2008).

29. For an economic analysis of one such "peripheral" market, see Grampp 1989. For a critique of the neoclassical paradigm, see Smelser and Swedberg 2005.

30. See, for instance, Bikhchandani, Hirshleifer, and Welch 1998.

31. All names of organizations and fashion labels are pseudonyms.

32. All interviews lasted between forty-five and ninety minutes and were tape-recorded. I coded and analyzed transcripts with Atlas.ti software, which enables researchers to inductively discover themes within and across transcripts.

33. Wacquant (2004, p. 6) uses the term "observing participant" to describe his research as an apprentice boxer. For more on ethnography and ethical dilemmas in this fieldwork, see the appendix.

34. Senior bookers explained that options developed in the 1960s, when the modeling industry expanded to meet the needs and manage the risks of the growing advertising industry; the first options were used to manage the busy schedules of early supermodels such as Lauren Hutton. See Godart and Mears (2009) for a discussion.

35. Reported in Callender 2005.

36. On cities and cultural production, see Currid 2007; Scott 2000. On fashion and the city, see Rantisi 2004.

37. On fashion as city branding, see Breward and Gilbert 2006; see also McRobbie 1998. For the *New York Times* survey of global Fashion Weeks, see Wilson 2008.

38. See Moore 2000 for an analysis of the different developmental trajectories of New York and London.

39. See Williams 1980, p. 185.

40. Bourdieu 1993b, pp. 137–38.
41. On sociology and magic, see Bourdieu 1993b. On sociology and front stage/backstage distinctions, see Goffman 1959.

CHAPTER 2

1. Anouck Lepere is a famous model whose partner is Jefferson Hack, cofounder of the prestigious London avant-garde magazine, *Dazed and Confused*.
2. See Bourdieu 1993a, p. 162. There are many such social configurations, from political and economic fields to industrial fields, each one guided by an internal logic and fierce competition for particular capitals. Within the field of cultural production, there are loosely distinct fields of photography, literature, art, and so on. Even within fashion, the high-fashion modeling field is distinct from children, art, and glamour (erotica) modeling, because each has its own principles of operations and orienting logics of play.
3. See Zelizer 2004. Circuits of commerce are not the same as "circuits of culture," an analytic framework to deconstruct meanings of cultural objects from production, consumption, regulation, representation, and identity, born out of cultural studies in the UK (Du Gay and Pryke 2002).
4. Sociologists have made leaps showing how markets are embedded in social networks (Granovetter 1985), and plenty of research documents social ties in fashion markets (Crane 2000; Godart and Mears 2009). But the most interesting questions I'm concerned with focus on the *contents* of these networks—the shared practices, understandings, and meanings among them.
5. While a dressmaker named Gagelin is credited as the first to have employed a house mannequin to walk around the premises of his salon modeling shawls, Charles Frederic Worth increased the number of house mannequins available to try on dresses for clients (see Evans 2001, 2005).
6. On the suspiciousness of scandal and fashion models, see Evans 2001; Maynard 2004. On fears of artifice in makeup practices, see Halttunen 1986. For Coco's early mannequins, see Quick 1997.
7. For a similar history in Australia, see Maynard 2004.
8. Paris was slower to introduce modeling agencies in 1959, since couture houses employed their own *mannequins de cabine*, full-time "house models," for shows and photographic work (Evans 2005).
9. As documented in Koda and Yohannan 2009.
10. See Arnold 2001; Crane 2000.
11. See Davis 1992; Hebdige 1979.
12. In Evans 2001, p. 299.
13. See Crane 2000; Okawa 2008.
14. Based on historical accounts of the industry, it seems that magazines and fashion houses gradually shifted in this period from a system of informal patronage and semipermanent employment to one of freelance work relations, similar to the shift in the film industry from studio-based employment to freelance capacities (Blair 2001; see also Evans 2001; Gross 1995). Showroom models today are the last vestiges of semipermanent modeling arrangements.
15. In Koda and Yohannan 2009.

16. See Nixon 1996.

17. Reported in Plunkett 2006.

18. On advertising, see Nixon 2003; Scott 2008.

19. Gross 1995; Soley-Beltran 2004.

20. Reported in Bertoni and Blankfeld 2010.

21. Elite Model Management, at www.elitemodel-world.com/ (accessed April 1, 2011).

22. Several news stories depict such phenomena. See, for instance, Dodes 2007; Lacey 2003; Nussbaum 2007. The movement of scouting networks in search of undiscovered talent deserves further research. Bookers and clients drew upon the national stereotypic "sexy" Latina, the "hungry" and desperate Russian, or the Western European woman who comes from a "normal home" during interviews, and scouts likely hold similar stereotypical notions of national difference. Such comments suggest the power of cultural stereotypes to shape global flows of labor.

23. See Wissinger 2007.

24. The Census Bureau of Labor Statistics estimates that about 1,510 persons held jobs in the United States as models in 2009, but this is an unreliable estimate since it includes artists' models with fashion models and discounts undocumented models. See www.bls.gov/oes/current/oes419012.htm (accessed April 1, 2011).

25. See McDougall 2008.

26. Reported in Model Health Inquiry 2007.

27. For example, *America's Next Top Model, Make Me a Supermodel, Manhunt: The Search for America's Most Gorgeous Male Model*, and *The Janice Dickinson Modeling Agency*.

28. See www.usefeetv.com. Although the British Actors' Equity (the UK equivalent of America's SAG, the Screen Actors Guild) advises performers and agents against accepting buyouts, this is an increasingly common practice.

29. Reported in Blakeley 2007b.

30. A concept attributed to Pierre Bourdieu; see especially Bourdieu 1984, 1993a.

31. Or, as Viviana Zelizer puts it in her description of the historical uses of money, "not all dollars are equal or interchangeable." See Zelizer 1994, p. 5.

32. See Aspers 2005; Entwistle 2009. On economic disinterestedness, see Bourdieu 1993a.

33. Launched in 1980, *i-D* had a circulation of about 78,000 in 2011. It estimates that 86 percent of readers fall within UK standard magazine ABC1 socioeconomic groupings, which include the upper middle class, middle class, and lower middle class (49 percent are upper middle and middle class). Available at www.i-donline.com (accessed April 1, 2011).

34. Ruggerone 2006.

35. Also noted in Bourdieu 1996.

36. On the art–commerce distinction, see Berger 1973.

37. Bourdieu 1996.

38. See Zelizer 2004.

39. See Moore 2000. Fittings in London pay about £60/hour and are not nearly as frequent as in New York, which has more than 5,000 fashion showrooms,

more than any other city in the world. See New York City Economic Development Corp. on "Fashion" at www.nycedc.com/BusinessInNYC/IndustryOverviews/Fashion/Pages/Fashion.aspx (accessed April 1, 2011).

40. Hourly rate estimates are based on rough percentages of Metro models who work for high, medium, and low rates per job type. For catalog work, 25 percent of catalogs pays $5,000/day, and 75 percent pays $2,000/day, thus the average rate of pay of $2,750 over eight hours is $343.75. For advertising, 5 percent of print advertising pays $500,000, 80 percent of advertising work pays $50,000, and 10 percent pays $1,000.

41. Simmel, quoted in Zelizer 1994, p. 19. On the *franc symbolique,* ibid., p. 20.

42. Mauss [1924] 1990.

43. Reported in Trebay 2009.

44. Reported in Plunkett 2006. See also Evans 2005 for a historical discussion.

45. See Crane 2000; see especially Moore 2000, p. 268.

46. On path dependence, see Arthur 1989. See also Moore 2000 on London fashion as an example.

47. Doherty is a rock star with messy hair and member of the London band The Libertines. He is frequently mentioned in the popular press as a drug addict and the former boyfriend of top model Kate Moss.

48. Data on New York fashion from NYC Economic Development Corporation, "Fashion Industry Snapshot 2011." See www.nycedc.com/Fashion (accessed April 1, 2011). On London, see Model Health Inquiry 2008.

49. Rates reported in Model Health Inquiry 2008. See www.britishfashioncouncil.com and also www.associationofmodelagents.org/. New York does not have a comparable organization, although informal price setting was alleged in a 2002 class-action anti-trust lawsuit, *Fears v. Wilhelmina Model Agency, Inc., et al.,* which legally prohibits agencies from "conspiring" to set collective rates in the United States.

50. For a comparison of the New York and London markets, see Rantisi 2004.

51. Documented by Moore 2000.

52. Fashion cities also have different payment schemes related to national labor laws. In France, for instance, models must be at least sixteen years old to work, and they must be paid for their work in wages, not in trade.

53. See Kawamura 2005.

54. See White 1981.

55. Monthly billings at any agency fluctuate widely, increasing or decreasing by as much as half of an average monthly gross amount.

56. Now conventional practice, this double 20 percent commission began in the late 1990s, when owners of major New York agencies announced a collective increase in models' commissions from 10 to 20 percent, in addition to the new 20 percent service fee charged to clients. In 2002, a group of ex-models filed suit against ten major agencies alleging anti-trust violation by agents, which they accused of conspiring to fix prices on commissions charged to mod-

els' and clients. Under New York State law, talent managers, which modeling agencies claim to be, have no caps on commissions, unlike employment agencies, which are limited to 10 percent. The class-action lawsuit *Fears v. Wilhelmina Model Agency, Inc.* intended to return the additional 10 percent of models' commissions to any models represented by the ten agencies from 1998 to 2004. The agents settled at nearly $22 million in 2005, after reportedly wrecking the personal finances of at least one agency owner, as well as sending the New York branch of Elite Models into bankruptcy. Being a nomadic and disorganized labor force, however, only a small proportion of the models eligible for settlement filed for their claims, and the court was left with $6 million in unclaimed fees, which it dispersed among charities for uninsured and eating-disordered women (see Liptak 2007). See *Fears v. Wilhelmina Model Agency, Inc., et al.* 02 Civ. 4911 (HB) (S.D.N.Y. May 5, 2005).

57. Entwistle also notes that market actors make calculations to balance being perceived as "cutting edge" and being commercially successful, and she finds this balancing act at work in both a modeling agency and among buyers for the British department store Selfridges (2009).

58. These average estimates come from interviews with models and interviews with bookers and management at both agencies.

59. Scene's most recent jackpot was a luxury-brand fragrance campaign worth €70,000, plus 10 percent each year for four years; it grossed over €420,000 in commission.

60. In New York, bookers estimate that the median earner—one in the middle of the curve, exempting those in debt and those making superstar earnings—makes roughly $60,000 a year.

61. Model Health Inquiry 2008.

62. See "Occupational Employment Statistics" (41-9012 Models) at www .bls.gov/oes/current/oes419012.htm (last accessed April 1, 2010).

63. Models must book 120 percent more than their debt before they can turn a profit, given the model commission of 20 percent automatically deducted from their rate of pay per job.

64. I walked in four London Fashion Week shows, for a total of £808 gross, or £202 ($350) a show.

65. I signed with Scene in London in July. I worked steadily for magazine clients for three months over the summer and left London with a debt of over £1,000. When I returned in the fall of two years later, I worked steadily for catalogs for two months. Thus over the course of sporadically working for over two years with Scene, I grossed a total of £6,430, and out of that amount paid £1,072 in commissions and £4,193 in expenses. I received my first, and only, check one year following, after finally coming out of the red with a net of £1,165, or about $2,000.

66. The method of studying the workplace as a participant observer entails researchers getting paid. In some scenarios, however, sociologists forgo full or partial payment out of ethical concerns to reciprocate to their research subjects. Such was the case in Rachel Sherman's ethnography of the luxury hotel industry, in which she became a service worker for a reduced wage (2007). Such arrangements can

have unintended consequences; as Sherman notes, she may have helped management undercut other workers' salaries. My participation came with a standard independent contractor agreement, and I viewed my earnings as a unique source of data on the payment structure of models' careers.

CHAPTER 3

1. See pioneers of the aesthetic labor concept Nickson et al. 2001; Warhurst et al. 2000; Witz, Warhurst, and Nickson 2003, and, more recently, in the United States, Williams and Connell 2010 on upscale retail workers. For a classic on emotional labor, see Hochschild 1983. For an overview of contemporary debates and research, see Wolkowitz 2006.

2. See Hamermesh and Biddle 1994. See Mills 1951 for a classic overview.

3. On Abercrombie and Fitch, see Greenhouse 2003; on "looking good," see Nickson et al. 2001.

4. On the aestheticization of labor in the post-Fordist economy, see Du Gay 1996; Lash and Urry 1994.

5. See Faulkner and Anderson 1987; Menger 1999.

6. See Neff et al. 2005.

7. Dean 2005; Entwistle and Wissinger 2006.

8. Entwistle and Wissinger (2006) argue that class is the least significant demographic criterion of entry, since models from all backgrounds have equal chances to succeed—and to fail. However, in addition to the unequal consequences of precarious labor for middle-class and working-class youth, class also shapes bodies. In the United States and in the UK, lower class status, dark skin, and being overweight are all correlated, which indirectly lowers the probability of poor and minority candidates to qualify for modeling. International scouting in poor areas likely offsets the embodied effects of class by making non-Western and non-white labor pools accessible to Western fashion producers.

9. Attributed to screenwriter William Goldman in Bielby and Bielby 1994.

10. Goffman 1959.

11. See Mears and Finlay 2005, pp. 328–29.

12. This is changing, however, as job tenure has dropped precipitously in the last three decades. For example, median job tenure fell 37 percent from 1983 to 2008 among men ages 45 to 54 years, from 12.8 years to 4.1 years. See U.S. DOL News Release 10-1278 (September 14, 2010). Visit www.bls.gov/news. release/pdf/tenure.pdf. For a discussion on the emotional toll of repeated job changes, see Sennett 1998.

13. See Wacquant 2004.

14. On gymnasts, see Johns and Johns 2000. On rowing, see Chapman 1997.

15. On stripping, see Murphy 2003; Wesely 2003.

16. Goffman 1959.

17. For parallel practices on the "care of the self," see Foucault 1988.

18. The minimum values (in inches) for the bust are 31; waist, 22; and hips, 32; the minimum for height is 5'6". Maximum values for the bust are 36; waist, 26; and hips, 36; the minimum for height is 5'11.5". This population comes from Metro's website featuring women ($n = 73$) in May 2004.

19. See Mears 2008.

20. As Entwistle and Wissinger (2006) argue, the freelance aesthetic laborer must be "always on."

21. Brid Costello, "Kate Moss: The Waif That Roared," *WWD Beauty Biz Issue,* November 13, 2009, www.wwd.com/beauty-industry-news/kate-moss -the-waif-that-roared-2367932?full=true (accessed April 1, 2011).

22. See Kessler-Harris 1990; Stacey 2004.

23. In Foucault and Gordon 1980, p. 155; see also Foucault 1977.

24. On the gaze in feminist theory, see Bordo 1993. On occupations that prompt self-surveillance, see Chapman 1997; Johns and Johns 2000; Wesely 2003.

25. Hochschild 1983, p. 7.

26. Goffman 1959.

27. Bourdieu 1984.

28. See West and Zimmerman 1987 for an account of how men and women "do gender."

29. See Sennett 1977.

30. See Pierce 1995, p. 72.

31. See McRobbie 2004 for a comparative study of creative workers in London.

32. See Peters 1997.

33. Aspers 2005 notes this among fashion photographers in Sweden; on low-wage retail workers as "worker-consumers," see Williams and Connell 2010; on new media industries, see Ross 2003.

34. For feminist debates about sex work, see Chapkis 1997; on makeup, see Peiss 1998.

35. Entwistle and Wissinger 2006.

36. Simmel 1957.

CHAPTER 4

1. Joss and her fellow casting clients in the industry had to adjust to digital images instead of Polaroids, since Polaroid announced its discontinuation of instant film in 2008, though the medium is now reportedly being reproduced by other companies.

2. Lears 1994; Zukin and Maguire 2004. See also Schudson 1984 on the history of advertising.

3. Bourdieu 1984; Featherstone 1991; Nixon and Du Gay 2002.

4. Crewe 2003; Salganik, Dodds, and Watts 2006.

5. In Bourdieu 1984, p. 6.

6. Style.com is a public catalog of designer collections sent down the runway in every major show. Importantly, the photographed designs are accompanied by the name of the models wearing them. I counted only women's ready-to-wear fashion because it is the dominant sector of the fashion industry, and women models receive the bulk of attention in the fashion press; Style.com reports collections from 172 designers for women's apparel, but just 63 designers for men's lines in the Spring/Summer 2007 season. See Godart and Mears 2009.

7. After removing missing data, as when a model's name does not appear in the image, less than 5 percent.

8. The mean number of shows per model is 6, with a minimum of 1 and a standard deviation of 10. The average number of models used per show is 25, with a maximum of 63 and a standard deviation of 10.

9. Blumer 1969, p. 280; for contrasting analyses of fashion as a class-driven diffusion process, see Simmel 1957; Veblen [1899] 2007.

10. See Lieberson 2000. On social influences of taste more generally, see Gladwell 2000; Salganik, Dodds, and Watts 2006.

11. Given their career ladders, fashion models generally exit the field by aging out and transitioning into acting or similar creative industry sectors with low education requirements, or they pursue degrees and change industries entirely.

12. I conducted a total of thirty-three in-depth interviews with bookers and staff working at agencies in New York and London. Of these, twenty-five were bookers, two were bookers' assistants, and six were business or accounts managers (see Table 4.1).

13. See Connell 1995. These symbolic meanings have structural and historical roots. For example, McRobbie (1998) argues that the disproportional presence of gay men and women in fashion design originates from the trade's early status as a low-wage feminine occupation in garment manufacture, a connotation that designers have been eager to shed. Today, cultural producers emphasize creative talents over manufacture and technical skills, and, McRobbie finds, some young fashion designers take pride in not being able to sew.

14. On product designers, see Molotch 2003.

15. Bloom 2007.

16. Aspers 2006.

17. See Nixon 1996. This expansion of attention around cultural intermediaries is reflected in the growth of reality TV shows featuring competitions among aspiring fashion stylists, hairstylists, and even fashion editors' *assistants*, which is a low-paying job.

18. On reputation in freelancing, see Blair 2001. Aspers (2001) finds a similar hedging among fashion photographers in Sweden.

19. Blakeley 2007a.

20. As cultural intermediaries, bookers envision consumers in order to appeal to them, a process Blaszczyk (2008) refers to as "imagining the consumer." But as Nixon (2003) notes, the first audience advertisers have in mind is themselves. While bookers imagine clients and clients' consumers, they of course must integrate their own preferences, for bookers also consume fashion.

21. Bourdieu 1984, p. 318.

22. Most magazine spreads are produced with the implicit aim of impressing advertisers, who wield considerable control over magazine content because they contribute far more revenue to publishing houses than reader subscriptions. See Crewe 2003; Evans et al. 1991; Steinem 1990.

23. The Q Score, in service since 1963 when it was developed by Marketing Evaluations Inc., is a tool for marketers to assess the familiarity and likability of a person or product. See www.qscores.com (accessed April 1, 2011).

24. See White 2002 on "decoupling." The history of advertising is itself a series of practitioners' attempts not to supply the market so much as to organize it. The science of advertising begins with practitioners imagining consumer needs and then filling them, thus constituting consumer demand in the process (Zukin and Maguire 2004).

25. Bourdieu 1993a.

26. Both agencies subscribe to dozens of magazines. For instance, Scene has twenty-six subscriptions, ranging from *10, 125, All Access, Another, Amica, Bon, Citizen K, Dazed and Confused, Exit, Elle* (UK and Italian), *Glamour, Flair, French, i-D, Issue One, Jalouse, Marie Claire* (UK and Italian), *Numero, Pop, V, Vogue* (UK, United States, France, China), *Wonderland,* and *W.*

27. Similar functions of status have been found in, for instance markets for jewelry and investment banking (Podolny 2005).

28. Two clients, a stylist and a photographer, explained that they deliberately try to *not* look at too many magazines so as not to corrupt their individual notions of good taste. These clients tended to be among the highest-status producers I talked to, and they were seemingly immune, or at least they wanted to *seem* immune, to the pressure to follow fashion trends.

29. Merton 1968.

30. Weber 1978.

31. See Bikhchandani, Hirshleifer, and Welch 1998.

32. Podolny 2005.

33. Trebay 2009.

34. See Beckert 1996, especially p. 819; see also Storper and Salais 1997.

35. This observation about the market for art is made in Velthuis 2005, p. 179.

36. This term is similar to what Nixon terms "cultures of commerce," which he defines as cultural meanings and values that define and set the conditions for business strategies to be enacted (2003, p. 35). On the importance of studying cultures of production, see Du Gay 1997 and Jackson et al. 2000.

37. See Bourdieu 1993b, "But Who Created the Creators?" pp. 139–48.

CHAPTER 5

1. Women are the greater focus of this chapter because they receive the overwhelming majority of media attention each Fashion Week season, and their presence in the modeling industry is greater than men's, the central problem of the next chapter.

2. Reported in Feitelberg 2007; Phillips 2007; Pilkington 2007.

3. Reported in Nikkhah 2007; Nussbaum 2007.

4. For feminist and intersectional critiques of fashion models' images, see Arnold 2001; Bordo 1993; Dyer 1993; Hill Collins 2004; hooks 1992. For an analysis of how ideas of race and sexuality shaped colonial discourses, see Stoler 1989.

5. Hill Collins 1990; West and Fenstermaker 1995.

6. See, for example, Bordo 1993; Hesse-Biber 2007; Wolf 1991.

7. See Smith 1990, p. 187. Capitalizing on the growing awareness of unrealistic beauty ideals, in 1997, The Body Shop ran an ad campaign with the slogan,

"There are 3 million women who don't look like supermodels and only eight who do." This commercial use of women's empowerment was a precursor to the much-lauded (and commercially triumphant) "Dove Real Beauty" campaign of recent years, which has featured "real women."

8. On trends in slimming body standards, see Fay and Price 1994; for a review of the literature see Hesse-Biber 2007. While this evidence suggests an increasingly slender aesthetic for the female form, consumer niches have grown since the 1960s, such that a greater variety of shapes and sizes, for instance, in hip-hop videos and niche-audience magazines, is more visible in the public sphere than ever before.

9. Fox 1997.

10. Ogden et al. 2004.

11. On men's increasing use of cosmetic surgery, for instance see Davis 2002.

12. See, for instance, Trebay 2008.

13. Ogden et al. 2004.

14. After removing missing data, less than 5 percent.

15. Reported in Feitelberg 2007.

16. Described in Haidarali 2005.

17. Documented in Gross 1995.

18. *Life* 1969.

19. Arnold 2001; Baumann 2008; hooks 1992.

20. Arnold 2001, p. 96.

21. Dyer 1993; Gilman 1985; Hill Collins 1990, 2004; hooks 1992.

22. On sexual imagery and colonialism, see Stoler 1989. Most recently, Baumann 2008 has found that women tend to have lighter complexions in magazine advertisements than men, and that darker-toned white female models are more frequently and more overtly sexualized than lighter-toned white female models. Baumann argues that hypersexual connotations of dark complexions exist independent of racial meanings, but my contention is that skin tone, sexuality, and race are all intertwined categories of cultural meanings.

23. Hall 1997.

24. Reported in Bannerman 2006.

25. Reported in Austen 2008.

26. The magazines included in this analysis were *Marie Claire, W, Vogue, Harper's Bazaar, Glamour, Cosmopolitan, Allure, Lucky,* and *Elle,* in "Where Are All the Black Models? Let's Start by Asking Anna Wintour," by Anna Holmes 2007, http://jezebel.com/gossip/maghag/where-are-all-the-black-models-lets-start-by-asking-anna-wintour-310667.php (accessed April 1, 2011).

27. For a popular version of this argument, see Frank 2004.

28. See Evans 2005.

29. Reported in Quick 1997.

30. Reported in Phillips 2007.

31. See, for example, Model Health Inquiry 2007.

32. See Evans 2005.

33. Reported in Trebay 2008.

34. For a similar process in technology markets, see Arthur 1989.

35. Becker 1995.

36. See Dimaggio and Powell 1983 on isomorphism.

37. For a strikingly similar line of reasoning behind editorial men's increasingly small suit sizes, see Trebay 2008.

38. Reported in Trebay 2008.

39. See McRobbie 1998; Wilson 2005.

40. For a discussion of fashion and gay men in the 1980s, see Bordo 1999; Nixon 1996.

41. Exact counts of non-white male models were not available at Scene, which dropped their men's board eighteen months before my interviews; however, bookers estimated that there were less than five ethnic minorities at any given moment on the men's board of fifty.

42. Reported in Lacey 2003.

43. Market data from 2005 (the time of conducting the interviews) comes from Target Market News 2005.

44. See David et al. 2002.

45. Some evidence suggests that advertisers also value black fashion consumers less than white consumers. Major marketers have been slow to purchase ad space in black niche magazines. For instance, *Essence* magazine, with a circulation of 1.1 million, reportedly attracts a disproportionately smaller number of advertisers compared to white women's fashion titles with similar circulation figures (see Moses 2007).

46. Bobo et al. 1997.

47. Warren and Twine 1997.

48. For one such discussion, see Kaplan 2008, www.salon.com/mwt/feature/2008/11/18/michelles_booty/ (accessed April 1, 2011).

49. hooks 1992, p. 73.

50. See Entman and Book 2000.

51. Reported in Glassman 2007.

52. See, for example, Rhodes et al. 2005. See Bloomfield 2006 for a press report.

53. On racial implications of mixed-race images, see Brown 1997; Streeter 2003.

54. See hooks 1992; Streeter 2003.

55. See Haney-López 1996.

56. Arnold 2001, p. 96.

57. See Bonilla-Silva 2003.

58. Reported in Lambert 1987.

59. Williams 1989 builds this argument.

60. Reported in Horyn 2007.

61. Bordo 1993.

62. Granovetter 1985.

63. See Dyer 1993.

CHAPTER 6

1. For a feminist analysis of women's harassment, see Bordo 1999, pp. 265–80.

2. Based on median weekly earnings of full-time employees in the United States, women continue to earn less money than men at about eighty cents to

the dollar (U.S. DOL 2010). Estimates vary depending on what measure is used and by union affiliation, education, tenure, geographic region and especially industry. As of 2011, women earned less than men at the higher levels of income distribution, but earned more than men in part-time work, and in occupations such as stock clerks and order fillers, bill and account collectors, and combined food preparation and serving workers, women earn slightly more than men, based on data from the Bureau of Labor Statistics and the Current Population Survey. See www.bls.gov/cps/earnings.htm (accessed April 1, 2011).

3. England 1992; Reskin 1993.

4. On women and aesthetic labor, see Wolkowitz 2006; on sexuality and the workplace, see Entwistle 2000; on gendered organizations, see Acker 1990; Kanter 1977; Williams 1995.

5. An occupation is a "female job" if it has a concentration of women at or above the national labor force concentration of women, which is about 50 percent in the United States. A nontraditional occupation for women is one in which women comprise 25 percent or less of total employment. The BLS counts about 84 percent concentration of women in modeling, but this count included artist models and product demonstrators. See table 2, "Median usual weekly earnings of full-time wage and salary workers, by detailed occupation and sex, 2009 annual averages" in U.S. DOL 2010.

6. Men earn considerably more in fashion shows in Milan (about $5,000/ show) than in New York.

7. However, twentieth-century menswear advertising did include quite a bit of homoerotic charge. See Jobling 2005.

8. On Cardin, see Cunningham 2001; Mort 1996; Nixon 1996. On the expansion of men's agencies in New York, see Bender 1967.

9. For a social history of the Marlboro man, see Brown 2008.

10. For a review of expanding menswear markets, see Crewe 2003 and Nixon 1996 on men's magazines; Entwistle 2004 on male modeling.

11. Williams 1995.

12. For an economic sociology analysis on gender and markets, see England and Folbre 2005.

13. See, for example, Acker 1990; Browne 2006; England 1992; Kanter 1977; Kessler-Harris 1990; Williams 1995.

14. Connell 1995. For an overview of intersectionality theory, see Hill Collins 1990.

15. MacKinnon 1987, pp. 24–25.

16. For an overview of women and the gaze, see Berger 1973; Bordo 1993; Mulvey 1989. On the gendered beauty premium, see Hamermesh and Biddle 1994; Stacey 2004.

17. See Dressel and Petersen 1982 on male strippers and Escoffier 2003 on male actors in pornography.

18. See Messner 2002 on gender and sports; see Clarey 2007 on Wimbledon prize monies.

19. See Almeling 2007.

20. West and Zimmerman 1987, p. 141.

21. See Berger 1973; Mulvey 1989.

22. Although, as Jobling (2005) documents, between 1900 and 1940, advertisers in Britain spent considerable amounts of money in press promotions for men's underwear, often deploying provocative and erotically charged images. However, these ads relied on illustrations of the male form, rarely using photographs until the 1960s, on grounds of decorum. As one editor remarked in a 1963 issue of industry journal *Advertiser's Weekly*: "To show [undergarments] on the masculine form is to reveal it in its most undignified and ridiculous garb" (in Jobling 2005, p. 124).

23. On magazine titles and direct-mailing lists, see SRDS 2005. NPD Group, based on the Consumer Tracking Service, estimated that in 2010, women's apparel generated $107 billion compared to men's $52 billion. See NPD Group 2011.

24. Reported in Coleman 2005.

25. According to Summary Health Statistics from the Department of Health and Human Services, 60 percent of men are current regular drinkers compared with 42 percent of women. Twenty-three percent of men are current smokers compared with 19 percent of women. See Pleis et al. 2009.

26. See Target Market News 2005.

27. By one estimate, reported in *Life* magazine in 1969, black models earned half of whites' rates for photographic work. See Bender 1967; *Life* 1969.

28. For a historical account see Kessler-Harris 1990; this point is also discussed in Zelizer 2005.

29. See McRobbie 1998; for a journalistic account see Wilson 2005. On "gay for pay," see Escoffier 2003.

30. Phillips 2006, p. 24. Though men's wages are equal to women's, men's work opportunities are limited, as the cultural preference for female nudes translates into a lower demand for male art models.

31. This insight comes from Entwistle 2004.

32. Simmel [1911] 1984.

33. Stacey 1987.

34. England 1992.

CHAPTER 7

1. For example, Crane 2000.

2. An interesting example of such progress and resistance was Fashion Week Fall 2009, held in the spring of 2009 just after Obama's inauguration. New York designers appeared to use a greater ethnic mix of models than in recent seasons, while Milan designers hired few minority women. See *New York* magazine at http://nymag.com/daily/fashion/2009/02/new_york_runways_more_diverse.html#comments; http://nymag.com/daily/fashion/2009/03/why_is_milan_so_whitewashed.html (accessed April 1, 2011).

3. Storper 1997, p. 255.

4. Becker 1995.

APPENDIX

1. Noted by Gary Alan Fine 1993.

2. As Laura Grindstaff (2002) notes in her ethnography of daytime talk shows, covert ethnographers, like the deceitful talk show producers she studied, get more unpredictability in the quality and reliability of their data than if they work openly and honestly and construct trusting relationships with their participants.

3. Fine 1993.

4. Glaser and Strauss 1967.

5. Fine 1993.

6. Goffman 1989.

7. Wacquant 2004, p. 6.

8. Stacey (1988). Stacey counters the feminist exaltation of ethnography as more egalitarian, since the ethnographer maintains a positional advantage to leave social settings whenever the time comes.

Bibliography

Abolafia, Michel. 1998. "Markets as Cultures: An Ethnographic Approach." In *The Laws of the Markets*, edited by Michel Callon, 69–85. Oxford: Blackwell.

Acker, Joan. 1990. "Hierarchies, Occupations, Bodies: A Theory of Gendered Organizations." *Gender and Society* 4:139–58.

Almeling, Rene. 2007. "Selling Genes, Selling Gender: Egg Agencies, Sperm Banks, and the Medical Market in Genetic Material." *American Sociological Review* 72:319–40.

Arnold, Rebecca. 2001. *Fashion, Desire, and Anxiety: Image and Morality in the 20th Century*. New Brunswick, NJ: Rutgers University Press.

Arthur, Brian. 1989. "Competing Technologies, Increasing Returns, and Lock-In by Historical Events." *The Economic Journal* 99:116–31.

Aspers, Patrik. 2005. *Markets in Fashion: A Phenomenological Approach*. London: Routledge.

———. 2006. "Contextual Knowledge." *Current Sociology* 54:745–63.

Austen, Ian. 2008. "Suits; Models Too Thin? A Store Says Yes." *New York Times*, August 31.

Bannerman, Lucy. 2006. "Paul Smith Says Skinny Will Go Out of Fashion." *The Times* (London), September 20.

Baumann, Shyon. 2008. "The Moral Underpinnings of Beauty: A Meaning-Based Explanation for Light and Dark Complexions in Advertising." *Poetics* 36:2–23.

Becker, Gary Stanley. 1976. *The Economic Approach to Human Behavior*. Chicago: University of Chicago Press.

Becker, Howard S. 1982. *Art Worlds*. Berkeley: University of California Press.

———. 1995. "The Power of Inertia." *Qualitative Sociology* 18:301–9.

Beckert, Jens. 1996. "What Is Sociological about Economic Sociology? Uncertainty and the Embeddedness of Economic Action." *Theory and Society* 25:803–40.

Bender, Marylin. 1967. "The Male Model: From Prop to Cynosure." *New York Times*, August 21.

Berger, John. 1973. *Ways of Seeing*. New York: Viking.

Bertoni, Steven, and Karen Blankfeld. 2010. "The World's Top-Earning Models." *Forbes*, May 13. www.forbes.com/2010/05/12/top-earning-models -business-entertainment-models.html (accessed April 1, 2011).

Bielby, William T., and Denise D. Bielby. 1994. "All Hits Are Flukes: Institutionalized Decision Making and the Rhetoric of Network Prime-Time Program Development." *American Journal of Sociology* 99:1287–313.

Bikhchandani, Sushil, David Hirshleifer, and Ivo Welch. 1998. "Learning from the Behavior of Others: Conformity, Fads, and Informational Cascades." *Journal of Economic Perspectives* 12:151–70.

Blair, Helen. 2001. "'You're Only as Good as Your Last Job': The Labour Process and Labour Market in the British Film Industry." *Work, Employment and Society* 15:149–69.

Blakeley, Kiri. 2007a. "How to Be a Supermodel." *Forbes*, October 3. www .forbes.com/2007/10/02/modeling-moss-bundchen-biz-media_cz_kb_ 1003supermodels.html (accessed April 1, 2011).

———. 2007b. "The World's Top-Earning Models." *Forbes*, July 16. www .forbes.com/2007/07/19/models-media-bundchen-biz-media-cz_kb_ 0716topmodels.html (accessed April 1, 2011).

Blaszczyk, Regina Lee. 2008. *Producing Fashion: Commerce, Culture, and Consumers*. Philadelphia: University of Pennsylvania Press.

Bloom, Julie. 2007. "A Synergetic Pas de Deux for Dance and Fashion." *New York Times*, September 5.

Bloomfield, Steve. 2006. "The Face of the Future: Why Eurasians Are Changing the Rules of Attraction." *The Independent*, January 15.

Blumer, Harold. 1969. "Fashion: From Class Differentiation to Collective Selection." *Sociological Quarterly* 10:275–91.

Bobo, Lawrence, James R. Kluegel, and Ryan A. Smith. 1997. "Laissez-Faire Racism: The Crystallization of a Kinder, Gentler, Antiblack Ideology." In *Racial Attitudes in the 1990s: Continuity and Change*, edited by Steven A. Tuch and Jack K. Martin, 15–44. Westport, CT: Praeger.

Bonilla-Silva, Eduardo. 2003. *Racism without Racists: Color-blind Racism and the Persistence of Racial Inequality in the United States*. Lanham, MD: Rowman & Littlefield.

Bordo, Susan. 1993. *Unbearable Weight: Feminism, Western Culture, and the Body*. Berkeley: University of California Press.

———. 1999. *The Male Body: A New Look at Men in Public and in Private*. New York: Farrar, Straus and Giroux.

Bourdieu, Pierre. 1984. *Distinction: A Social Critique of the Judgment of Taste*. Cambridge, MA: Harvard University Press.

————. 1993a. *The Field of Cultural Production: Essays on Art and Literature.* New York: Columbia University Press.

————. 1993b. *Sociology in Question.* London and Thousand Oaks, CA: Sage.

————. 1996. *The Rules of Art: Genesis and Structure of the Literary Field.* Stanford, CA: Stanford University Press.

Breward, Christopher, and David Gilbert. 2006. *Fashion's World Cities.* Oxford and New York: Berg.

Brown, Elspeth. 2008. "Marlboro Men: Outsider Masculinities and Commercial Modeling in Postwar America." In *Producing Fashion: Commerce, Culture, and Consumers,* edited by Regina Lee Blaszczyk, 187–206. Philadelphia: University of Pennsylvania Press.

Brown, Linda Joyce. 1997. "Assimilation and the Re-Racialization of Immigrant Bodies: A Study of *TIME*'s Special Issue on Immigration." *The Centennial Review* 41:603–8.

Browne, Jude. 2006. *Sex Segregation and Inequality in the Modern Labour Market.* Bristol, UK: Policy Press.

Caballero, Marjorie J., and Paul J. Solomon. 1984. "Effects of Model Attractiveness on Sales Response." *Journal of Advertising* 13:17–23.

Callender, Cat. 2005. "The Model Maker." *The Independent,* September 29.

Caves, Richard E. 2000. *Creative Industries: Contracts between Art and Commerce.* Cambridge, MA: Harvard University Press.

Center for an Urban Future. 2005. "Creative New York." New York: City Futures. www.nycfuture.org (accessed April 1, 2011).

Chapkis, Wendy. 1997. *Live Sex Acts: Women Performing Erotic Labor.* New York: Routledge.

Chapman, G. E. 1997. "Making Weight: Lightweight Rowing, Technologies of Power, and Technologies of the Self." *Sociology of Sport Journal* 14:205–23.

Cialdini, Robert B., and Noah J. Goldstein. 2004. "Social Influence: Compliance and Conformity." *Annual Review of Psychology* 55:591–621.

Clarey, Christopher. 2007. "Wimbledon to Pay Women and Men Equal Prize Money." *New York Times,* February 22.

Coleman, David. 2005. "Gay or Straight? Hard to Tell." *New York Times,* June 19.

Connell, R. W. 1995. *Masculinities: Knowledge, Power and Social Change.* Berkeley: University of California Press.

Craig, Maxine Leeds. 2002. *Ain't I a Beauty Queen? Black Women, Beauty, and the Politics of Culture.* New York: Oxford University Press.

Crane, Diana. 2000. *Fashion and Its Social Agenda: Class, Gender, and Identity in Clothing.* Chicago: University of Chicago Press.

Crewe, Ben. 2003. *Representing Men: Cultural Production and Producers in the Men's Magazine Market.* Oxford: Berg.

Cunningham, Thomas. 2001. "Before Cardin, There Was No Designer Fashion for Men." *Daily News Record,* December 31.

Currid, Elizabeth. 2007. *The Warhol Economy: How Fashion, Art, and Music Drive New York City.* Princeton, NJ: Princeton University Press.

Darling-Wolf, Fabienne. 2001. "Gender, Beauty, and Western Influence: Negotiated Femininity in Japanese Women's Magazines." In *The Gender Challenge* to the Media: Diverse Voices from the Field, edited by Elizabeth L. Toth and Linda Aldoory, 277–311. Cresskill, NJ: Hampton Press.

David, Prabu, Glenda Morrison, Melissa A. Johnson, and Felicia Ross. 2002. "Body Image, Race, and Fashion Models: Social Distance and Social Identification in Third-Person Effects." Communication Research 29:270–94.

Davis, Fred. 1992. Fashion, Culture, and Identity. Chicago: University of Chicago Press.

Davis, Kathy. 2002. "'A Dubious Equality': Men, Women and Cosmetic Surgery." Body and Society 8:49–65.

Dean, Deborah. 2005. "Recruiting a Self: Women Performers and Aesthetic Labor." Work, Employment and Society 19:761–74.

DiMaggio, Paul J., and Walter W. Powell. 1983. "The Iron Cage Revisited: Institutional Isomorphism and Collective Rationality in Organizational Fields." American Sociological Review 48:147–60.

Dodes, Rachel. 2007. "Strike a Pose, Count Your Pennies." Wall Street Journal, February 3.

Dressel, Paula L., and David M. Petersen. 1982. "Becoming a Male Stripper—Recruitment, Socialization, and Ideological Development." Work and Occupations 9:387–406.

Du Gay, Paul. 1996. Consumption and Identity at Work. London and Thousand Oaks, CA: Sage.

Du Gay, Paul, and Michael Pryke, eds. 2002. "Cultural Economy: An Introduction." In Cultural Economy: Cultural Analysis and Commercial Life, 1–20. London: Sage.

Dyer, Richard. 1993. The Matter of Images: Essays on Representations. London and New York: Routledge.

England, Paula. 1992. Comparable Worth: Theories and Evidence. New York: Aldine de Gruyter.

England, Paula, and Nancy Folbre. 2005. "Gender and Economic Sociology." In The Handbook of Economic Sociology, edited by Neil J. Smelser and Richard Swedberg, 627–49. Princeton, NJ: Princeton University Press.

Entman, Robert M., and Constance L. Book. 2000. "Light Makes Right: Skin Color and Racial Hierarchy in Television Advertising." In Critical Studies in Media Commercialism, edited by Robin Andersen and Lance Strate, 214–24. New York: Oxford University Press.

Entwistle, Joanne. 2000. The Fashioned Body: Fashion, Dress, and Modern Social Theory. Malden, MA: Polity Press, in association with Blackwell.

———. 2004. "From Catwalk to Catalogue: Male Models, Masculinity and Identity." In Cultural Bodies: Ethnography and Theory, edited by Helen Thomas and Jamilah Ahmen, 55–75. Malden, MA, and Oxford: Blackwell.

———. 2009. The Aesthetic Economy of Fashion: Markets and Value in Clothing and Modeling. London: Berg.

Entwistle, Joanne, and Elizabeth Wissinger. 2006. "Keeping Up Appearances: Aesthetic Labour and Identity in the Fashion Modelling Industries of London and New York." Sociological Review 54:773–93.

Escoffier, Jeffrey. 2003. "Gay for Pay: Straight Men and the Making of Gay Pornography." Qualitative Sociology 26:531–53.

Etcoff, Nancy L. 1999. *Survival of the Prettiest: The Science of Beauty.* New York: Doubleday.

Evans, Caroline. 2001. "The Enchanted Spectacle." *Fashion Theory: The Journal of Dress, Body & Culture* 5:271–310.

———. 2005. "Multiple, Movement, Model, Mode: The Mannequin Parade 1900–1929." In *Fashion and Modernity*, edited by Christopher Breward and Caroline Evans, 125–45. Oxford and New York: Berg.

Evans, Ellis D., Judith Rutberg, Carmela Sather, and Charli Turner. 1991. "Content Analysis of Contemporary Teen Magazines for Adolescent Females." *Youth & Society* 23:99–120.

Faulkner, Robert R., and Andy B. Anderson. 1987. "Short-Term Projects and Emergent Careers: Evidence from Hollywood." *American Journal of Sociology* 92:879–909.

Fay, Michael, and Christopher Price. 1994. "Female Body Shape in Print Advertisements and the Increase in Anorexia Nervosa." *European Journal of Marketing* 28:5–14.

Featherstone, Mike. 1991. *Consumer Culture and Postmodernism*. London and Newbury Park, CA: Sage.

Feitelberg, Rosemary. 2007. "Little Diversity in Fashion: African-Americans Bemoan Their Absence in Industry." *Women's Wear Daily*, September 17.

Fine, Gary Alan. 1993. "Ten Lies of Ethnography: Moral Dilemmas of Field Research." *Journal of Contemporary Ethnography* 22:267–94.

Foucault, Michel. 1977. *Discipline & Punish: The Birth of the Prison*. New York: Pantheon Books.

———. 1988. *The History of Sexuality Volume 3: The Care of the Self*. New York: Vintage Books.

Foucault, Michel, and Colin Gordon. 1980. *Power/Knowledge: Selected Interviews and Other Writings, 1972–1977*. New York: Pantheon Books.

Fox, Kate. 1997. "Mirror, Mirror: A Summary of Research Findings on Body Image." Social Issues Research Center. www.sirc.org/publik/mirror.html (accessed April 1, 2011).

Frank, Robert H., and Philip J. Cook. 1995. *The Winner-Take-All Society: How More and More Americans Compete for Ever Fewer and Bigger Prizes, Encouraging Economic Waste, Income Inequality, and an Impoverished Cultural Life*. New York: Free Press.

Frank, Thomas. 2004. *What's the Matter with Kansas? How Conservatives Won the Heart of America*. New York: Metropolitan Books.

Freeman, Alan. 2010. London's Creative Workforce, 2009 Update. Working Paper 40, Greater London Authority. www.london.gov.uk/priorities/art-culture/cultural-metropolis (accessed April 1, 2011).

Gilman, Sander L. 1985. *Difference and Pathology: Stereotypes of Sexuality, Race, and Madness*. Ithaca, NY: Cornell University Press.

Gladwell, Malcolm. 2000. *The Tipping Point: How Little Things Can Make a Big Difference*. Boston: Little, Brown.

Glaser, Barney, and Anselm Strauss. 1967. *The Discovery of Grounded Theory Strategies for Qualitative Research*. Chicago: Aldine.

Glassman, Sara. 2007. "Model Minnesotan." *Star Tribune*, March 15.

Godart, Frederic, and Ashley Mears. 2009. "How Do Cultural Producers Make Creative Decisions? Lessons from the Catwalk." *Social Forces* 88:671–92.

Goffman, Erving. 1959. *The Presentation of Self in Everyday Life*. Garden City, NY: Doubleday.

———. 1989. "On Fieldwork." Transcribed by Lyn H. Lofland. *The Journal of Contemporary Ethnography* 18:123–32.

Grampp, William Dyer. 1989. *Pricing the Priceless: Art, Artists, and Economics*. New York: Basic Books.

Granovetter, Mark. 1985. "Economic Action and Social Structure: The Problem of Embeddedness." *American Journal of Sociology* 91:481–510.

Greenhouse, Steven. 2003. "Going for the Look, but Risking Discrimination." *New York Times*, July 13.

Grindstaff, Laura. 2002. *The Money Shot: Trash, Class, and the Making of TV Talk Shows*. Chicago: University of Chicago Press.

Gross, Michael. 1995. *Model: The Ugly Business of Beautiful Women*. New York: W. Morrow.

Haidarali, Laila. 2005. "Polishing Brown Diamonds: African American Women, Popular Magazines, and the Advent of Modeling in Early Postwar America." *Journal of Women's History* 17:10–37.

Hall, Stuart. 1997. *Representation: Cultural Representations and Signifying Practices*. London and Thousand Oaks, CA: Sage, in association with the Open University.

Halperin, Ian. 2001. *Bad & Beautiful: Inside the Dazzling and Deadly World of Supermodels*. New York: Citadel Press.

Halttunen, Karen. 1986. *Confidence Men and Painted Women: A Study of Middle-Class Culture in America, 1830–1870*. New Haven, CT: Yale University Press.

Hamermesh, Daniel S., and Jeff E. Biddle. 1994. "Beauty and the Labor-Market." *American Economic Review* 84:1174–94.

Haney Lopez, Ian. 1996. *White by Law: The Legal Construction of Race*. New York: New York University Press.

Hartmann, Heidi I. 1981. "The Family as the Locus of Gender, Class, and Political Struggle: The Example of Housework." *Signs* 6:366–94.

Hebdige, Dick. 1979. *Subculture: The Meaning of Style*. London: Methuen.

Hesse-Biber, Sharlene. 2007. *The Cult of Thinness*. New York: Oxford University Press.

Hill Collins, Patricia. 1990. *Black Feminist Thought: Knowledge, Consciousness, and the Politics of Empowerment*. Boston: Unwin Hyman.

———. 2004. *Black Sexual Politics: African Americans, Gender, and the New Racism*. New York: Routledge.

Hirsch, Paul M. 1972. "Processing Fads and Fashions: An Organization Set Analysis of Cultural Industry Systems." *American Journal of Sociology* 77:639–59.

Hochschild, Arlie Russell. 1983. *The Managed Heart: Commercialization of Human Feeling*. Berkeley: University of California Press.

hooks, bell. 1992. *Black Looks: Race and Representation*. Boston: South End Press.

Horyn, Cathy. 2007. "Designers in a Time of Many Dresses, Some Terrific." *New York Times*, September 13.

Jackson, Peter, Michelle Lowe, Daniel Miller, and Frank Mort. 2000. *Commercial Cultures: Economies, Practices, Spaces*. Oxford: Berg.

Jobling, Paul. 2005. *Man Appeal: Advertising, Modernism and Men's Wear*. Oxford and New York: Berg.

Johns, David P., and Jennifer S. Johns. 2000. "Surveillance, Subjectivism, and Technologies of Power: An Analysis of the Discursive Practices of Weight-Performance Sport." *International Review for the Sociology of Sport* 35:219–34.

Kalleberg, Arne L. 2009. "Precarious Work, Insecure Workers: Employment Relations in Transition." *American Sociological Review* 74:1–22.

Kalleberg, Arne L., Barbara F. Reskin, and Ken Hudson. 2000. "Bad Jobs in America: Standard and Nonstandard Employment Relations and Job Quality in the United States." *American Sociological Review* 65:256–78.

Kanter, Rosabeth Moss. 1977. *Men and Women of the Corporation*. New York: Basic Books.

Kaplan, Erin Aubry. 2008. "First Lady Got Back." Salon.com, November 18. www.salon.com/mwt/feature/2008/11/18/michelles_booty/ (accessed April 1, 2011).

Karpik, Lucien. 2010. *Valuing the Unique: The Economics of Singularities*, translated by Nora Scott. Princeton, NJ: Princeton University Press.

Kawamura, Yuniya. 2005. *Fashion-logy: An Introduction to Fashion Studies*. Oxford and New York: Berg.

Kessler-Harris, Alice. 1990. *A Woman's Wage: Historical Meanings and Social Consequences*. Lexington: University Press of Kentucky.

Knight, Frank H. [1921] 1957. *Risk, Uncertainty and Profit*. New York: Kelley & Millman.

Koda, Harold, and Kohle Yohannan. 2009. *The Model as Muse: Embodying Fashion*. New Haven, CT: Yale University Press.

Lacey, Marc. 2003. "In Remotest Kenya, a Supermodel Is Hard to Find." *New York Times*, April 22.

Lambert, Bruce. 1987. "Rockettes and Race: Barrier Slips." *New York Times*, December 26.

Lash, Scott, and John Urry. 1994. *Economies of Signs and Space*. London: Sage.

Lears, T. J. Jackson. 1994. *Fables of Abundance: A Cultural History of Advertising in America*. New York: Basic Books.

Lieberson, Stanley. 2000. *A Matter of Taste: How Names, Fashions, and Culture Change*. New Haven, CT: Yale University Press.

Life. 1969. "Black Models Take Center Stage." October 17.

Liptak, Adam. 2007. "Doling Out Other People's Money." *New York Times*, November 26.

MacKinnon, Catharine A. 1987. *Feminism Unmodified: Discourses on Life and Law*. Cambridge, MA: Harvard University Press.

March, James G., and Johan P. Olsen. 1979. *Ambiguity and Choice in Organizations*. Bergen, Norway: Universitetsforlaget.

Massoni, Kelley. 2004. "Modeling Work: Occupational Messages in *Seventeen* Magazine." *Gender & Society* 18:47–65.

Mauss, Marcel. [1924] 1990. *The Gift: The Form and Reason for Exchange in Archaic Societies.* New York: W.W. Norton.

Maynard, Margaret. 2004. "Living Dolls: The Fashion Model in Australia." *The Journal of Popular Culture* 33:191–205.

McDougall, Paul. 2008. "Congressman Wants Foreign Models off Tech Visas." *Information Week,* June 12.

McRobbie, Angela. 1998. *British Fashion Design: Rag Trade or Image Industry?* London: Routledge.

———. 2002. "From Clubs to Companies: Notes on the Decline of Political Culture in Speeded Up Creative Worlds." *Cultural Studies* 16:516–31.

———. 2004. "Making a Living in London's Small-Scale Creative Sector." In *Cultural Industries and the Production of Culture,* edited by Dominic Power and Allen J. Scott, 130–44. New York and London: Routledge.

Mears, Ashley. 2008. "Discipline of the Catwalk: Gender, Power and Uncertainty in Fashion Modeling." *Ethnography* 9:429–56.

Mears, Ashley, and William Finlay. 2005. "Not Just a Paper Doll: How Models Manage Bodily Capital and Why They Perform Emotional Labor." *Journal of Contemporary Ethnography* 34:317–43.

Menger, Pierre-Michel. 1999. "Artistic Labor Markets and Careers." *Annual Review of Sociology* 25:541–74.

Merton, Robert. 1968. "The Matthew Effect in Science." *Science* 159:56–63.

Messner, Michael A. 2002. *Taking the Field: Women, Men, and Sports.* Minneapolis: University of Minnesota Press.

Mills, C. Wright. 1951. *White Collar: The American Middle Classes.* New York: Oxford University Press.

Model Health Inquiry. 2007. Interim Report. Unpublished report by the British Fashion Council, London, July 11. www.britishfashioncouncil.com/ (accessed April 1, 2009).

———. 2008. "Model Health Certificates: Feasibility Study." Unpublished final report to the British Fashion Council, August 15. www.britishfashioncouncil .com/ (accessed April 1, 2009).

Molotch, Harvey L. 2003. *Where Stuff Comes From: How Toasters, Toilets, Cars, Computers, and Many Others Things Come to Be as They Are.* New York: Routledge.

Moore, Christopher M. 2000. "Streets of Style: Fashion Designer Retailing within London and New York." In *Commercial Cultures: Economies, Practices, Spaces,* edited by Peter Jackson, Michelle Lowe, Daniel Miller, and Frank Mort, 261–78. Oxford: Berg.

Mort, Frank. 1996. *Cultures of Consumption: Masculinities and Social Space in Late Twentieth-Century Britain.* London and New York: Routledge.

Moses, Lucia. 2007. "Black Women's Titles Continue Mainstream Struggle." *Mediaweek.com,* September 10. www.mediaweek.com/mw/esearch/ article_display.jsp?vnu_content_id=1003637076 (accessed April 1, 2011).

Mulvey, Laura. 1989. *Visual and Other Pleasures.* Bloomington: Indiana University Press.

Murphy, Alexandra G. 2003. "The Dialectical Gaze: Exploring the Subject-Object Tension in the Performances of Women Who Strip." *Journal of Contemporary Ethnography* 32:305–35.

Neff, Gina, Elizabeth Wissinger, and Sharon Zukin. 2005. "Entrepreneurial Labor among Cultural Producers: 'Cool' Jobs in 'Hot' Industries." *Social Semiotics* 15:307–34.

Negus, Keith. 1999. *Music Genres and Corporate Cultures*. London and New York: Routledge.

Nickson, Dennis, Chris Warhurst, Anne Witz, and Anne Marie Cullen. 2003. "The Importance of Being Aesthetic: Work, Employment and Service Organization." In *Customer Service: Empowerment and Entrapment*, edited by Andrew Sturdy, Irena Grugulis, and Hugh Willmott, 170–90. Basingstoke: Palgrave.

Nikkhah, Roya. 2007. "Dame Vivienne Attacks 'Racist' Magazines." *The Telegraph* (London), October 15.

Nixon, Sean. 1996. *Hard Looks: Masculinities, Spectatorship and Contemporary Consumption*. New York: St. Martin's Press.

———. 2003. *Advertising Cultures: Gender, Commerce, Creativity*. London and Thousand Oaks, CA: Sage.

Nixon, Sean, and Paul Du Gay. 2002. "Who Needs Cultural Intermediaries?" *Cultural Studies* 16:495–500.

NPD Group. 2011. "NPD Reports on the U.S. Apparel Market for 2010: Encouraging Signs Within." Press release, February 10. www.npd.com/press/releases/press_110210.html (accessed April 1, 2011).

Nussbaum, Emily. 2007. "The Incredible Shrinking Model." *New York* magazine, February 18.

NYCEDC. 2007. "NYC Fashion Industry Snapshot." New York.

Ogden, Cynthia L., Cheryl D. Fryar, Margaret D. Carroll, and Katherine M. Flegal. 2004. "Mean Body Weight, Height, and Body Mass Index, United States, 1960–2002." Centers for Disease Control and Prevention, Advance Data from Vital and Health Statistics.

Okawa, Tomoko. 2008. "Licensing Practices at Maison Christian Dior." In *Producing Fashion: Commerce, Culture and Consumers*, edited by Regina Lee Blaszczyk, 82–110. Philadelphia: University of Pennsylvania Press.

Peiss, Kathy Lee. 1998. *Hope in a Jar: The Making of America's Beauty Culture*. New York: Metropolitan Books.

Peters, Tom. 1997. "The Brand Called You." *Fast Company* 10, August. www.fastcompany.com/magazine/10/brandyou.html (accessed April 1, 2011).

Peterson, Richard, and David Berger. 1975. "Cycles in Symbol Production: The Case of Popular Music." *American Sociological Review* 40:158–73.

Phillips, Sarah R. 2006. *Modeling Life: Art Models Speak about Nudity, Sexuality, and the Creative Process*. Albany: State University of New York Press.

Phillips, Tom. 2007. "Everyone Knew She Was Ill." *The Observer*, January 14.

Pierce, Jennifer L. 1995. *Gender Trials: Emotional Lives in Contemporary Law Firms*. Berkeley: University of California Press.

Pilkington, Ed. 2007. "Supermodels Launch Anti-Racism Protest." *The Guardian*, September 15.

Plattner, Stuart. 1996. *High Art Down Home: An Economic Ethnography of a Local Art Market.* Chicago: University of Chicago Press.

Pleis J. R., J. W. Lucas, and B. W. Ward. 2009. "Summary Health Statistics for U.S. Adults: National Health Interview Survey, 2008." National Center for Health Statistics. Vital Health Stat Series 10, Number 242.

Plunkett, Jack W. 2006. *Plunkett's Retail Industry Almanac 2006.* Houston, TX: Plunkett Research, Ltd.

Podolny, Joel M. 2005. *Status Signals: A Sociological Study of Market Competition.* Princeton, NJ: Princeton University Press.

Quick, Harriet. 1997. *Catwalking: A History of the Fashion Model.* Edison, NJ: Wellfleet Press.

Rantisi, Norma. 2004. "The Designer in the City and the City in the Designer." In *Cultural Industries and the Production of Culture,* edited by Dominic Power and Allen J. Scott, 91–109. New York and London: Routledge.

Reskin, Barbara. 1993. "Sex Segregation in the Workplace." *Annual Review of Sociology* 19:241–70.

Rhodes, G., K., K. Lee, R. Palermo, M. Weiss, S. Yoshikawa, P. Clissa, T. Williams, M. Peters, C. Winkler, and L. Jeffrey. 2005. "Attractiveness of Own-Race, Other-Race and Mixed-Race Faces." *Perception* 34:319–40.

Rosen, Sherwin. 1983. "The Economics of Superstars." *American Economic Review* 71:845–58.

Ross, Andrew. 2003. *No-Collar: The Humane Workplace and Its Hidden Costs.* New York: Basic Books.

Ruggerone, Lucia. 2006. "The Simulated (Fictitious) Body: The Production of Women's Images in Fashion Photography." *Poetics* 34:354–69.

Salganik, Matthew J., Peter Sheridan Dodds, and Duncan J. Watts. 2006. "Experimental Study of Inequality and Unpredictability in an Artificial Cultural Market." *Science* 311:854–56.

Schudson, Michael. 1984. *Advertising, the Uneasy Persuasion: Its Dubious Impact on American Society.* New York: Basic Books.

Scott, Allen J. 2000. *The Cultural Economy of Cities: Essays on the Geography of Image-Producing Industries.* London and Thousand Oaks, CA: Sage.

Scott, William R. 2008. "California Casual: Lifestyle Marketing and Men's Leisurewear, 1930–1960." In *Producing Fashion: Commerce, Culture and Consumers,* edited by Regina Lee Blaszczyk, 169–86. Philadelphia: University of Pennsylvania Press.

Sennett, Richard. 1977. *The Fall of Public Man.* New York: Knopf.

———. 1998. *The Corrosion of Character: The Personal Consequences of Work in the New Capitalism.* New York: Norton.

Sherman, Rachel. 2007. *Class Acts: Service and Inequality in Luxury Hotels.* Berkeley: University of California Press.

Simmel, Georg. [1911] 1984. "Flirtation." In *Georg Simmel: On Women, Sexuality, and Love,* translated and edited by Guy Oakes, 133–52. New Haven, CT: Yale University Press.

———. 1957. "Fashion." *American Journal of Sociology* 62:541–58.

Skov, Lisa. 2002. "Hong Kong Fashion Designers as Cultural Intermediaries: Out of Global Garment Production." *Cultural Studies* 16:553–69.

Smelser, Neil J., and Richard Swedberg. 2005. "Introducing Economic Sociology." In *The Handbook of Economic Sociology*, edited by Neil J. Smelser and Richard Swedberg, 3–25. Princeton, NJ: Princeton University Press.

Smith, Dorothy. 1990. *Texts, Facts, and Femininity: Exploring the Relations of Ruling*. London: Routledge.

Soley-Beltran, Patricia. 2004. "Modelling Femininity." *European Journal of Women's Studies* 11:309–26.

SRDS. 2005. "The Lifestyle Market Analyst: A Reference Guide for Consumer Market Analysis." Des Plaines, IL: Standard Rate and Data Service.

Stacey, Judith. 1987. "Sexism by a Subtler Name? Post-industrial Conditions and Postfeminist Consciousness in the Silicon Valley." *Socialist Review* 96:7–28.

———. 1988. "Can There Be a Feminist Ethnography?" *Women's Studies International Forum* 11:21–27.

———. 2004. "Cruising to Familyland: Gay Hypergamy and Rainbow Kinship." *Current Sociology* 52:181–97.

Steinem, Gloria. 1990. "Sex, Lies, and Advertising." *Ms.* magazine, July/August.

Stoler, Ann L. 1989. "Making Empire Respectable: The Politics of Race and Sexual Morality in 20th-Century Colonial Cultures." *American Ethnologist* 16:634–60.

Storper, Michael. 1997. *The Regional World: Territorial Development in a Global Economy*. New York: Guilford Press.

Storper, Michael, and Robert Salais. 1997. *Worlds of Production: The Action Frameworks of the Economy*. Cambridge, MA: Harvard University Press.

Streeter, Caroline A. 2003. "The Hazards of Visibility: 'Biracial' Women, Media, Images, and Narratives of Identity." In *New Faces in a Changing America*, edited by Herman L. DeBose and Loretta I. Winters, 301–22. Thousand Oaks, CA: Sage.

Target Market News. 2005. The Buying Power of Black America Report. Chicago, The Black Consumer Market Authority.

Thompson, John B. 2005. *Books in the Digital Age: The Transformation of Academic and Higher Education Publishing in Britain and the United States*. Cambridge and Malden, MA: Polity Press.

Trebay, Guy. 2008. "The Vanishing Point." *New York Times*, February 7.

———. 2009. "Testing Her Strong Suit." *New York Times*, February 11.

U.S. DOL. 2010. "Highlights of Women's Earnings in 2009." Report 1025, Bureau of Labor Statistics. www.bls.gov/cps/earnings.htm (accessed April 1, 2010).

Van Rees, Kees. 1983. "Advances in the Empirical Sociology of Literature and the Arts: The Institutional Approach." *Poetics* 12:285–310.

Veblen, Thorstein. [1899] 2007. *The Theory of the Leisure Class*. New York: Oxford University Press.

Velthuis, Olav. 2005. *Talking Prices: Symbolic Meanings of Prices on the Market for Contemporary Art*. Princeton, NJ: Princeton University Press.

Wacquant, Loïc. 2004. *Body & Soul: Notebooks of an Apprentice Boxer*. Oxford and New York: Oxford University Press.

Warhurst, Chris, Dennis Nickson, Anne Witz, and Anne Marie Cullen. 2000. "Aesthetic Labour in Interactive Service Work: Some Case Study Evidence from the 'New' Glasgow." *Service Industries Journal* 20:1–18.

Warren, Jonathan W., and France Winddance Twine. 1997. "White Americans, the New Minority? Non-Blacks and the Ever-Expanding Boundaries of Whiteness." *Journal of Black Studies* 28:200–218.

Weber, Max. 1978. *Economy and Society: An Outline of Interpretive Sociology*. Berkeley: University of California Press.

Wesely, Jennifer K. 2003. "Exotic Dancing and the Negotiation of Identity: The Multiple Uses of Body Technologies." *Journal of Contemporary Ethnography* 32:643–69.

West, Candace, and Sarah Fenstermaker. 1995. "Doing Difference." *Gender & Society* 9:8–37.

West, Candace, and Don Zimmerman. 1987. "Doing Gender." *Gender & Society* 1:125–51.

White, Harrison C. 1981. "Where Do Markets Come From?" *American Journal of Sociology* 87:517–47.

———. 2002. *Markets from Networks: Socioeconomic Models of Production*. Princeton, NJ: Princeton University Press.

Williams, Christine L. 1995. *Still a Man's World: Men Who Do "Women's" Work*. Berkeley: University of California Press.

Williams, Christine L., and Catherine Connell. 2010. "'Looking Good and Sounding Right': Aesthetic Labor and Social Inequality in the Retail Industry." *Work and Occupations* 37:349–77.

Williams, Patricia. 1989. "The Obliging Shell: An Informal Essay on Formal Equal Opportunity." *Michigan Law Review* 87:2128–51.

Williams, Raymond. 1980. *Problems in Materialism and Culture: Selected Essays*. London: New Left Books.

Wilson, Elizabeth. 1985. *Adorned in Dreams: Fashion and Modernity*. London: Virago.

———. 1992. "The Invisible Flaneur." *New Left Review* 191:90–110.

———. 2007. "A Note on Glamour." *Fashion Theory: The Journal of Dress, Body & Culture* 11:95–107.

Wilson, Eric. 2005. "In Fashion, Who Really Gets Ahead?" *New York Times*, December 8.

———. 2008. "The Sun Never Sets on the Runway." *New York Times*, September 7.

Wissinger, Elizabeth. 2007. "Modelling a Way of Life: Immaterial and Affective Labour in the Fashion Modelling Industry." *Ephemera: Theory and Politics in Organization* 7:250–69.

Witz, Anne, Chris Warhurst, and Dennis Nickson. 2003. "The Labour of Aesthetics and the Aesthetics of Organization." *Organization* 10:33–54.

Wolf, Naomi. 1991. *The Beauty Myth: How Images of Beauty Are Used Against Women*. New York: W. Morrow.

Wolkowitz, Carol. 2006. *Bodies at Work*. London: Sage.

Woodward, Ian, and Michael Emmison. 2001. "From Aesthetic Principles to Collective Sentiments: The Logics of Everyday Judgements of Taste." *Poetics* 29:295–316.

Zaloom, Caitlin. 2006. *Out of the Pits: Traders and Technology from Chicago to London.* Chicago: University of Chicago Press.

Zelizer, Viviana. 1994. *The Social Meaning of Money.* New York: Basic Books.

———. 2004. "Circuits of Commerce." In *Self, Social Structure, and Beliefs: Explorations in Sociology,* edited by Jeffrey C. Alexander, Gary T. Marx, and Christine L. Williams, 122–44. Berkeley: University of California Press.

———. 2005. *The Purchase of Intimacy.* Princeton, NJ: Princeton University Press.

Zukin, Sharon, and Jennifer Smith Maguire. 2004. "Consumers and Consumption." *Annual Review of Sociology* 30:173–97.

Index

TEXT
10/13 Sabon

DISPLAY
Sabon

COMPOSITOR
Westchester Book Group

INDEXER
Carol Frenier

PRINTER AND BINDER
Maple-Vail Book Manufacturing Group

UNIVERSITY OF CALIFORNIA PRESS GRATEFULLY
ACKNOWLEDGES THE FOLLOWING GENEROUS DONORS
TO THE AUTHORS IMPRINT ENDOWMENT FUND OF THE
UNIVERSITY OF CALIFORNIA PRESS FOUNDATION.

Wendy Ashmore
Clarence & Jacqueline Avant
Diana & Ehrhard Bahr
Nancy & Roger Boas
Robert Borofsky
Beverly Bouwsma
Prof. Daniel Boyarin
Gene A. Brucker
William K. Coblentz
Joe & Wanda Corn
Liza Dalby
Sam Davis
William Deverell
Frances Dinkelspiel & Gary Wayne
Ross E. Dunn
Carol & John Field
Phyllis Gebauer
Walter S. Gibson
Jennifer A. González
Prof. Mary-Jo DelVecchio Good & Prof. Byron Good
The John Randolph Haynes & Dora Haynes Foundation / Gilbert Garcetti
Daniel Heartz
Leo & Florence Helzel / Helzel Family Foundation
Prof. & Mrs. D. Kern Holoman
Stephen & Gail Humphreys
Mark Juergensmeyer
Lawrence Kramer
Mary Gibbons Landor
Constance Lewallen
Raymond Lifchez
David & Sheila Littlejohn
Dianne Sachko Macleod
Thomas & Barbara Metcalf
Robert & Beverly Middlekauff
Jack & Jacqueline Miles